A GUIDE TO FIELD IDENTIFICATION

BIRDS
OF NORTH AMERICA

by
CHANDLER S. ROBBINS, BERTEL BRUUN,
and HERBERT S. ZIM

illustrated by ARTHUR SINGER

GOLDEN PRESS • NEW YORK
Western Publishing Company, Inc.
Racine, Wisconsin

PREFACE TO THE REVISED EDITION

In addition to those persons to whom we expressed our appreciation for their assistance in preparation of the First Edition, we thank the many birders who have taken the trouble to make suggestions for improving this enlarged Revised Edition. Regrettably, it is not possible to thank each one individually on this page. We do extend our special thanks, however, to Eirik A. T. Blom, Daniel Boone, Michael C. J. Carey, James King, R. Guy McCaskie, Jay M. Sheppard, Lester L. Short, Paul W. Sykes, Jr., Robert B. Weeden, and Claudia Wilds for their extensive and detailed written comments on field marks and geographic range. We also thank John L. Confer, Elizabeth D. Darlington, Charles R. Smith, Daniel R. Gray III, and Dorothy W. McIlroy for having read and commented upon portions of the manuscript. Richard W. Stallcup kindly read the entire species account and offered many valuable suggestions. Portions of the manuscript were critically read by R. Michael Erwin, Mark R. Fuller, and Marshall Howe of the U.S. Fish and Wildlife Service, and the new range maps were reviewed and corrected by Danny Bystrak.

We thank John Bull of the American Museum of Natural History for making available study skins to the artist and authors, and we thank George Watson and David Bridge of the U.S. National Museum for the use of skins in their North American collection.

C. S. R.
B. B.
H. S. Z.

CONTENTS

The sequence of orders and families below follows the latest revision in classification by the American Ornithologists' Union, rather than conforming to page-number sequence. Departures from this sequence have been made within the book to enhance its usefulness as a field guide; see p. 10.

4

INTRODUCTION

Birds, of all wild creatures, generate the most interest because of the large number of colorful species, their cheerful songs, and especially their long semiannual migrations that bring the thrill of the unexpected to the alert bird watcher.

For many, interest in birds and other wildlife begins by feeding wild birds in winter, by being involved in a scout project, visiting a bird sanctuary, or watching a television program. Many birders enjoy competing with themselves or their friends through the annual, life, or locality lists of birds they have identified. Because most North American species are migratory, observers anywhere on this continent have an opportunity to find a great variety of species close to home. The senior author is one of more than 275 people who have identified over 600 species in North America; and from his 2½ acre suburban Maryland yard he has seen 193 species, or more than a quarter of the birds in this book.

After learning to name birds on sight, there is further challenge and pleasure in recognizing them by their songs and calls, in learning where to find the various species, and in participating in a variety of amateur activities that contribute to scientific studies. These activities include photography, organized bird counts, banding, atlasing, and intensive studies of individual species.

This guide will help you identify all of the 650 species that nest in North America north of Mexico (including Greenland), all the vagrants that occur with any regularity, and nearly all the accidentals from other continents that one might hope to find here in a lifetime of birding. Special emphasis is given to the different plumages of each species, to characteristic behaviors that enable the expert to identify birds to family or species at a distance, and to typical song patterns. Maps show spring arrival dates as well as breeding and winter ranges.

Revised Edition. As bird watching has grown over the years since publication of the first edition of this guide, so too has our field knowledge of birds. In this enlarged Revised Edition there are more birds, more pages, more illustrations, and more than 600 all-new range maps based on the latest data. The text has been extensively revised throughout to incorporate new knowledge, and to update nomenclature (the common and scientific names for birds) and taxonomy (how birds are classified). Art revisions range from small color improvements and helpful additional details (flight silhouettes, rump patterns, plumages, heads) to entirely new plates and many more paintings of individual birds. Special features of this guide that have been retained include full-color illustrations of birds in typical habitats; text, art, Sonagrams, and maps next to each other on facing pages; accent marks to assist with pronunciation of scientific names; measurements from live birds in natural poses; and comparison plates of related species.

Map based on Life Areas of N.A., by John W. Aldrich, *Journal of Wildlife Management*, Oct. 1963

SCOPE This guide covers a continental land mass of over 9 million square miles. Geographically and climatically, North America ranges through a rich variety of subtropical, temperate, and arctic environments. Mapped above are the major natural vegetative regions, which depend on latitude, altitude, rainfall, and other factors. The distribution of birds tends to fit into these natural areas and even more closely into the specific habitats that they include. Bear these natural regions in mind when using the range maps.

Arctic-Alpine	Pacific Rain Forest	Mesquite-Grassland
Open Boreal	East Deciduous Forest	Pinyon-Juniper
Closed Boreal	Grasslands	Chaparral-Oak Woodland
No. Hardwood-Conifer	Oak-Savannah	Southern Evergreen
Aspen Parkland	Northern Desert Scrub	Mexican Pine and Pine-Oak
Montane Woodland	Southern Desert Scrub	Tropical Areas (combined)

American Robin

Wilson's
Storm-Petrel

Bridled Tern

BREEDING BIRDS About 650 species of native and introduced birds nest regularly north of Mexico. All are included in this guide.

REGULAR VISITORS An additional 60 species, such as seabirds from the southern hemisphere and landbirds from eastern Asia, Mexico, and the West Indies, migrate or wander regularly to North America.

CASUAL AND ACCIDENTAL VISITORS About 100 foreign species stray occasionally into our region, especially in western Alaska, extreme southern United States, Newfoundland, or Greenland. Those considered most likely to occur again are included.

BIRDS IN THIS BOOK Of the 28 orders of living birds, 21 are represented north of Mexico. Of the 170 families, 65 occur regularly in North America and are treated in this book. Most of the birds included here have been found in North America at least five times in the present century and can be expected to occur again.

The inclusion of Greenland in this edition has added only three regularly breeding species, but the tremendous increase in field work in the outer Aleutian Islands has revealed that many Asiatic species formerly considered only Accidental Visitors to North America are in reality regular migrants through that part of Alaska. A few of them, such as the White-tailed Eagle, are even nesting in the Aleutians. Hence, many new Alaskan species have been added.

Included as Breeding Birds are those introduced species that are breeding regularly. Four gamebird species, the Chukar, Gray Partridge, Black Francolin, and Ring-necked Pheasant, are so established. Other recent additions include several parrot species and the Melodious Grassquit. Omitted are extinct species, introduced birds released experimentally or on a small scale, and escaped birds that are not established and spreading.

Hybrids between closely related species sometimes occur in the wild. Three of the most spectacular and best-known hybrids are included. Observers should also watch for *albinism*, which occurs occasionally in most species of wild birds. Pure white or pale brown forms are rare. Most frequently the normal plumage is modified by white feathers on the wings or tail or in patches on the body. Dark-colored *melanistic* birds occasionally appear, especially among the hawks, but this condition is rare in other species.

NAMES OF BIRDS In this book each species is designated by its common name and by its scientific name.

Common names. Some common birds have many local names. For example, the Northern Bobwhite is called partridge in many parts of the South, as is the Ruffed Grouse in much of the North. The latest English names of the American Birding Association (*A.B.A. Checklist,* 2nd ed., 1982) are used in this guide. Some widely used alternate names are listed in the index. Most of the recent changes in English nomenclature have been made to avoid confusion with birds with similar names in other parts of the world.

Scientific names. Each species of bird is assigned a Latin or scientific name, which is understood and accepted worldwide. These Latin names are often descriptive and indicate avian relationships better than common names. Changes in classification are made as new light is shed on relationships among different species. The scientific names used in this guide (including accent marks to aid in pronunciation) are those adopted by the American Ornithologists' Union (*A.O.U. Check-list of North American Birds,* 5th ed. and supplements through 1982).

Each scientific name consists of two parts—the genus name, followed by the species name, as in *Párus carolinénsis* (Carolina Chickadee). Closely related species belong to the same genus, closely related genera (the plural of genus) to the same family, and closely related families to the same order. Sometimes intermediate groups—such as subfamilies and tribes—are recognized as well. All birds belong to the class Aves.

The largest order of birds (Passeriformes), the perching birds, includes about 60 families worldwide, and 23 in North America. Its members show much variation in appearance and habits, though all have characteristics in common that put them in a single order. Our several species of buntings, for example, all belong to the family Emberizidae. The Indigo Bunting *(Passerína cyánea)* is closely related to the Lazuli Bunting *(Passerína amoéna),* but it is very different in appearance and habits from the Lark Bunting *(Calamospíza melanócorys)* and the Snow Bunting *(Plectróphenax nivális).*

Some species are subdivided into subspecies (races or geographic forms), which adds a third word to the scientific name. The Florida race of Carolina Chickadee is called *Párus carolinénsis ímpiger.* As most subspecies cannot be told in the field, very few are included in this guide.

Taxonomy. Scientific names, because they reveal relationships, are the very foundation of taxonomy, or the classification of birds. The Scissor-tailed and Fork-tailed Flycatchers (p. 204), for example, have recently been merged in the genus *Tyrannus* (p. 206), showing their close relationship with the kingbirds. In general, the taxonomic sequence in this book follows a "natural" or evolutionary order, progressing from the least to the more advanced families—with some exceptions (see **How to Use This Book,** p. 10).

HOW TO USE THIS BOOK

The following information will aid you in using your field guide. Begin to use the book before you go birding; get familiar with its general layout and special features such as taxonomic sequence, silhouettes, comparison plates, and maps.

Scientists classify birds (or group them) according to their relationships; changes in the classification of birds occur as we learn more about them. (For instance, the Black-backed Wagtail, once considered simply a "race" of White Wagtail, is now recognized as a full, distinct species.) The Table of Contents should be consulted for the currently accepted taxonomic sequence for orders and families. Some departures have been made in the sequence used within the book in order to set up comparisons. For instance, heron allies and flamingos have been placed with the similarly shaped cranes.

1. Sequence. For the most part, water birds occupy the first half of this guide, landbirds the second. Specifically, the sequence is as follows, with a few exceptions: seabirds, waterfowl, hawks, upland gamebirds, wading birds, gull-like birds, miscellaneous landbirds, and songbirds.

2. First flip to the proper section of the guide, then use the **silhouettes** (located at the beginning of most families and some other groups) to narrow your choice to within a few pages. Silhouettes of birds in the group illustrated are in black. Those of birds of similar shape, which might be confused with species illustrated, are in blue.

3. Once you have arrived at the proper group of species, look for **comparison plates,** which are available for the larger groups of closely related birds: waterfowl (p. 64), hawks (p. 82), shorebirds (p. 108), gulls (p. 150), terns (p. 158), perching bird families (p. 202), spring warbler heads (p. 268), fall warblers (p. 294), and sparrows (p. 326).

4. Learn to recognize common **families** and other **groups** by such characteristics as size, shape, posture, habits, length and shape of bills and tails, and length of legs, and practice locating them quickly in the guide. Brief introductory paragraphs that summarize field characteristics common to each order and family and to some other groups are marked with blue squares or dots.

5. Once you are in the proper family, you will rely mostly on *plumage* characters or minor differences in the bill, tail, body size, or actions. A quick glance at the *maps* will rule out species not likely to be found in your area; and during the song season, a glance at the *Sonagrams* may help to verify an identification.

6. Focus attention on the bird's *head*. An expert can identify most species by the head alone. Examine carefully the shape and color of the bill and its length relative to the head. Look for a dark line through the eye and a light stripe over the eye or a pale ring around the eye. How wide and how conspicuous are these markings? Is there a median line through the crown? What color is the throat? And are there other distinctive markings on the head?

7. Check routinely for *wing bars, tail spots, streaking* on breast or back, and *rump patches*.

8. Look for *distinctive actions* such as tail wagging or flicking, manner of walking, hopping, feeding, or flying. Compare the *habitat* with that shown in the illustration.

9. Illustrations feature the adult male, usually in breeding plumage. Next, the female. Immatures (im.) are illustrated when noticeably different from adults (ad.). Juvenile (juv.) plumage is shown for some species. Birds not labeled are adults in which sexes are similar. Otherwise ♂ indicates the male, ♀ the female. Most birds typically seen in flight are illustrated in a flying position. If birds have very different summer and winter plumages, these are also shown. The color phases of a few species are given and comparison illustrations call attention to similar species on a different page.

10. In *fall* and *winter* the majority of individuals of many species will be in dull plumage, so from August through March give special attention to pictures of these plumages.

11. The text attempts to evaluate the *abundance* of most species of breeding birds and regular visitors within their principal geographic range. Remember that at the edge of a species' range its abundance decreases rapidly.

When modified by the word *local*, the terms below indicate relative abundance in a very restricted area.

An *abundant* bird is one very likely to be seen in large numbers every time by a person visiting its habitat at the proper season.

A *common* bird may be seen most of the time or in smaller numbers under the same circumstances.

An *uncommon* bird may be seen quite regularly in small numbers in the appropriate environment and season.

A *rare* bird occupies only a small percentage of its preferred habitat or occupies a very specific limited habitat. It is usually found only by an experienced observer.

12. The **habitats** given in the text are generally those preferred during the nesting season. Some winter habitat preferences also are given if different from those in the breeding season. During migration, most species may be found in a much broader range of habitats, but even then birds typical of wetland habitats in the nesting season show a strong preference for wetlands in other seasons as well, plains birds prefer plains, and woodland birds seek shelter in trees.

13. The **range maps** use North America as a base except for species with restricted ranges. The breeding or summer range is red, winter range blue. Areas where the species occurs all year are purple. Areas where birds pass only during migration are shown by red hatching: slanting *up* from left to right for spring, *down* for fall, or cross-hatching for both. Black lines show average first arrival dates in spring; dashed blue or red lines bound areas where some species occasionally extend their range in winter or summer.

The maps are based on the most recent maps in State and Provincial publications, supplemented by data from Audubon Christmas Bird Counts and the Breeding Bird Survey of the U.S. Fish and Wildlife Service.

KEY TO RANGE MAPS

▨	breeding or summer range	——	arrives March 1
▨	winter range	·····	arrives April 1
▨	all year	– – –	arrives May 1
/////	spring migration	.–.–.	arrives June 1
\\\\\	fall migration	- - -	extended winter range
⋈⋈	spring and fall migration	- - -	extended summer range

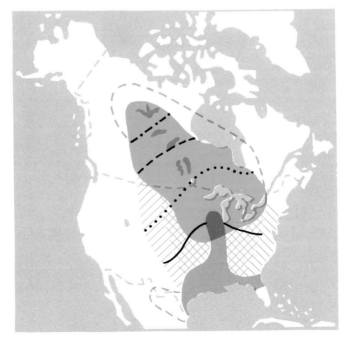

14. A number of **abbreviations** have been used to save space and convey information quickly. Besides such common abbreviations as months, states, and provinces, you will also find: feet: ', inches: ", length: L, wingspan: W, adult: ad., immature: im., juvenile: juv., and number of songs given per minute: x/min. ♂ indicates the male, ♀ the female.

15. The **measurements** of total length are original figures based on actual field measurements, from the tip of the bill to the tip of the tail, of thousands of live birds hand-held in natural positions. These live measurements are shorter than conventional ones (of dead birds, stretched "with reasonable force"). The single figure given for length (L) is a median or average figure for the adult male, rounded to the nearest ¼ inch in small birds and to the nearest ½ inch or 1 inch in larger birds. Individual birds may be 10 percent longer or shorter. Thus a bird recorded at L 10" will normally appear between 9 and 11 inches long. If the sexes differ appreciably in size this is usually mentioned. On larger flying or soaring birds an average wingspan (W) measurement also is given, in inches.

SCRUB JAY

16. Besides verbal descriptions of **songs** and their normal cadence (number of songs given per minute), songs or calls of many species are pictured by Sonagrams (see the next two pages). This technique gives a true "picture" of an actual song recorded in the wild. Although there are both individual and geographical differences in songs of any given species, the species patterns are so characteristic that an experienced observer can identify a familiar species almost instantly by its song alone. The Sonagrams reproduced in this guide were carefully selected to represent typical individuals of each species.

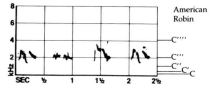

BIRD SONGS are valuable aids in identification. Many experts can identify most songbirds by song. Words cannot describe bird songs adequately, nor can songs be shown accurately on a musical staff. By methods developed by the late Dr. Peter Paul Kellogg of the Laboratory of Ornithology, Cornell University, bird songs can be recorded in the field and then reproduced either audibly or visually (Sonagrams). Tapes or phonograph records are ideal for learning bird songs at home, and with a little practice, Sonagrams are handy for field use.

Sonagrams contain a great deal more information than a few descriptive words, and anyone with an interest in learning to identify birds by their songs will find it well worth the trouble to learn to use them.

With a little practice you can visualize from Sonagrams the approximate pitch of an unfamiliar bird song (in relation to a species you know); the quality (clear, harsh, buzzy, mechanical); the phrasing (separate notes, repetitions, trills, continuous song, or phrases); the tempo (even, accelerating, or slowing); the length of individual notes and of the entire song; and changes in loudness. A good way to learn to use Sonagrams is to compare them with the songs of live birds or with recordings. Even more helpful is to compare the Sonagrams with recordings played at half speed (16 rpm instead of 33 rpm); half speed also drops the pitch one octave and makes it possible for persons with hearing difficiency to hear very high-pitched songs.

This is the first field guide in which Sonagrams have appeared. The typical Sonagram in this book shows 2½ seconds of song. Pitch, usually up to six kilocycles per second (kilohertz), is marked in the left margin at two kHz intervals. For pitch comparison, middle C of the piano and the four octaves above middle C are indicated in the right margin of the enlarged robin Sonagram above. Middle C has a frequency of 0.262 kHz. The frequency doubles with each succeeding octave: C' is 0.523, C" is 1.046, C" ' is 2.093, and C" " (top note on the piano) is 4.186 kHz.

Knowledge of music is not necessary for reading Sonagrams. Even a tone-deaf person can detect the differences in pattern, timing, and quality. First, study Sonagrams of some familiar sounds and of birds you know well. Then use Sonagrams to make comparisons and to remind yourself of the sound patterns of different species.

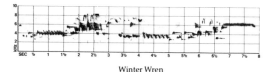

Winter Wren

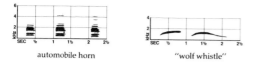

automobile horn   "wolf whistle"   Eastern Meadowlark

Three toots on an automobile horn are easily read. The "wolf whistle" shows how a whistle appears as a single narrow line that rises and falls as pitch changes. Compare it with the Eastern Meadowlark. A ticking clock has no recognizable pitch, but each tick appears in the Sonagram as a vertical line, indicating a wide frequency range. Compare the clock ticks with the Sedge Wren Sonagram. Very high-pitched songs (6-12 kHz) are shown on an extra high Sonagram; older people may not hear these. Some birds, such as thrashers, have very long songs, of which only a typical portion is shown. For some others with typical songs that exceed 2½ seconds (Purple Finch, House Wren), a shorter complete song is used.

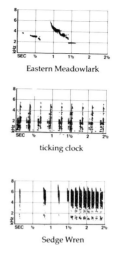

ticking clock

Sedge Wren

Purple Finch

Study some common songs. The Northern Bobwhite's (p. 92) consists of a faint introductory whistle, a short loud whistle, and a longer upward-slurred note that is not as pure as the preceding whistle. The Black-capped Chickadee's "phoebe" song (p. 228) consists of 2 or 3 whistles you can easily imitate. The first note is a full tone higher than the next. Buzzy songs and calls (Grasshopper Sparrow, Common Nighthawk) and buzzy elements of complex songs cover a broad frequency range on the Sonagrams. Many songs have overtones or harmonics that give a richness of quality. These appear as generally fainter duplicates at octaves above the main or fundamental pitch. High-pitched harmonics are "drowned out" by the louder lower notes. Birds, like people, have individual and geographical differences in their voices; yet any typical song is distinctive enough to be recognized by an experienced observer.

RECORDINGS

Many excellent phonograph records (some also available on cassette tapes) can be purchased from the following sources:
Laboratory of Ornithology, 159 Sapsucker Woods Rd., Ithaca, NY 14850
Federation of Ontario Naturalists, 187 Highbourne Rd., Toronto, Ont.
John William Hardy, 1615 NW 14th Ave., Gainesville, FL 32605
Dover Publications, 180 Varick St., New York, NY 10014
Sveriges Radio, Stockholm, Sweden, one of many European sources

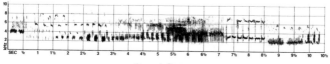

Brewer's Sparrow

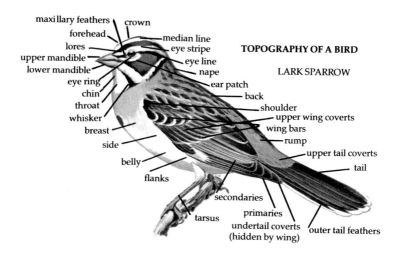

TOPOGRAPHY OF A BIRD

LARK SPARROW

maxillary feathers
crown
forehead
median line
eye stripe
upper mandible
eye line
lower mandible
nape
eye ring
ear patch
chin
back
throat
shoulder
whisker
upper wing coverts
breast
wing bars
side
rump
belly
upper tail coverts
flanks
tail
secondaries
primaries
tarsus
undertail coverts
(hidden by wing)
outer tail feathers
lores

DESCRIBING BIRDS is hardly necessary if you identify a species at sight with the help of a friend or a guidebook. However, use of the correct descriptive terms becomes important with birds that you cannot immediately identify. Then you will want to make detailed notes on appearance and behavior. The accuracy of such notes will be augmented by the use of the terms illustrated above and below. Your description and notes submitted to an expert or used in checking other references may solve your identification problem.

The use of correct terminology will also aid you in making comparisons and in checking variations in color and pattern of local birds. Knowing the terminology helps focus your attention on specific parts of a bird as you observe it. Sometimes such details as an incomplete eye ring or the color of the undertail coverts will clinch an identification.

PARTS OF WING

DUCK WING from below

axillars
wrist
leading edge of wing
wing linings

DUCK WING from above
upper wing coverts
speculum

primaries

secondaries

underwing coverts

scapulars

primaries
secondaries

trailing edge of wing

BIRD WATCHING AND BIRD STUDY

Persons who live in suburbs or rural locations can enjoy bird watching right at home. Planting for shelter and providing food and water will attract many species to a small suburban yard.

Birds are most easily found in parks, sanctuaries, wood margins, open areas, and shores. National Parks, National Monuments, and Wildlife Refuges are excellent places to observe birds. State and private sanctuaries, local parks, and zoos can also prove helpful and stimulating. Prism binoculars (6 to 8 power, with central focus) are almost essential. A spotting 'scope (12 to 30 power) is useful for working with water birds. Camera fans will want a 35mm camera with focal plane shutter, a telephoto lens, and tripod.

Walk slowly and quietly. Do not wear brightly colored clothing. Your parked car can serve as a blind and birds will approach closer than if you are on foot. If you are quiet and partly concealed, you can often attract songbirds and draw them close to you by repeatedly "pshshing" or "squeaking" (sucking air through your lips) or noisily kissing the back of your hand. Some species will respond to crude imitations of their song or to playing back bird songs on a portable tape recorder; but be careful not to disturb birds during their nesting season.

Local bird clubs, Audubon groups, or ornithological societies are found in every state and Canadian province, especially in the larger cities. These clubs hold meetings, lectures, and field trips. For help in locating these and other nature societies consult Rickert's *Guide to North American Bird Clubs*, the Conservation Directory of the National Wildlife Federation, your state conservation department, a library or newspaper. Many larger cities or universities have museums with bird collections, and study here can greatly aid field recognition. Many tours are run specifically for bird study. The National Audubon Society Workshops have outstanding programs in nature education.

National organizations and their **publications** are:

American Birding Association, Box 4335, Austin, TX 78765; *Birding*.

American Ornithologists' Union, National Museum of Natural History, Smithsonian Institution, Washington, DC 20560; *Auk*.

Cooper Ornithological Society, Department of Zoology, University of California, Los Angeles, CA 90052; *Condor*.

Laboratory of Ornithology at Cornell University, 159 Sapsucker Woods Rd., Ithaca, NY 14583; *Living Bird Quarterly*.

National Audubon Society, 950 Third Ave., New York, NY 10022; *Audubon* and *American Birds*.

Wilson Ornithological Society, Museum of Zoology, University of Michigan, Ann Arbor, MI 48104; *Wilson Bulletin*.

■ **LOONS** (*Order* Gaviiformes, *Family* Gaviidae) are specialized for swimming and diving. Loons come ashore only to breed. They are silent in winter. In flight the head is lower than the body. The wingbeats are fast, uninterrupted by gliding. Common and Yellow-billed dive by sliding under; the other species hop up and forward to begin the plunge. Loons eat fish, crustaceans, and some water plants. Eggs, 2-3.

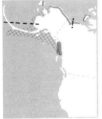

YELLOW-BILLED LOON
Gávia ádamsii

This largest, most northern loon breeds on tundra lakes. Adult's bill is straw-colored, including the straight upper ridge, which is always dark in Common Loon; lower mandible is sharply upturned. The white spots on back are larger and fewer than in Common. In winter, sides of head are lighter and browner than Common, brown of hind neck extends forward below eye, and shafts of primaries are white (dark in Common). The maxillary feathering extends farther above nostrils than on Common. Calls are similar.

COMMON LOON
Gávia ímmer

The most common loon in the East, breeding along lakes and rivers. Its yodel-like laugh is given frequently, near the nest and in flight. Varies considerably in size. Note its usually dark, evenly tapered bill and, in summer, its cross-banded back. In winter the head, neck, and back are darker than the Red-throated and Yellow-billed, and with less contrast than in Arctic. Migrate in small flocks.

ARCTIC LOON
Gávia árctica

Rare in the East, common in the West. Breeds on tundra lakes. The light gray crown and white stripes on the side of the throat are diagnostic. In winter the back, darkest of all loons, is gray with pale feather edgings. The bill is thinner than Common's and straight. The Arctic is so like a small Common Loon that identification in winter is risky outside its normal range unless the narrow chinstrap is seen. Call is an ascending whistle.

RED-THROATED LOON
Gávia stelláta

Common in its breeding range on both fresh and salt water, wintering mainly along the coast. Often migrates in flocks. Much slimmer than Arctic. Notice slender, upturned bill. In summer plumage the white stripes extend up the back of the head. Head and bill are habitually pointed slightly upward, even in flight. In winter the back is pale gray with tiny white spots. Call, a rapid quacking.

cormorant scaup merganser loon grebe

LOONS

YELLOW-BILLED LOON
L 25" W 60"

winter

summer

COMMON LOON
L 24" W 58"

winter

summer

ARCTIC LOON
L 18" W 47"

Pacific
race   summer

winter

summer

RED-THROATED LOON
L 17" W 44"

winter

summer

■ **GREBES** (*Order* Podicipediformes, *Family* Podicipedidae) are swimming and diving birds, smaller than loons, with flat lobes on their toes. The short legs are far back on the body; tail and wings are short. Flight is weak and hurried; taxi before becoming airborne. Head held low in flight. Grebes dive and pursue small aquatic animals. Courtship displays on the water are often elaborate, accompanied by wails and whistles. Nest in floating marsh vegetation; eggs, 2-9.

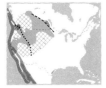

WESTERN GREBE
Aechmóphorus occidentális

Locally abundant, breeding in colonies in lake vegetation. Winters along the Pacific Coast and in some inland areas, often in large flocks. A large black and white grebe with a long, straight neck. The bill is much longer, yellower, and more needle-like than in other grebes. Summer and winter plumages alike.

RED-NECKED GREBE
Pódiceps grisegéna

An uncommon long-necked grebe. In ponds and lakes in summer; winters mainly in salt water. Light throat always contrasts with dark neck. Stockier appearance and heavy bill distinguish it from Western, shape and size from Horned and Eared Grebes.

HORNED GREBE
Pódiceps aurítus

This commonest grebe (except in Southwest) has a thin straight bill. Nests on lakes and ponds; winters in salt water and on Great Lakes, often in loose flocks. Told in winter from Red-necked and Eared Grebes by white face and neck. Rump low, arcs smoothly into water.

EARED GREBE
Pódiceps nigricóllis

A small grebe with thin upturned bill, high, rounded back, and rump usually held high, fluffed. It breeds in colonies and is common on shallow lakes. In winter, note slender neck, white ear and throat patches. Most winter in flocks on inland lakes.

PIED-BILLED GREBE
Podilýmbus pódiceps

Fairly common in shallow fresh water, rare in salt water. A small, solitary, stocky grebe with a high chicken-like bill. Rarely flies; escapes by diving or slowly sinking below the surface. Call, a series of low, slurred whistles.

LEAST GREBE
Tachybáptus domínicus

A tiny grebe with a slender dark bill. Uncommon; in southern Rio Grande Valley; rare and local farther north.

Pied-billed Grebe

GREBES

WESTERN GREBE
L 18″ W 40″

takeoff

courtship dance

winter

summer

RED-NECKED GREBE
L 13″ W 32″

Horned

head comparison

winter

summer

HORNED GREBE
L 9½″ W 24″

Eared

winter

summer

EARED GREBE
L 9″ W 23″

Eared

Pied-billed

winter

im.

summer

PIED-BILLED GREBE
L 9″

winter

summer

LEAST GREBE
L 6½″

■ **TUBENOSES** (*Order* Procellariiformes) have external tubular nostrils. They are birds of the sea, coming ashore on remote islands and shores only to breed. They nest in colonies; feed on squid, fish, and other marine life, usually at or near the surface. All have hooked beaks. The sexes are similar. Silent away from the breeding grounds. Lengths given are for birds in flight.

FAMILIES OF TUBENOSES OCCURRING OFF OUR COASTS

Albatrosses (Diomedeidae) Large birds, including the longest-winged species. Long, narrow wings, very heavy hooked beak.   p. 22

Fulmars, Shearwaters, and Large Petrels (Procellariidae) Large birds, though considerably smaller than the albatrosses. The bill is generally thinner, with a pronounced tooth at the end.   pp. 24-28

Storm-Petrels (Hydrobatidae) Small birds, scarcely larger than swallows. Bills are short and legs fairly long.   p. 30

● **ALBATROSSES** (*Family* Diomedeidae) are primarily Southern Hemisphere birds; three species breed north of the equator. They have tremendously long wingspreads (11' in the Wandering Albatross); glide low over the waves on stiffly held wings. Single egg laid on ground.

LAYSAN ALBATROSS   *Diomédea immutábilis*
This white-bodied albatross nests on mid-Pacific islands; occurs far offshore, but regularly in summer close to the Aleutians and less frequently, Oct. to June, south to southern California. The black mantle covers upper wings and back. Note wing pattern. Juveniles resemble adults. Seldom follows large ships.

YELLOW-NOSED ALBATROSS
          Diomédea chlororhýnchos
Very rare visitor to North Atlantic from southern oceans. Most occur in summer. Juveniles have black bill, are paler above, and have broader dark underwing margins. The slightly larger **Black-browed Albatross** (*Diomédea melanóphris*, L 30″ W 90″), an even rarer North Atlantic vagrant, resembles Yellow-nosed but adult has entire bill yellow and broader dark underwing margins. Juveniles have black bill, gray lower neck, and dark underwings.

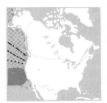

BLACK-FOOTED ALBATROSS   *Diomédea nígripes*
Our only regular all-dark albatross. Occurs as close as a mile off the Pacific Coast. Often rests on the water; feeds on squid and fish at night. Told from the dark Pacific shearwaters by larger size and heavier bill. Juveniles generally have less white. Often follows ships.

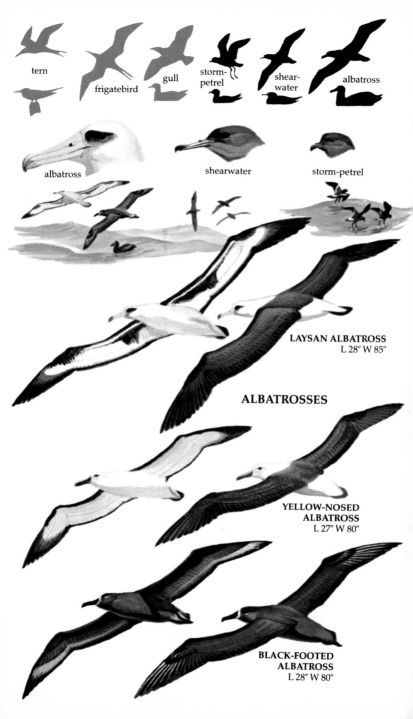

tern

frigatebird

gull

storm-petrel

shear-water

albatross

albatross

shearwater

storm-petrel

LAYSAN ALBATROSS
L 28″ W 85″

ALBATROSSES

YELLOW-NOSED ALBATROSS
L 27″ W 80″

BLACK-FOOTED ALBATROSS
L 28″ W 80″

● **FULMARS** (*Family* Procellariidae) strongly resemble gulls in appearance and in scavenging habits, but fly like shearwaters and typically are found far at sea. Nest colonially on high sea cliffs; lay 1 egg.

NORTHERN FULMAR
Fulmárus glaciális

A large gull-like tubenose. In its light color phase it can be told from gulls by the stiff flight, the habit of flapping and gliding, the heavy head and neck, the shorter tail, and, at close range, the tubular nostrils. Dark-phase birds are paler and grayer than Sooty Shearwaters (p. 26), have shorter, rounder wings and a broader tail. Fulmars follow ships, and readily accept offal.

● **SHEARWATERS** (*Family* Procellariidae) differ from fulmars in having longer, narrower wings, a narrower tail, and a longer, thinner bill. The flight pattern is similar—a few deep wingbeats and a long glide, usually close to the water. Their food is small fish and crustaceans. Nocturnal on breeding grounds. Lay a single egg.

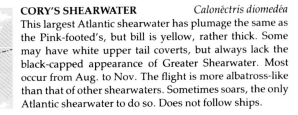

CORY'S SHEARWATER
Calonéctris diomedéa

This largest Atlantic shearwater has plumage the same as the Pink-footed's, but bill is yellow, rather thick. Some may have white upper tail coverts, but always lack the black-capped appearance of Greater Shearwater. Most occur from Aug. to Nov. The flight is more albatross-like than that of other shearwaters. Sometimes soars, the only Atlantic shearwater to do so. Does not follow ships.

PINK-FOOTED SHEARWATER
Púffinus creátopus

A large common Pacific tubenose; breeds in Chile. May be a pale subspecies of Flesh-footed (p. 26). Often seen in flocks with Sooty and Manx Shearwaters (pp. 26, 28). Larger than the Sooty, with slower wingbeats; much larger than the Manx, with less contrasting colors. Most common from May to Nov., but a few are seen all year round. Does not follow ships.

GREATER SHEARWATER
Púffinus grávis

A large, fairly common, Atlantic shearwater, breeding Nov.-Apr. in the Tristan da Cunha Islands. Black cap and white on tail are pronounced. In May and June it migrates north over the western Atlantic; in Oct. and Nov. south over the eastern Atlantic. Larger and heavier than either Audubon's (p. 28) or Manx (p. 28) Shearwaters. Often occurs in large flocks; follows ships.

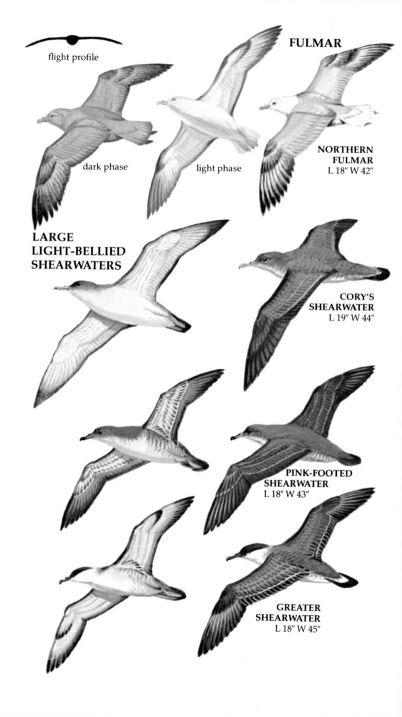

flight profile

FULMAR

NORTHERN FULMAR
L 18″ W 42″

dark phase

light phase

LARGE LIGHT-BELLIED SHEARWATERS

CORY'S SHEARWATER
L 19″ W 44″

PINK-FOOTED SHEARWATER
L 18″ W 43″

GREATER SHEARWATER
L 18″ W 45″

SOOTY SHEARWATER *Púffinus gríseus*
A large, dark, gray-brown bird of cool waters. Nests on subantarctic islands. Abundant in fall off West Coast, uncommon on East Coast. The only dark-bodied shearwater in the western Atlantic, and the only one in the Pacific with contrasting silvery wing linings. Bill is dark. Told from Flesh-footed Shearwater by dark body, smaller size, and faster wingbeats; from Short-tailed by longer, heavier bill and more gently sloping forehead.

SHORT-TAILED SHEARWATER *Púffinus tenuiróstris*
A fairly large, slender shearwater breeding in southern Australia. Told from Flesh-footed Shearwater by smaller size, shorter tail, dark legs, and dark bill. Generally separable from Sooty Shearwater by smaller bill, more rounded head, and uniform smoky-gray underwings, but a few of each species have the underwing pattern of the other. Uncommon, except abundant in Gulf of Alaska, May-July; off California flocks appear in late fall, later than the Sooty.

FLESH-FOOTED SHEARWATER *Púffinus carnéipes*
A very large species and a very rare and irregular visitor to the West Coast from South Pacific breeding grounds. Larger than the Sooty and Short-tailed Shearwaters, with a large, dark-tipped, pale pink bill and flesh-colored feet and legs. Entire plumage, including underwings, is blackish. Similar in shape and habits to the Pink-footed (p. 24), and considered by some to be conspecific. Compare with Heermann's Gull (p. 146).

BULLER'S SHEARWATER *Púffinus búlleri*
Regular, rare to uncommon, in fall from Monterey, California, north to British Columbia. A slender shearwater with a dark cap. Note the W-shaped pattern above, light wing tips below. Flight is lighter than that of Black-vented Shearwater (p. 28), and periods of gliding on more arched wings longer. The **Streaked Shearwater** (*Calonéctris leucomélas*, L 18" W 47"), a casual visitor from the western Pacific to Monterey Bay, California, most closely resembles the Pink-footed (p. 24), but is slimmer, has a more pronounced wing angle, dark eye contrasting with white face and crown, heavily streaked nape, scaly grayish back, and yellowish bill. Molting birds may show a long pale "U" around the rump.

SHEARWATERS

SOOTY SHEARWATER
L 16" W 43"

SHORT-TAILED SHEARWATER
L 15" W 39"

FLESH-FOOTED SHEARWATER
L 18" W 43"

BULLER'S SHEARWATER
L 15" W 40"

AUDUBON'S SHEARWATER *Púffinus lherminiéri*
A very small, rather common Atlantic shearwater; breeds in the Bahamas. Undertail coverts are dark, not white as in Manx Shearwater. Has longer tail and shorter wings than Manx, and wingbeats are correspondingly faster. It is most commonly seen in summer. Does not follow ships.

MANX SHEARWATER *Púffinus púffinus*
Uncommon on the Atlantic (where it very rarely breeds). It is much smaller than the Pink-footed Shearwater (p. 24) and its back and wings are dark, where the Buller's Shearwater (p. 26) has light areas. White undertail coverts distinguish it from smaller and shorter-winged Audubon's. Wingbeats and flight are fast. Does not follow ships.

Black-vented   Manx

BLACK-VENTED SHEARWATER *Púffinus opisthómelas*
Common in fall and winter off the Pacific Coast north to Santa Barbara, California. Like Manx but has black undertail coverts.

● **LARGE PETRELS,** also called Gadfly Petrels, are in the shearwater family. In flight and behavior they are intermediate between the shearwaters and the smaller storm-petrels. Their very fast flight resembles that of shearwaters, but the angle of the wing is like the storm-petrels'; fast high-soaring arcs are unique. These birds do not follow ships; they eat fish and shrimp. Nest in burrows; 1 egg.

BLACK-CAPPED PETREL *Pteródroma hasitáta*
Uncommon summer and fall visitor from West Indies to Gulf Stream off the Carolinas; casual farther north during storms. Dark above and light below, it can be confused only with Manx and Audubon's Shearwaters, neither of which has rump or hind neck white. Flight is distinctly different, with wings more angled, less rigid. **Cook's Petrel** (*Pteródroma coókii*, L 10" W 26"), casual 50+ miles off the California coast, has shape of Black-capped Petrel and color pattern suggesting Buller's Shearwater (p. 26), but has pale cap, white forehead and underwings, and white tail with dark center.

MOTTLED PETREL *Pteródroma inexpectáta*
A medium-sized petrel from New Zealand, a casual summer visitor to the Gulf of Alaska. Note the contrast between the throat and the belly. The heavy black bar on the underside of the wing is unique; from above, the light upper surface contrasts with the dark leading edge. When primaries are widely spread, light areas toward the tips of the upper wings appear.

SMALL SHEARWATERS
AND LARGE PETRELS

**AUDUBON'S
SHEARWATER**
L 11″ W 26″

**MANX
SHEARWATER**
L 13″ W 32″

**BLACK-
CAPPED
PETREL**
L 13″ W 35″

**MOTTLED
PETREL**
L 11½″

● **STORM-PETRELS** (*Family* Hydrobatidae) flutter and hop over the waves, pattering with webbed feet. Found singly or in flocks. Egg, 1.

BLACK STORM-PETREL   *Oceanódroma melánia*
Rather common off southern California in winter, common north to Monterey Bay, Sept.-Nov., local in summer. This largest black petrel has dark underwings, long legs, and a forked tail. Flight is deliberate, wingbeats deep, suggesting flight of Black Tern. Follows ships.

ASHY STORM-PETREL   *Oceanódroma homóchroa*
Common only locally, Apr.-Nov. Stocky build, medium size, brown color, pale wing coverts above and below. Flight is more fluttering than the larger Black Storm-Petrel's, wingbeats not going above the horizontal.

FORK-TAILED STORM-PETREL   *Oceanódroma furcáta*
Abundant in northern Pacific, where it breeds. This uniform pale gray bird has a light head, underparts, wing patch, and light underwing with dark leading edge. Tail is forked. Glides more than other petrels and has shallower wingbeat.

Fork-tailed

LEACH'S STORM-PETREL   *Oceanódroma leucórhoa*
Uncommon and local in summer. Medium-sized, dark, with a prominent white rump (white very restricted in southern California) and gray wing patch. Tail is forked, feet dark. Leach's has darker underwings than Ashy. Flight is erratic and nighthawk-like; Wilson's is moth-like.

Leach's

WILSON'S STORM-PETREL   *Oceanítes oceánicus*
Very common off Atlantic Coast, June-Sept. Dark brown with white rump, light wing patch, long legs, and yellow feet. Tail is rounded. Dances over the surface with wings held high. Often follows ships in loose flocks.

Wilson's

BAND-RUMPED STORM-PETREL *Oceanódroma cástro*
Casual on both coasts during storms. Almost identical to Leach's. Told by shape of white rump band, less deeply forked tail. Flight like small shearwater with much soaring.

LEAST STORM-PETREL   *Oceanódroma microsóma*
Rare north to San Diego in late summer. Note tiny size, short wedge-shaped tail, deep rapid wingbeats, and dark plumage.

STORM-PETRELS

storm-petrel at burrow

BLACK STORM-PETREL
L 8½″ W 18″

Ashy from below

ASHY STORM-PETREL
L 7″ W 16″

FORK-TAILED STORM-PETREL
L 7½″ W 18″

Leach's

LEACH'S STORM-PETREL
L 7½″ W 19″

Wilson's

BAND-RUMPED STORM-PETREL
L 8½″ W 18″

WILSON'S STORM-PETREL
L 6½″ W 16″

LEAST STORM-PETREL
L 5½″ W 13″

PELICANS AND THEIR ALLIES (*Order* Pelecaniformes) are large aquatic fish-eating birds with all four toes webbed. Most nest in large colonies and are silent outside breeding grounds. There are six families: Tropicbirds (Phaethontidae), Pelicans (Pelecanidae), Frigatebirds (Fregatidae), Gannets and Boobies (Sulidae), Cormorants (Phalacrocoracidae), and Anhinga (Anhingidae). Tropicbirds, Frigatebirds, Gannets, and Boobies lay one egg. The other families lay 3-5.

RED-BILLED TROPICBIRD   *Pháethon aethéreus*
Rare but regular visitor off southern California in fall, casual in North Atlantic; seldom seen close to shore. Adults usually have a long streamer tail, red bill. Immature's bill is yellow. Fishes by diving tern-like into the ocean. Flight is pigeon-like, with strong wingbeats.

WHITE-TAILED TROPICBIRD   *Pháethon leptúrus*
A casual visitor off the Southeast coast after storms. Similar to Red-billed but smaller, with a heavy black band on the wing in place of the black streaking, and a short eye line. Immature lacks the streamer tail and is barred with black above.

BROWN PELICAN   *Pelecánus occidentális*
A locally common breeder on both coasts, rarely found on fresh water. Adult has a light head and a gray-brown body. Immature is uniformly dull brown above, lighter below. An excellent flier, with a powerful stroking flight alternating with short glides, which often carry the bird only inches above the water. Flies with head drawn back to the shoulder; rarely soars. Small flocks fly in long lines. Dives into the water from heights of 30′ for small fish. Semi-tame birds often beg for food on fishing piers.

AMERICAN WHITE PELICAN
Pelecánus erythrorhýnchos
Locally common in breeding colonies of several hundred pairs on the West Coast and also on lakes. Black area of wing includes all the primaries and half of the secondaries. Flat, rounded plate on the bill is seen in breeding season only. Flight is an alternation of flapping and gliding. Migrates in long lines in V-formation and often soars at great heights. Fishes by wading or swimming in shallows, often in flocks, scooping up fish with its large bill. Does not dive. Some non-breeding birds spend the summer at their wintering grounds.

loon gull tropicbird pelican frigatebird gannet cormorant

TROPICBIRDS

RED-BILLED TROPICBIRD
L 34″ W 44″

Red-billed

WHITE-TAILED TROPICBIRD
L26″ W 37″

White-tailed

PELICANS

BROWN PELICAN
L 41″ W 90″

winter

diving

im.

summer

winter

fishing formation

AMERICAN WHITE PELICAN
L 50″ W 110″

im.

summer

MAGNIFICENT FRIGATEBIRD *Fregáta magníficens*
Common in summer in Florida Keys; occasional on Southeast, Gulf, and West coasts in fall and during storms. Note prominent crook in narrow wing, and long slender tail. Male's pouch is inflated during courtship. Robs gulls and terns in flight; also takes small fish and marine refuse from surface, but does not land on the water. Efficient glider, it soars to great heights without moving wings.

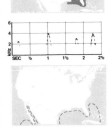

NORTHERN GANNET *Súla bassánus*
Common in summer near breeding islands; winters on the ocean; often visible from shore, especially during east winds. Note its double-ended silhouette. Dark wing tips on white body identify the adult. Nests in large colonies. Feeds by diving from 50' or more into the ocean. In migration, flies just above the water, often in lines. Alternately flaps stiffly and glides.

MASKED BOOBY *Súla dactylátra*
A regular summer visitor to Dry Tortugas, Florida; very rare on mainland. All the flight feathers and the face are black; the skin near the bill is slaty. Immature is dark above with a pale band around the neck. A tropical gannet, it is larger than the other two boobies but smaller than the Gannet, which it resembles in habits.

RED-FOOTED BOOBY *Súla súla*
Very rare visitor to Caribbean and West Coast. There are two color phases. White phase is like small Gannet with black secondaries. Dark phase is brown. Intermediates have white tail.

BROWN BOOBY *Súla leucogáster*
A regular visitor to the Gulf Coast, rare in California. Upper parts uniformly dark. Immature lacks the sharp white and brown contrast below. Resembles Gannet in habits and behavior.

BLUE-FOOTED BOOBY *Súla neboúxii*
A casual visitor to Salton Sea, California, and the lower Colorado River. From above, note the white patch on the upper back and (in adult) the large white rump. Underwings are dark. Birds of all ages have blue feet. Bluish bill of adult is diagnostic. Behavior, gannet-like.

FRIGATEBIRD

MAGNIFICENT FRIGATEBIRD
L 35" W 90"

♂

im.

♀

♂

subadult

NORTHERN GANNET
L 31" W 70"

ad.

gannet

im.

BOOBIES

RED-FOOTED BOOBY
L 24" W 60"

ad.

MASKED BOOBY
L 27" W 68"

im.

white phase

im.

dark phase

ad.

ad.

BROWN BOOBY
L 23" W 56"

im.

ad.

BLUE-FOOTED BOOBY
L 26" W 64"

im.

36

● **CORMORANTS AND ANHINGAS** are fish eaters that swim with bill tilted upward, dive from the surface, and swim under water. They often perch with wings half open to dry. Fly silently in V.

GREAT CORMORANT   *Phalacrócorax cárbo*
Our largest cormorant and the only one with a white throat patch. Bill is yellower and heavier than Double-crested Cormorant's. In breeding season adult has a white flank patch; immature has belly whiter than neck.

BRANDT'S CORMORANT   *Phalacrócorax penicillátus*
A common, short-tailed, crestless Pacific cormorant. The throat is dark (blue in breeding season) with dull yellow margin behind. The immature is dark below, as is the smaller immature Pelagic, but has a large pale Y on its breast. In flight note straight neck, big head.

DOUBLE-CRESTED CORMORANT
Phalacrócorax aurítus
Widespread; found on inland lakes and rivers as well as coastally. The throat pouch is orange; the crests seldom are visible. Immatures are white on the breast, dark on the belly. In flight large head is held higher than neck.

PELAGIC CORMORANT   *Phalacrócorax pelágicus*
A small, common thin-billed Pacific bird. The throat pouch and face are dull red. In spring it has a double crest and a white flank patch. Immature is all dark without pale Y. In flight small head merges with slender, straight neck.

OLIVACEOUS CORMORANT   *Phalacrócorax olivǎceus*
A small, rather common, unwary bird with slender bill; just reaches southern La. and southern Ariz. Brown wing contrasts with irridescent blackish body.

Pelagic Cormorant

RED-FACED CORMORANT   *Phalacrócorax úrile*
Resident in the Aleutians. It resembles the Pelagic but has more and brighter red on the face and a blue pouch. Immature is told from Pelagic by the longer bill.

Olivaceous Cormorant

ANHINGA   *Anhínga anhínga*
Common in fresh-water swamps, ponds, and lakes, where it spears fish. Often swims with only head and neck exposed. Long straight bill, long tail, and white wing and back plumes differentiate it from cormorants. Usually seen singly, but may soar very high in flocks.

Anhinga

Double-crested Cormorant

CORMORANTS

GREAT CORMORANT
L 30″ W 60″

im.

Great Cormorant

BRANDT'S CORMORANT
L 29″ W 50″
head only

Double-crested

DOUBLE-CRESTED CORMORANT
L 27″ W 50″

im.

PELAGIC CORMORANT
L 22″ W 40″

OLIVACEOUS CORMORANT
L 22″ W 40″

RED-FACED CORMORANT
L 28″ W 48″

Pelagic

head only

im.

♀

♂

♀

partially submerged

ANHINGA
L 28″ W 47″
ANHINGA

drying wings

■ **WATERFOWL** (*Order* Anseriformes, *Family* Anatidae) in North America are divided into eight tribes: one each for swans and geese, and six for ducks. Waterfowl are aquatic, with webs between the three front toes. They have long necks and narrow pointed wings, and most have short legs. They differ from loons and grebes in having flattened bills with tooth-like edges that serve as strainers. Their flattened bodies are well insulated with down feathers. Young hatch down-covered and can walk and swim a few hours after hatching.

Tundra Swan

Canada Goose

Mallard

SWANS, the largest of the water-fowl, are characterized by long necks—longer than their bodies. American species, all white, are graceful in the air and on water. They patter along the surface when taking flight. The young are brownish. Swans tip for aquatic plants in shallow water. Eggs, 3-10. p. 40

GEESE are intermediate between swans and ducks in size and other characterisics, but form a distinctive group. Sexes are alike. Geese are heavier and longer-necked than ducks. They molt once a year, as do swans. Legs of most are placed farther forward than in ducks and swans. This is an adaptation for grazing. Eggs, 3-8. pp. 42-44

SURFACE-FEEDING DUCKS are smaller than swans and geese and have flatter bills and shorter legs. Surface-feeding ducks are birds of ponds, lakes, and slow rivers, where they feed on water plants. They fly strongly and take off with a sudden upward leap. In flight their secondary wing feathers show a bright patch—the speculum. They nest on the ground (except Wood Duck); eggs, 5-12. pp. 46-52

WHISTLING-DUCKS form a connecting link between ducks and the larger waterfowl. They are long-legged, long-necked ducks. They fly somewhat like geese. Whistling-Ducks live along lakes and ponds and feed on water plants by tipping. They also graze like geese and occasionally damage crops. Lay 10-15 eggs. p. 52

Black-bellied Whistling-Duck

BAY DUCKS (*Genus Aythya*) fall into a single tribe (all have a lobed hind toe). Expert divers, their legs are set far back. Bay ducks breed along northern lakes, and most winter in huge rafts (flocks) in tidal estuaries or along ice-free coasts. Feed mainly on aquatic plants. Most nest on the ground; lay 4-14 eggs. p. 54

Ring-necked Duck

SEA DUCKS belong to the same tribe as mergansers. In taking off, they patter along the surface. Sea ducks dive deeper than bay ducks and feed more on mollusks. Sea ducks breed more along the coast than on inland lakes. In winter they are more strictly coastal than the bay ducks. Nest on the ground; eggs, 4-8. pp. 56-60

Common Eider

STIFF-TAILED DUCKS are little, chunky, southern ducks living in lakes and fresh-water bays. Their rather long stiff tails give them their name. Eggs, 5-11. p. 62

Ruddy Duck

MERGANSERS have long slender bills modified for seizing fish. Mergansers take off slowly, as sea ducks do. Nest in hollow trees (except Red-breasted). Eggs, 6-18. p. 62

Red-breasted Merganser

● **SWANS** (*Subfamily* Anserinae, *Tribe* Cygnini) are heavy, white, long-necked birds of lake and river shores. They dip head and neck into the water to feed on bottom vegetation; also browse on shore grasses. Sexes are similar. Immatures are grayish brown. Swans have a deep, ponderous flight, with neck extended. Fly in V-formation or in lines.

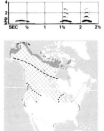

MUTE SWAN *Cýgnus ólor*

An Old World species introduced into eastern North America and commonly seen in parks. It breeds locally in the wild. When swimming, neck is held in a graceful S-curve; the secondary wing feathers are often raised. The dull rose bill of the immature is black at the base. Voice, a low grunt, is seldom heard. Wingbeats of flying birds produce a diagnostic hum.

TUNDRA SWAN *Cýgnus columbiánus*

Our most common swan, formerly called Whistling Swan; breeds in the Far North and winters in large flocks in shallow fresh or brackish water. When swimming, it is told from the Mute Swan by its silhouette. The neck is held straight, the bill level; secondaries are not raised. The adult's black bill often shows a bright yellow spot that the Trumpeter lacks. Bill profile typically more concave and head rounder than Trumpeter. The immature is light gray-brown; its bill is pink, dusky only at the tip. The call, a muffled, musical whistle, resembles honking of the Canada Goose (p. 42). The Old World race, *C. c. béwickii*, is a very rare visitor to Alaska and the Northwest coast. The adult can be recognized by its bill, which has a yellow base.

WHOOPER SWAN *Cýgnus cýgnus*

Very rare visitor to Alaska and Greenland. Resembles Trumpeter Swan but adult has extensive yellow base to its large bill.

TRUMPETER SWAN *Cýgnus buccinátor*

Increasingly common in Yellowstone Park, Wyoming, in Red Rocks Lake, Montana, and in parts of the Canadian Rockies. Rare outside its breeding range, but found along West Coast in winter. Best told by voice or by flat head and bill profile and large size. Immatures have black base and tip to their pink bill. Call is a loud, low-pitched trumpeting: a low note followed by about 3 on a higher pitch.

SWANS

pelican   Mallard   eider   goose   swan

threat
posture

im.

MUTE SWAN
L 40″ W 90″

WHOOPER SWAN
L 46″ W 92″
heads only

im.

ad.

im.

Old World race
of Tundra Swan

TUNDRA SWAN
L 36″ W 80″

im.

TRUMPETER SWAN
L 45″ W 90″

● **GEESE** (*Tribe* Anserini) are large plump birds with long necks, short legs, and broad round-tipped bills. They feed on grains, grass sprouts, and some marine vegetation, and fly with deep, powerful wingbeats. Geese usually migrate in noisy flocks, in V-formation or in long undulating lines. Sexes look alike.

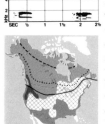

CANADA GOOSE *Bránta canadénsis*

The most common and best-known goose, identified by the black head and neck and broad white cheek. It breeds on lake shores and coastal marshes. Gathers in large flocks after the breeding season and grazes in open fields within commuting distance of water. Migrates by day and by night. There are at least ten recognized subspecies, which differ greatly in size and slightly in color. The characteristic honking is well known; the smaller races have a cackling call.

BRANT *Bránta bérnicla*

A small, locally common, dark goose with a short neck and lacking the white cheek of the Canada Goose. Note the sharp contrast between dark wings and light sides. White neck mark is lacking in the immature. Eastern birds are light-bellied. Western birds, formerly known as Black Brants, have black on breast and belly and more extensive white neck marking. Flight is rapid, usually low over the water, often in flocks strung out in a long line. Breeds in the Arctic; winters in coastal bays. Food is aquatic plants such as eel grass, taken by tipping. Once nearly extinct, it is now regaining its former numbers. Voice is a soft *rronk*.

Brant eastern race

BARNACLE GOOSE *Bránta leucópsis*

An Old World species, occurring casually along the East Coast in fall, generally in flocks with other geese. Recognized by entire white face. Immature is like adult. Nests in Greenland and arctic Europe, winters in Europe. Call is a series of rapid short barks.

Brant western race

EMPEROR GOOSE *Chén canágica*

A small gray goose, breeding along marshy shores in Alaska and wintering along the Alaskan coast. A few stragglers get as far south as coastal northern California. Note the adult's orange legs and the white tail and dark undertail coverts of both adult and immature. Call is a loud *kla-ga kla-ga kla-ga*.

GEESE 1

CANADA GOOSE
L 16-25″ W 50-68″

large race

small race

im.

BRANT
L 17″ W 46″

eastern race

eastern

im.

western

western race

EMPEROR GOOSE
L 18″ W 53″

BARNACLE GOOSE
L 18″ W 56″

im.

GREATER WHITE-FRONTED GOOSE   *Ánser álbifrons*
A common gray goose usually in large flocks on its main wintering grounds, but rare east of the Mississippi. This is our only goose with irregular black markings on light gray underparts, and the only one south of Alaska with orange or yellow legs. The adult's white face is a good close-up field mark. Immature is best told from immature Blue Goose by yellow bill, yellow legs, and call, a high, squealing *wah wah wah wah*, or *tu-lu*, *tu-lu*.

BEAN GOOSE   *Ánser fabális*
Rare spring visitor to western Aleutians. Resembles immature Greater White-fronted Goose, but heavier black bill with orange band near tip is diagnostic.

PINK-FOOTED GOOSE   *Ánser brachyrhýnchus*
Breeds in Greenland, migrating to Europe. Pink feet and pink area on otherwise black bill are diagnostic.

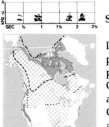

SNOW GOOSE (including **BLUE GOOSE**)
Chén caeruléscens
Locally abundant in large flocks. The adult white phase is pure white with black wing tips. Both the adult and the pale gray immature are very similar to the rare Ross' Goose, from which they may be told by the larger size and heavier bill. The blue phase is abundant in the eastern Great Plains, uncommon east of Mississippi River. The adult has the head, neck, and legs of the white phase and the dark body of the Greater White-fronted Goose. The immature is almost identical with the immature Greater White-fronted, but has gray-brown bill and legs. Hybrids between the color phases have a dark back, but are much lighter on the underparts. Call, a short, muffled *haw-haw, haw-haw*, suggests Tundra Swan's (p. 40).

white phase

ROSS' GOOSE   *Chén róssii*
The smallest and rarest North American goose. It breeds in the Arctic, winters almost exclusively in the Central Valley of California. It is very similar to the Snow Goose, with which it occurs, but it averages smaller. The short bill lacks the dark streak. At very close range, the adult's bill shows warty basal protuberances. The immature is paler gray than the immature Snow and the legs are pinker. There is a rare black form. The call is a weak *aw-aw*, rarely heard.

blue phase

GEESE 2

GREATER WHITE-FRONTED GOOSE
L 20″ W 60″

im.

BEAN GOOSE
L 21″ W 60″

PINK-FOOTED
GOOSE
L 19″ W 60″

blue phase

im.

SNOW
GOOSE
blue phase
L 19″ W 59″

Snow Goose

im.

SNOW
GOOSE
white phase
L 19″ W 59″

im.

ROSS' GOOSE
L 16″ W 51″

• **SURFACE-FEEDING DUCKS** (*Tribe* Anatini) are the common ducks that dabble and tip in the shallows of fresh- and salt-water marshes. Surface feeders are agile fliers that take off nearly vertically. Mostly do not dive, but young and molting adults will dive when in danger. Sexes have different plumages. Most species have a bright distinctive rectangle of color (the speculum) on the hind edge of each wing. In early summer the males assume a drab "eclipse" plumage; a second molt restores the colorful plumage by early fall. Though chiefly vegetarians, they eat some mollusks, insects, and small fish.

MALLARD
Ánas platyrhýnchos

This wide-ranging bird is the most abundant duck in the Mississippi Valley and is increasing in the East; it is common in ponds and fresh-water marshes. Male is told by its green head, white neck band, and rusty breast. Female is mottled brown. Both have a blue speculum, broadly bordered in front and back with white.

The Mexican race, *A. p. díazi*, formerly considered a separate species, used to be a shy, rare, and local resident in the upper Rio Grande Valley of New Mexico. It interbred so extensively with the nominate race that no pure *diazi* now exist north of Mexico. Very similar to female Mallard. Recognized in flight by its darker tail and, at close range, by unmarked yellow-green bill of male and dark ridge on upper mandible of female. Mallards often flock with Black Ducks. Voice, a loud quack.

AMERICAN BLACK DUCK
Ánas rúbripes

The most abundant surface-feeding duck on the Atlantic Coast; found in shallow coastal waters and in ponds. Note in all plumages the white wing linings that contrast with the dark body, and the violet-blue speculum with only a trace of a white border. The pale head shows more contrast to the dark body than in the female Mallard. Bill of male is not mottled. Voice same as Mallard's.

MOTTLED DUCK
Ánas fulvígula

Common resident in fresh and brackish marshes. Intermediate in plumage between the Black Duck and female Mallard, it has a distinct white border behind the speculum, but not in front. Also told from Mallard by darker tail, pale head, and yellower bill. In winter, Mallards and Black and Mottled Ducks use the same marshes. In Jan. Mottled Ducks are paired; Gulf Coast wintering Blacks and Mallards generally are not. Voice is like Mallard's.

SURFACE-FEEDING DUCKS 1

Mallard takeoff

landing

feeding

MALLARD
L 16" W 36"

♂

♀

♀

♂

♀

Mexican

Mexican race

♂

♀

AMERICAN BLACK DUCK
L 16" W 36"

♂

♀

MOTTLED DUCK
L 15"

♂

♀

NORTHERN PINTAIL $\acute{A}$*nas ac$\acute{u}$ta*

Abundant in West, common in East. Found on lakes, ponds, and bays, where it is seen in huge flocks except in the breeding season. Pintails are slim and very agile, with slender pointed wings. Note the male's sharp tail plumes, white underparts, and dark head. The female has a longer neck and a longer, more pointed tail than other mottled ducks. The speculum is metallic brown with a white rear border. Call is a short whistle.

WHITE-CHEEKED PINTAIL $\acute{A}$*nas baham$\acute{e}$nsis*

A straggler in the Southeast from the West Indies. Resembles female Northern Pintail but has white cheeks, and a mottled red bill. Sexes are similar.

GADWALL $\acute{A}$*nas str$\acute{e}$pera*

Uncommon. Seen most often with Common Pintail and wigeons, it rarely congregates in large flocks. Unlike other surface-feeding ducks, the Gadwall dives regularly. Note the male's plain head, dark bill, gray body, and dark tail coverts. The Black Duck (p. 46) is browner, with yellow bill. The female is lighter brown than the Black, and usually shows white in the wing when swimming. The speculum of both sexes is white with some brown and black, the feet are yellow. Call, very low and reedy.

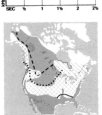

AMERICAN WIGEON $\acute{A}$*nas americ$\acute{a}$na*

A common duck, feeding largely on aquatic vegetation, occasionally coming ashore to eat shoots of grains and grasses. Recognized by large white patch on the forewing, most distinct in male. Except in the breeding season, wigeons congregate in large flocks. Unlike most ducks, they fly in tight flocks and not in long open V's. The male also shows a white crown and flanks and dark tail coverts. The female at rest is told from female Gadwall by pale gray head and bluish bill. Call is of 2 or 3 short whistles, the last one lower pitched.

EURASIAN WIGEON $\acute{A}$*nas pen$\acute{e}$lope*

This Old World duck is a regular visitor to the northern coasts of North America, though never in large numbers. Usually seen with the similar American Wigeon. Male Eurasian has rusty head and gray sides; American is opposite. Female is duller on the side and browner on the head than female American. In flight note darker axillars. Call is a high, descending whistle.

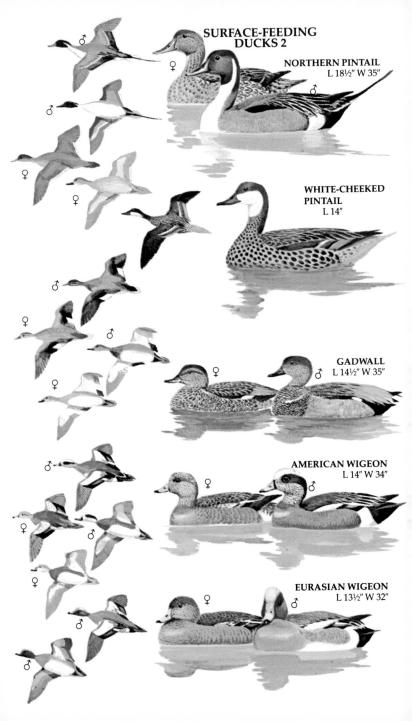

SURFACE-FEEDING DUCKS 2

NORTHERN PINTAIL
L 18½" W 35"

**WHITE-CHEEKED
PINTAIL**
L 14"

GADWALL
L 14½" W 35"

AMERICAN WIGEON
L 14" W 34"

EURASIAN WIGEON
L 13½" W 32"

NORTHERN SHOVELER
Ánas clypeáta

Abundant in the central and western part of its range; found mainly in shallow water. Identify both sexes by the flat head, long spatulate bill, and large blue wing patch. On the water it rides low in front, bill held downward. Quacks like a Mallard; also a low clucking.

BLUE-WINGED TEAL
Ánas díscors

A small, common, shy duck of ponds, marshes, and protected bays. Flies rapidly in small, tight flocks. Both sexes have a light blue area on the forward edge of the wing, and a green speculum. Male has white facial crescent. Male peeps; female quacks softly. Sonagram below.

CINNAMON TEAL
Ánas cyanóptera

Common in the West, in the same habitat as the Blue-winged Teal, which it resembles in behavior. Male is cinnamon red on head and underparts. Female is told from female Blue-winged by more Shoveler-like bill and more distinct facial markings. Voice is like Blue-winged's.

FALCATED TEAL
Ánas falcáta

Very rare visitor to Alaska. Male unmistakable. Female resembles female Gadwall, but speculum is dark green; in flight is like female Eurasian Wigeon (p. 48).

GARGANEY
Ánas querquédula

Very rare visitor to Alaska and East and West coasts. Notice male's conspicuous head stripe. Female resembles female Blue-winged Teal, but has much paler and less blue on wing.

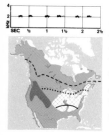

GREEN-WINGED TEAL
Ánas crécca

Common on small ponds and lakes, and also prefers fresh water in winter. Male is told by its dark head and the vertical white stripe on the side. Female resembles female Blue-winged, but has a smaller bill and lacks the large blue wing patches. It flies fast in small, tight flocks. Male of Old World races (rare visitors to both coasts) can be told by the white horizontal line above the wing and the more distinct head markings. Call, a short whistle.

BAIKAL TEAL
Ánas formósa

Casual visitor to Alaska. Note male's distinctive face pattern. Female is told from Green-winged Teal by distinct white patch at base of bill. Both sexes have a green speculum with a white border.

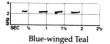

Blue-winged Teal

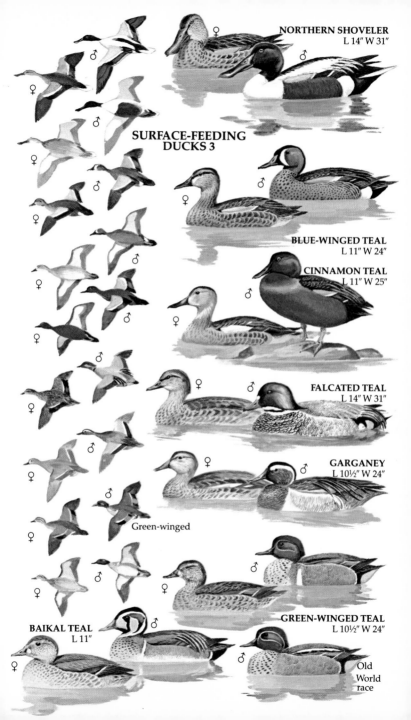

NORTHERN SHOVELER
L 14″ W 31″

SURFACE-FEEDING DUCKS 3

BLUE-WINGED TEAL
L 11″ W 24″

CINNAMON TEAL
L 11″ W 25″

FALCATED TEAL
L 14″ W 31″

GARGANEY
L 10½″ W 24″

Green-winged

GREEN-WINGED TEAL
L 10½″ W 24″

BAIKAL TEAL
L 11″

Old World race

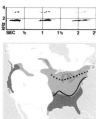

WOOD DUCK (*Tribe* Cairinini) *Aix spónsa*

This is a common duck of open woodland around lakes and along streams. The large head, the short neck, and the long square tail are good field marks. No other duck has the long slicked-back crest. The dull-colored female has a white eye ring. Males in eclipse plumage resemble the female, but have much white under the chin. Flight is rapid; Wood Ducks dodge agilely between the trees. They feed on plant materials, from duckweed to acorns (which are crushed in the gizzard), and some insects. Nesting is in natural tree cavities, but Wood Ducks also use nest boxes. The call is a distinctive rising whistle.

• **WHISTLING-DUCKS** (*Subfamily* Anserinae, *Tribe* Dendrocygnini), formerly called Tree Ducks, are not all arboreal. The sexes look alike. When these shy birds are alarmed, they raise their heads and look around, as geese do. Flight is strong, the wingbeats rather slow. In flight the feet project beyond the tail; head and feet droop down below the body line. In landing, they extend their head and feet downward until the bill nearly touches the ground. They are particularly fond of corn, but other seeds are eaten, as are acorns. Feeding is at night. Whistling-Ducks do not dive. Call, series of shrill whistles.

FULVOUS WHISTLING-DUCK *Dendrocýgna bícolor*

Rather common in marshlands within its range, also in rice fields and sometimes ponds. In all plumages has a deep tawny yellow head and underparts, with a dark back and wings. The bill is dark, almost black; legs and feet have a dull bluish tone. Use the white rump and white side markings as secondary field marks. The white streakings on the neck are not always visible. The bird is not often seen because of its nocturnal feeding habits. It rarely perches in trees and never nests in them.

BLACK-BELLIED WHISTLING-DUCK
Dendrocýgna autumnális

Rather common within its breeding range but only a straggler outside. It is found in much the same habitat as the Fulvous, though to a larger degree in wooded country. The best field marks are the black underparts and the large white areas on the wings. The bill is red, yellow, and blue, and the feet are pink. Female is duller. It frequently perches in trees and sometimes nests in holes in the trunk or in forks in the branches.

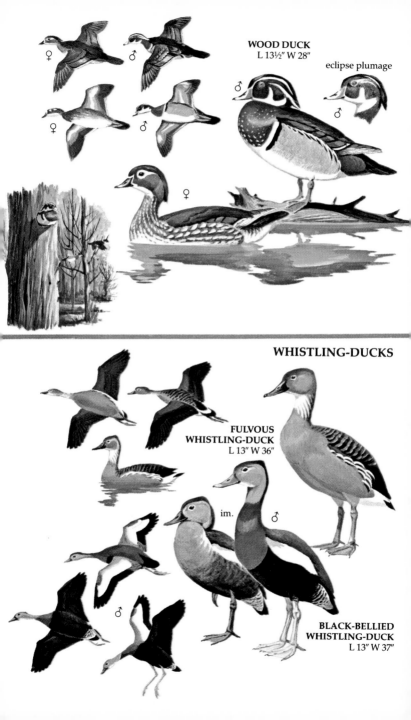

WOOD DUCK
L 13½″ W 28″

eclipse plumage

♀ ♂

♀ ♂

♂ ♂

♀

WHISTLING-DUCKS

**FULVOUS
WHISTLING-DUCK**
L 13″ W 36″

im. ♂

♂

**BLACK-BELLIED
WHISTLING-DUCK**
L 13″ W 37″

54

● **BAY DUCKS** (*Subfamily* Anatinae, *Tribe* Aythyini) commonly winter in protected coastal bays and river mouths. They dive from the surface, swim under water, and eat more animal food than surface-feeding ducks. They run along the surface to take off. Calls are short low croaks.

REDHEAD   *Aýthya americána*
This common duck summers on ponds and lakes and winters in tidewater, often mixing with other bay ducks. The male has a large round head, light bill, dark breast, and white underparts. The female's rounded head, plain bluish bill, and lack of conspicuous eye ring and white face patch distinguish it from the Ring-necked Duck and scaups. The **Common Pochard** (*Aýthya ferína*, L 13″) is a very rare visitor to Alaska. Closely resembles Redhead, but male has lighter gray back and sides, and head shape and bill suggest Canvasback.

CANVASBACK   *Aýthya valisinéria*
This locally abundant duck winters more in saltier waters than does the Redhead. It mixes less with other bay ducks, though it is often found near them. Both sexes resemble the Redhead, but are noticeably lighter-backed and larger, and have a distinctly flattened head profile.

RING-NECKED DUCK   *Aýthya colláris*
Common in woodland ponds. In winter more confined to fresh water than other bay ducks. The vertical white stripe on the side and solid black back are best field marks of the male. Female can be told by its distinct narrow white eye ring, ringed bill, and broad gray wing stripe. The **Tufted Duck** (*Aýthya fulígula*, L 12″), casual on northern coasts, lacks vertical stripe on side, has white wing stripes; female lacks distinctive facial markings.

GREATER SCAUP   *Aýthya maríla*
Locally common, usually in salt water. Long white wing stripe and rounded head help distinguish both sexes from Lesser Scaup. Head color of males not reliable but Greater shows contrast in shade between neck and breast. Female scaups are told by the white face. Call, *scaup*.

LESSER SCAUP   *Aýthya affínis*
Abundant, especially inland. White wing stripe is shorter than in Greater Scaup. At very close range the smaller "nail" with narrow black area at the tip of the shorter and flatter bill is diagnostic.

BAY DUCKS

REDHEAD
L 14½″ W 33″

CANVASBACK
L 15″ W 34″

TUFTED DUCK
head
L 12″

RING-NECKED DUCK
L 12″ W 28″

GREATER SCAUP
L 13″ W 31″

Greater Scaup

Lesser Scaup

LESSER SCAUP
L 12″ W 29″

● **SEA DUCKS** (*Tribe* Mergini, part) are heavy, rather large, short-necked diving ducks typically seen along coasts. In winter they often occur in large flocks, frequently of mixed species. Most live on mollusks.

COMMON GOLDENEYE *Bucéphala clángula*
Common in lakes and rivers in forested country, where it nests in cavities or even nest boxes. Winters along the coast and on lakes and rivers. Note the round dark head, puffy crest, wing patch, and loud musical whistling of the wings. The male has a round white facial spot, the female a white collar. Usually goldeneyes are in pairs or small flocks. Flight is very fast. When feeding, they prefer deeper water than the bay ducks. Call suggests Common Nighthawk's (p. 182).

BARROW'S GOLDENEYE *Bucéphala islándica*
Rather common in the West; winters on coasts and rivers. Male is told from Common Goldeneye by white facial crescent, purple head, and blacker sides. The crest tends to be more flattened and pointed to the rear. Female has less white on wing than Common, darker head, abrupt forehead; and in spring and early summer the short bill may be entirely yellow, not black with a yellow tip. Eats crustaceans. Wings produce loud whining sound.

BUFFLEHEAD *Bucéphala albéola*
Summers on wooded lakes and rivers; common in winter in tidewater, generally in loose flocks. Unlike other diving ducks, it takes off without running along the water surface. The male is distinguished by the large white patch on its puffy greenish head. Small white cheek patch of the female also is diagnostic. In flight it is told from goldeneyes by whiter head (male), the small wing patch (female), and the lack of wing whistle.

HARLEQUIN DUCK *Histriónicus histriónicus*
Uncommon and shy. Summers on swift rivers and along arctic shores. Winters in the heavy surf along rocky coasts. Male is recognized by its dark and light pattern (appears dark at a distance), small size, and long tail. Female is smaller and darker than goldeneyes, lacks the white wing patch in flight, and has distinct head spots. Seldom found with other ducks, though occasionally with scoters (p. 60). Harlequin often swims with its long tail tilted upward or slowly raises and lowers it.

winter
♀

COMMON GOLDENEYE
L 13″ W 31″

♀ winter

BARROW'S GOLDENEYE
L 13″ W 31″

♀ Common ♂

♀ Barrow's ♂

BUFFLEHEAD
L 10″ W 24″

♀ ♂

♀ ♂

Bufflehead

courtship display

SEA DUCKS

HARLEQUIN DUCK
L 12″ W 26″

♂

♀

♀ ♂

♀ ♂

COMMON EIDER
Somatéria mollíssima

Abundant, but winters so locally in huge rafts (off Chatham, Massachusetts, and in Alaska) that it is rare at other coastal locations. At close range the female and immature male can be told from other eiders by the sloping profile and by the long slender frontal shield, which extends much farther up the forehead than in the other eiders (twice as far above nostril as in King Eider). Male in first winter is intermediate between female and first spring plumage shown. The wingbeats are rather slow and deliberate, and it flies with the head held low. Flocks fly in lines a few feet over the surface. Call is a low, slurred moan.

KING EIDER
Somatéria spectábilis

Rare in U.S. but common in the Far North. The King Eider behaves very much like the Common Eider, with which it often occurs. The black back, white foreparts, and heavily shielded bill are good field marks for the male. The large white wing patches are unlike those of any other sea duck. The female is told from scoters (p. 60) by its uniform head coloration and stocky build, from Common Eider by the bill profile (see bottom of p. 59) and richer brown plumage. Not so strictly confined to salt water. Immatures migrate farther south than adults.

SPECTACLED EIDER
Somatéria físcheri

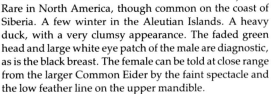

Rare in North America, though common on the coast of Siberia. A few winter in the Aleutian Islands. A heavy duck, with a very clumsy appearance. The faded green head and large white eye patch of the male are diagnostic, as is the black breast. The female can be told at close range from the larger Common Eider by the faint spectacle and the low feather line on the upper mandible.

STELLER'S EIDER
Polystícta stélleri

This small Asiatic eider is uncommon where it occurs along the Alaskan coast. Its shape is like Mallard's (p. 46), but bill is stubbier and tail longer. Black collar of male continues down back as a dark line. The female is a uniform dark brown except for a blue speculum bordered with white as in the Mallard (p. 46). Both sexes have a tiny rounded crest. Their wings whistle in flight like goldeneyes'. Unlike other eiders, male helps rear the young.

EIDERS

♀ ♂ ♂ 1st spring

♂ ♀ ♂

COMMON EIDER
L 17″ W 41″

♂ 1st spring

♂ ♀ ♂

KING EIDER
L 16″ W 37″

♂

♂

♀ ♂

SPECTACLED EIDER
L 15″ W 36″

♂

♂

♂

♀ ♂

STELLER'S EIDER
L 12″ W 29″

Steller's
♀

Common

King

Common Eider

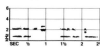

OLDSQUAW
Clángula hyemális

Abundant within its range. Summers on tundra lakes. Winters in loose flocks in deep lakes, along coasts, and often far out to sea. It is the only duck with distinctly different breeding and winter plumages, and the only diving duck that is dark in front and white behind at the water line. The distinctive needle-like tail plumes of the male are shared only by the Northern Pintail (p. 48), which has no white on the face or black on the breast. In flight the Oldsquaw, quite short and stocky, is the only white-headed duck with all-dark wings. Its flight is fast and it migrates chiefly at night. A very vocal duck, it is often noticed by its yodel-like whistle before it is seen.

BLACK SCOTER
Melanítta nígra

The least common scoter in most areas, but locally abundant on its Alaskan breeding grounds and along the coast in winter. The male is our only all-black duck. (Other scoters may appear all black at a distance.) Note the plump, short-necked scoter body and the prominent yellow protuberance on its black bill. Bills of other male scoters are orange. In good light the dark cap and gray face of the female may be seen. The female may have some yellow around the nostril. Wing linings of both sexes flash silvery in flight. Legs and feet are black (orange or pink in other scoters).

WHITE-WINGED SCOTER
Melanítta fúsca

Often abundant. Found in mixed flocks with other scoters. This largest scoter is the one most likely to be found inland. The male has a dark protuberance on the bill, which is otherwise orange. In both sexes the best field mark is the contrast between dark body and white wing patch (not always visible when swimming). In good light female lacks contrasting dark crown of the other scoters. Rides on the water in tight flocks; flies in loose flocks over short distances, in long lines when migrating.

SURF SCOTER
Melanítta perspicilláta

In many places the most common scoter. The male has a long, thick-based, multicolored bill and prominent white markings on nape and forehead. The female is told from the Black Scoter by the two white cheek spots and from the White-winged by lack of wing patches. The agile Surf seldom flies in line formation.

OLDSQUAW, SCOTERS

summer

winter

OLDSQUAW
L 15″ W 30″

♀ ♂ ♀ ♂ ♂ ♀ ♀

BLACK SCOTER
L 14″ W 33″

♂ ♀ ♀ ♂

WHITE-WINGED SCOTER
L 16″ W 38″

ad. ♀ ♂ im. ♀ ♂

SURF SCOTER
L 14″ W 33″

im. ♀ ♂ ad. ♀ ♂

scoters at sea

• **MERGANSERS** (*Tribe* Mergini, part) are fish-eating diving ducks with a long thin bill serrated on the sides. Flight is rapid, with the body held very straight and horizontal. All have a white wing patch.

SMEW   *Mergéllus albéllus*
Very rare winter visitor to northern coasts. Associates with other diving ducks in lakes and sheltered bays.

HOODED MERGANSER   *Lophódytes cucullátus*
Uncommon; in wooded lakes and streams. Male's dark sides and black-bordered white cockade tell it from the Bufflehead (p. 56). Note female's bushy crest, dark face and body, and merganser bill. Call is low and toneless.

RED-BREASTED MERGANSER   *Mérgus serrátor*
Common, especially along seacoasts in winter. Both sexes have the shaggy crest. The male is told by the reddish-brown chest patch. Females, which have more crest than female Common Merganser, lack contrast between head and throat. Call, low, short quacks.

COMMON MERGANSER   *Mérgus mergánser*
A large, common, fresh-water species, seldom found in salt water. Longer and slimmer than goldeneyes (p. 56), and the male is whiter behind. The male's green head, which seldom appears crested, often looks black. The female has more of a crest; the distinct white throat and sharp contrast between neck and breast distinguish it from the female Red-breasted. Call, low, short quacks.

• **STIFF-TAILED DUCKS** (*Tribe* Oxyurini) are small and stubby, with a short thick neck. In swimming the tail is often held up at a jaunty angle. They dive and sometimes sink slowly, as grebes do.

RUDDY DUCK   *Oxyúra jamaicénsis*
Common in summer on lakes and ponds with floating vegetation, in winter on estuaries, lakes, and rivers. Wings are short and rounded; flight fast, uneven, with rapid wingbeats. Identified by white cheeks under the dark cap and by the long uptilted tail. Usually silent.

MASKED DUCK   *Oxyúra domínica*
A casual visitor to the southeastern U.S. from West Indies and Mexico. Largely in fresh water; nests in marshes. Note male's black face and large white wing patch. Recognize female by dark face lines, white wing patches.

MERGANSERS

SMEW
L 13" W 26"

♀

♂

♀

crest lowered

♀

♂

♂

HOODED MERGANSER
L 13" W 26"

♂

♀

♀

♀

RED-BREASTED MERGANSER
L 16" W 33"

♀

♀

♂

STIFF-TAILED DUCKS

COMMON MERGANSER
L 18" W 37"

winter

♂

♂

summer

♂

♀

♀

♀

RUDDY DUCK
L 11" W 23"

courtship display

♀

♂

♂

♀

MASKED DUCK
L 10" W 20"

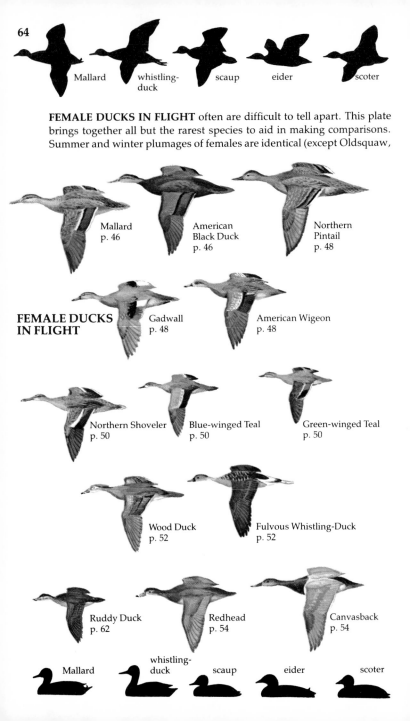

64

Mallard whistling-duck scaup eider scoter

FEMALE DUCKS IN FLIGHT often are difficult to tell apart. This plate brings together all but the rarest species to aid in making comparisons. Summer and winter plumages of females are identical (except Oldsquaw,

Mallard
p. 46

American
Black Duck
p. 46

Northern
Pintail
p. 48

**FEMALE DUCKS
IN FLIGHT**

Gadwall
p. 48

American Wigeon
p. 48

Northern Shoveler
p. 50

Blue-winged Teal
p. 50

Green-winged Teal
p. 50

Wood Duck
p. 52

Fulvous Whistling-Duck
p. 52

Ruddy Duck
p. 62

Redhead
p. 54

Canvasback
p. 54

Mallard whistling-duck scaup eider scoter

merganser   Ruddy Duck   loon   coot   alcid

p. 60). Immatures usually are similar in plumage to females. Different species often flock together. Note the wing pattern, the most important field mark.

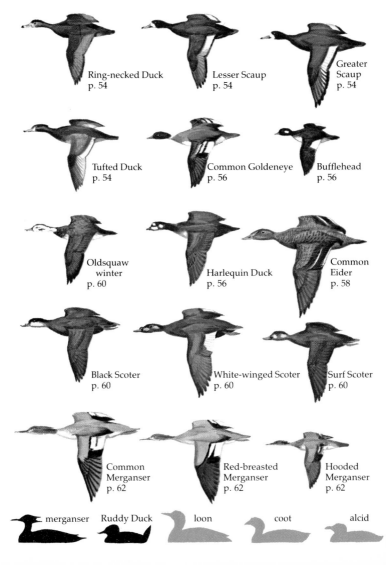

Ring-necked Duck
p. 54

Lesser Scaup
p. 54

Greater Scaup
p. 54

Tufted Duck
p. 54

Common Goldeneye
p. 56

Bufflehead
p. 56

Oldsquaw
winter
p. 60

Harlequin Duck
p. 56

Common Eider
p. 58

Black Scoter
p. 60

White-winged Scoter
p. 60

Surf Scoter
p. 60

Common Merganser
p. 62

Red-breasted Merganser
p. 62

Hooded Merganser
p. 62

merganser   Ruddy Duck   loon   coot   alcid

■ **VULTURES, HAWKS, AND FALCONS** (*Order* Falconiformes) are diurnal flesh eaters. Most have a heavy, sharp, hooked bill, and strong, curved talons, and take live prey; some are scavengers. Sexes are usually alike, females larger than males. Immatures differ from adults. There is much individual variation, and several species have dark forms.

FAMILIES OF VULTURES, HAWKS, AND FALCONS

Vultures (Cathartidae) Large, blackish, broad-winged birds with a naked head, usually scavengers. Generally silent. Eggs, 1-3.   p.66

Kites, Hawks, Eagles, and Ospreys (Accipitridae) Subdivided into:

Kites: southern birds with pointed wings (rounded in Hook-billed and Snail Kites); food is insects, snails, snakes. Eggs, 1-5.   p.68

Accipiters: medium to small bird hawks; strong fliers with comparatively short rounded wings, long tail. Eggs, 3-5.   p. 70

Harriers: mouse hawks with long wings and tail. Eggs, 4-6.   p. 70

Buteos and Eagles: medium-sized to very large soaring hawks with broad wings and a fairly short tail. Eggs, 1-5.   pp. 72-78

Ospreys: Long-winged hawks with conspicuous crook at wrist. Hover, then dive for fish. Eggs, 4-6.   p. 78

Caracaras and Falcons (Falconidae) Subdivided into:

Caracaras: long-legged scavengers. Eggs, 2-4.   p. 78

Falcons: strong, fast fliers with pointed wings, long slender tail; eat birds, mammals, insects. Eggs, 3-6.   p. 80

TURKEY VULTURE   *Cathártes áura*

A common carrion eater, scavenging in fields and along roadsides. Soars in wide circles, holding its two-toned wings in a broad V and tilting quickly from side to side. Immature has a black head. Feeding vultures are soon joined by others flying in from beyond human vision.

BLACK VULTURE   *Córagyps atrátus*

Common on southern farms and ranch lands. Recognized at a great distance by its short-tailed, longer-necked silhouette, horizontal wing position, and relatively weak, heavy flight, an alternation of laborious, deep flapping and short glides. White patches near wing tips are distinctive. This carrion eater often invades settlements to feed on garbage and small animals.

CALIFORNIA CONDOR   *Gýmnogyps califirniánus*

Almost extinct; limited to small area in mountains of southern California. Immature lacks the striking underwing pattern, but shares the massive beak and very stable soaring flight on long wide wings held in a straight line.

vulture buteo gull kite falcon accipiter pigeon

VULTURES

im.

TURKEY VULTURE
L 25″ W 72″

flight profile

BLACK VULTURE
L 22″ W 54″

flight profile

CALIFORNIA CONDOR
L 45″ W 120″

im.

flight profile

- **KITES** are medium-sized hawk-like birds. All are graceful on the wing, capable of swift flight and effortless soaring; hover while hunting. They do not dive (stoop), as do other hawks, but slip downward, feet first, to seize their prey before swooping (kiting) upward.

BLACK-SHOULDERED KITE
Elánus caerúleus

Rare but increasing; in open country, grasslands, and marshes. Adult is told by the long white tail and black wing patch, the immature by the long white tail and pointed wings. Adult plumage is acquired during first winter. In flight wings are held with tips downward, gull fashion. Often hovers. Eats rodents and insects.

MISSISSIPPI KITE
Ictínia mississippiénsis

Uncommon but increasing; in brushlands and open woods near water. Adults recognized by plain gray underparts and pale head; immature by its graceful, almost swallow-like flight and notched black tail (barred below). Often seen in flocks when feeding or migrating. Eats insects caught in the air and on the ground.

SWALLOW-TAILED KITE
Elanoídes forficátus

Fairly common in swamps, marshes, riverbanks, and open forests. This most graceful of all North American hawks is told in all plumages by the striking black and white pattern and swallow tail. Immature is like adult, but speckled. Somewhat gregarious. In hunting, drifts along slowly just a few feet above treetops or low over the ground with outstretched wings and tail in constant balancing motion. Often feeds in flight.

HOOK-BILLED KITE
Chondrohíerax uncinátus

Very rare south Texas breeder. Male is dark gray with gray-barred underparts, female dark brown, rufous-barred below. Note the long oval wings, prominently barred beneath, and long barred tail. (Not illustrated.)

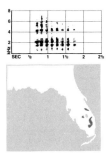

SNAIL KITE
Rostrhámus sociábilis

A South American species. A very rare but tame resident at Lake Okeechobee and Loxahatchee Refuge, Florida. Tail of male is distinctive. Easily told from Northern Harrier (p. 70) by broad wings, dark body, and by white on tail, not just rump. Flight is floppy, not kite-like. Feeds solely on a fresh-water snail (*Pomacea*), which it removes from shell with its long hooked beak. Nests, usually in loose colonies, are a few feet above water.

KITES

BLACK-SHOULDERED KITE
L 14½″ W 40″

im.

im.

im.

im.

MISSISSIPPI KITE
L 12½″ W 36″

SWALLOW-TAILED KITE
L 21″ W 50″

♂

♀

♂

SNAIL KITE
L 15″ W 44″

♀

- **ACCIPITERS** feed mainly on birds and small mammals. These long-tailed hunters with short rounded wings fly rapidly with short wing-beats interrupted by glides. Females are much larger than males.

NORTHERN GOSHAWK   *Accípiter gentílis*
An uncommon to rare hawk of northern forests, large enough to prey on grouse and squirrels. Recognized by its size (larger than crow), its gray or blue-gray underparts, and in all plumages the broad white eye stripe. Note also the white fluffy undertail coverts often present. Tail is less rounded than in Cooper's Hawk. Call, a long series of short high *kak*s.

COOPER'S HAWK   *Accípiter coóperii*
Uncommon; in open woodlands and wood margins. Best told from Sharp-shinned Hawk by comparatively rounded tail, large head, white terminal tailband, and slower wingbeat. As in other accipiters, the immature shows rich brown streaking. A very fast and powerful hawk. Call, a series of 15-20 *kak*s. Sonagram below.

SHARP-SHINNED HAWK   *Accípiter striátus*
Fairly common over most of North America in open woodlands and wood margins. The tail is narrower and more square-cut than Cooper's; sometimes even notched. This smallest accipiter preys on small birds up to the size of pigeons. Like other accipiters, it migrates during all daylight hours; flies just above treetops in early morning, often soars high at midday. In the East greatly outnumbers Cooper's during migration. Call like Cooper's, but shriller, with quality of American Kestrel's (p. 80).

- **HARRIERS** are slim with long rounded wings and long tails. In hunting they glide swiftly a few feet above the ground, holding their wings above the horizontal. Sexes differ greatly in color.

NORTHERN HARRIER   *Círcus cyáneus*
A slim common hawk of grasslands and marshes; feeds largely on rodents. The white rump is prominent. Shares hunting grounds with Rough-legged Hawk (p. 72), which is much heavier and shorter-tailed. In gliding, the wings, long and narrow, but not as pointed as a falcon's, are held above the horizontal. Flies a few feet above the ground, tilting from side to side. Migrating birds fly high, often soar. Typical call, about 10 short, sharp whistles.

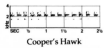

Cooper's Hawk

ACCIPITERS

NORTHERN GOSHAWK
L 19" W 42"

♂

im. ♀

im. ♀

♂

im. ♀

♂

COOPER'S HAWK
L 15½" W 28"

♀

im. ♀

♀

im. ♀

♂

im. ♀

SHARP-SHINNED HAWK
L 10½" W 21"

HARRIER

NORTHERN HARRIER
L 16½" W 42"

♀

♂

♀

♂

hovering

● **BUTEOS,** the largest subfamily of the Accipitridae, are the soaring hawks, which circle overhead and drop upon their prey in a steep dive. Broad rounded wings, a robust body, and a broad fanned tail distinguish them. Usually lone hunters, but two species migrate in flocks. In migration they tend to follow mountain ridges and shorelines.

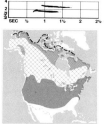

ROUGH-LEGGED HAWK *Búteo lagópus*

An uncommon open-country bird living almost entirely on rodents. The broad dark band on the white tail, black at the bend of the wing, and the black belly are the best field marks. There are two color phases and much individual variation. Some adults have only brown barring on the belly. Tail and wings are longer than in other buteos except the Ferruginous Hawk. Often hovers. Call, a thin whistle usually slurred downward.

FERRUGINOUS HAWK *Búteo regális*

Uncommon hawk of the Great Plains; feeds entirely on rodents. Note V of dark legs against belly of light phase (this contrast is lacking in the immature). The head is usually light in contrast with the darker rusty back. The tail is always very light, and unbanded except for subterminal mottling on the immature. The primaries are light and black-tipped. The dark phase is rare. Hovers. Call is similar to Rough-legged's.

RED-TAILED HAWK *Búteo jamaicénsis*

A well-known and common buteo; nests in woodlands, feeds in open country. The uniformly colored tail of the adult—reddish above, light pink beneath—and the dark belly band are the best field marks. The tail of the immature is finely barred. Body is heavier than other buteos', plumage extremely variable. Flying head-on, light wrist area gives impression of a pair of "headlights." Often perches on poles or treetops, rarely hovers. Harlan's race, recently merged with Red-tailed, is an uncommon buteo of the plains and one of the most difficult hawks to identify. In all plumages it strongly resembles typical Red-tailed, but the tail is mottled dark on white, with a terminal band—never barred. The primaries, always black-tipped, are finely barred, unlike those of Rough-legged and Ferruginous Hawks. Two color phases interbreed, and the offspring show a mingling of characteristics. Some western birds resemble Harlan's, but lack the dark terminal tailband. Red-tailed Hawks prey on rabbits and rodents. Call is a high scream, often imitated by jays.

Harlan's race

BUTEOS 1

hovering

dark phase

light phase

ROUGH-LEGGED HAWK
L 19" W 52"

flight profile

light phase

dark phase

FERRUGINOUS HAWK
L 20" W 54"

light phase

dark phase

RED-TAILED HAWK
L 18" W 48"

im.

Harlan's race

dark phase

light phase

dark phase

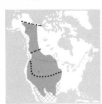

SWAINSON'S HAWK
Búteo swaínsoni

A dark-breasted western hawk; especially common on the plains. The head, back, primaries, and chest are dark, contrasting in the adult light phase with the light belly. Note the heavy terminal band on the long, finely barred tail. The rare dark phase appears all black except for the face, the underwing coverts, and the banded tail. Glides with rather pointed wings slightly uptilted; migrates in flocks, forming "kettles." Feeds largely on gophers and rats. Usually perches near ground. Call is a thin whistle usually slurred downward.

BROAD-WINGED HAWK
Búteo platýpterus

A woodland species, common and rather tame. Adult is easily recognized by the broad–barred tail. Immature, with characteristic buteo shape, has white underwing surface contrasting with black tips on primaries. It lacks the belly band of the much larger Red-tailed Hawk (p. 72). Shape in flight is like Red-tail's. Head-on, light cere suggests single, central "headlight." The Broad-wing hunts from a perch, flashing into action upon appearance of a large insect, mouse, or small reptile. It characteristically migrates in large flocks, forming "kettles." Call is a thin whistle suggesting Eastern Wood-Pewee's (p. 216).

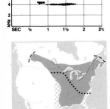

RED-SHOULDERED HAWK
Búteo lineátus

One of the most common hawks in the Southeast, breeding in moist woodlands, often close to cultivated fields. Note the reddish shoulder patches, uniformly colored underparts, translucent "windows" at the base of the primaries, and narrow white bands on the dark tail. Wings and tail are comparatively longer than those of Red-tailed or Broad-winged Hawks. Red-shoulders often hunt from a perch for rodents, insects, and small birds. Call often imitated by Blue Jay.

HARRIS' HAWK
Parabúteo unicínctus

A very dark Southwest buteo; common in mesquite brushland, less so in deserts. Slimmer and longer tailed than most buteos. Tail of adult is black with white on tip and base. Chestnut on shoulder and thigh is diagnostic. Immature resembles Red-shouldered immature, but tail has more white at tip and base. Gregarious. Preys on rodents, lizards, and small birds. Call is loud and rasping.

Red-shouldered

light phase

BUTEOS 2

SWAINSON'S HAWK
L 18″ W 49″

light phase

dark phase

Swainson's
Hawk
im.

**BROAD-WINGED
HAWK**
L 13″ W 33″

im.

**RED-SHOULDERED
HAWK**
L 16″ W 40″

im.

HARRIS' HAWK
L 18″ W 43″

im.

COMMON BLACK-HAWK   *Buteogállus anthracínus*
This black buteo is rare in U.S. In flight the dangling yellow legs, the two white bands on the tail, and the white base of the outer primaries identify the adult. Immatures are best identified by their buffy under-wings and wide-winged silhouette. The wings and tail are wide, even for a buteo. Flight is alternate flapping and gliding. From woodlands near water it hunts land crabs, toads, and crayfish, its commonest foods.

ZONE-TAILED HAWK   *Búteo albonotátus*
A black buteo of wooded canyons and rivers. Both adults and immatures seem to mimic Turkey Vulture (p. 66) in plumage and in habit of soaring, with wings frequently tilted in a V. The white tailbands of adult are often partly concealed. The wings are longer and slimmer than most buteos'. Flight is slow and sluggish. Eats small mammals, reptiles, and birds.

WHITE-TAILED HAWK   *Búteo albicaudátus*
A rather common hawk of the border, south to Argentina, in grasslands and the edge of the desert. The adult is told by light gray appearance and a very prominent black terminal band on the white tail. The immature is dark, almost eagle-like in color, with an unmarked grayish tail. The wings are held in a V when soaring, and the tail is short. Feeds on small animals.

SHORT-TAILED HAWK   *Búteo brachyúrus*
A small resident buteo of swamps and coastal areas, rare and local in the U.S. In both color phases the head and back are dark and the tail is black with three white bands. Short tail gives it chunky appearance. Buffy-breasted immature resembles immature Broad-winged Hawk (p. 74). Note pure white or jet black wing linings of adult. Feeds on lizards, snakes, and rodents.

GRAY HAWK   *Búteo nítidus*
A small gray buteo found mostly south of the Mexican border. Rare and local in U.S. in woods along streams. Flight is rapid and direct. The all-gray adult can be told from the White-tailed Hawk by the three wide black bands on the tail. Whitish rump is characteristic of both adult and immature. Lizards are its preferred food. Has a variety of loud, high, slurred calls.

SOUTHERN BUTEOS

im.

COMMON BLACK-HAWK
L 20″ W 48″

im.

ZONE-TAILED HAWK
L 19″ W 47″

im.

WHITE-TAILED HAWK
L 21″ W 48″

dark phase

light phase

SHORT-TAILED HAWK
L 14″ W 35″

im.

GRAY HAWK
L 15″ W 35″

im.

GOLDEN EAGLE *Áquila chrysáetos*

Uncommon (rare East) in remote mountains, tundra, grasslands, and deserts. The golden neck feathers are seen only at close range. The broad white tailband and white wing patches of the immature are good field marks. Note its buteo flight and large wing surface. Legs are feathered to the toes. Feeds mostly on rodents. Call, rapid sharp chips.

BALD EAGLE *Haliaéetus leucocéphalus*

Rare (locally more common) along shores. White head and tail make adult unmistakable. Immatures are brown, mottled irregularly with white until their fourth year. Bill is much heavier than Golden Eagle's, and legs are feathered halfway down the tarsus. Flies with deep strokes, soars on flattened wings. Note large head, short tail. Chief food is fish. Call is similar to Golden Eagle's, but softer. **White-tailed Eagle** (*Haliaéetus albicílla*, L 32"), all brown with white, wedge-shaped tail, nests in Greenland and western Aleutians. The immature resembles immature Bald Eagle, but has more wedge-shaped tail.

● **OSPREY** (fish hawk) occurs worldwide. Fish, the only prey, are taken at or just below the surface. The birds hover, often 50' to 150' high, then suddenly plunge, sometimes going completely under the water. Often nest on artificial platforms.

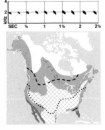

OSPREY *Pandíon haliáetus*

Uncommon; along seacoasts, lakes, and rivers. Conspicuous crook in long wings and black wrist mark confirm identification of adults and young at great distances. Plumage is dark above, white below. Except when migrating at a height, they flap more than they sail. Wingbeats are slow and deep. Wings are held in an arched position. Call, a series of loud, clear whistles.

● **CARACARAS AND FALCONS**, though dissimilar in looks and behavior, are closely related. Caracaras are tropical carrion eaters.

CRESTED CARACARA *Polybórus pláncus*

This uncommon and local long-legged scavenger of prairies and open scrublands spends much time on the ground. In flight the large head and beak, long neck, white throat, and long black-banded white tail set it apart from vultures, with which it associates. Call, a low rattle.

EAGLES

GOLDEN EAGLE
L 32″
W 78″

im.

ad.

flight profile

BALD EAGLE
L 32″ W 80″

im.

flight profile

OSPREY

OSPREY
L 22″ W 54″

flight profile

Bald Eagle
im.

Osprey

CRESTED CARACARA
L 21″ W 48″

Black Vulture
for comparison

Osprey fishing

CARACARA

im.

Crested
Caracara

Turkey Vulture
for comparison

● **FALCONS** are streamlined hawks with long pointed wings, large heads, and tails that narrow at the tip. They are rapid on the wing, with a direct, choppy, powerful flight, though they sometimes soar with the tail spread open.

GYRFALCON *Fálco rustícolus*
An arctic bird, rarely wandering south of Canada. White phase is mostly in Greenland, black in western Canada, and the more common gray phase in between. Preys on birds and rodents. Has a slow wingbeat and fast flight. Note the large size and pale facial markings.

PRAIRIE FALCON *Fálco mexicánus*
A light brown falcon of the plains, sometimes found in wooded areas. Black axillars (base of underwings) are diagnostic. Plumage is much paler than Peregrine Falcon's, head markings much less distinct. Flight is strong, rapid, and usually low. Call, a series of short loud notes.

PEREGRINE FALCON *Fálco peregrínus*
A rare local falcon of coasts, mountains, and woods. Being reintroduced in several areas. Best field-marks are facial pattern, dark cap, and large size. Flight is fast; only Prairie Falcon is swifter. Rarely soars. It preys almost entirely on birds. Call, a long series of slurred notes.

MERLIN *Fálco columbárius*
This uncommon small dark falcon of open areas is told by the absence of a black facial pattern and by prominently barred tail and long pointed wings. Flight is direct with steady wingbeats, often low over the ground; seldom soars. It often captures shorebirds, pigeons, mice, and insects. Call is a series of sharp *biks*. Sonagram below.

AMERICAN KESTREL *Fálco sparvérius*
The smallest and most common falcon in open and semi-open country. The only small falcon with two "whiskers" on each side of face and the only one with a rusty back. Hunts from poles, wires, or trees; frequently hovers. Eats insects primarily. Call, a sharp *killy killy killy*.

APLOMADO FALCON *Fálco femorális*
Rare; along the Mexican border. Tail is proportionately longer and wider than on most falcons. Note the distinctive white line below the black cap.

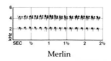

Merlin

FALCONS

black
phase
im.

white
phase

gray
phase

GYRFALCON
L 20″ W 48″

**PRAIRIE
FALCON**
L 16″ W 40″

Prairie Falcon

im.

♀

Peregrine
Falcon

♂

**PEREGRINE
FALCON**
L 15″ W 40″

♂

♀

♂

MERLIN
L 12″ W 23″

♂

♀

♀

♂

**AMERICAN
KESTREL**
L 8½″ W 21″

♂

Kestrel
hovering

ad.

im.

**APLOMADO
FALCON**
L 14″ W 35″

HAWKS IN FLIGHT are best studied at concentration spots during migration. In some places more than 1,000 buteos and accipiters can be seen in one day. Hawks tend to move along shores rather than cross large bodies of water. Concentrations may be seen along lake and ocean shores and along mountain ridges, where updrafts will aid their flight. Some good places to observe hawk migrations are:

Hawk Mountain, Kempton, Pa., all hawks	spring and fall
Great Lakes, south shores, all hawks	Mar. and Apr.
Great Lakes, north shores, all hawks	Sept. and Oct.
Cape May, N.J., accipiters, falcons, Osprey	Sept. and Oct.
Point Diablo, Marin Co., Calif., hawks, kites	Aug., Sept., Oct.

LONG-TAILED HAWKS

Gyrfalcon
p. 80

Northern Goshawk
p. 70

Peregrine Falcon
p. 80

Cooper's Hawk
p. 70

Prairie Falcon p. 80

Sharp-shinned Hawk
p. 70

Merlin
p. 80

Northern Harrier
p. 70

American Kestrel
p. 80

Mississippi Kite
p. 68

DARK BUTEOS

LIGHT BUTEOS

83

Rough-legged Hawk
p. 72

dark phase

Rough-legged
Hawk p. 72

light phase

Ferruginous Hawk
p. 72

dark phase

Ferruginous
Hawk p. 72

light phase

Red-tailed Hawk
p. 72

dark phase

Red-tailed
Hawk p. 72

light phase

Harlan's race
Red-tailed Hawk
p. 72

Red-
shouldered
Hawk p. 74

light phase

Swainson's Hawk
p. 74

dark phase

Swainson's
Hawk p. 74

Broad-winged
Hawk p. 74

84

■ **GALLINACEOUS BIRDS** (*Order* Galliformes) are heavy-bodied, chicken-like land birds. All have a short heavy bill with the upper mandible strongly decurved. The wings are short and rounded. Tails vary from short to very long. Legs are rather long. Their flight is not fast, but they can burst into full flight with rapid wingbeats from a sitting position. When flushed, seldom fly more than a few hundred feet. All are capable runners that forage on the ground for seeds and insects. Males of most species are more colorful than the females. Males of many species have elaborate courtship displays that include strutting, raising or spreading of specialized feathers on the head, neck, and tail, and the inflating of air sacs in the neck. Beating of the air with their wings or the release of air from the air sacs produces characteristic courtship sounds. They are mainly non-migratory.

FAMILIES AND SUBFAMILIES OF GALLINACEOUS BIRDS

Chachalacas and relatives (*Family* Cracidae) Large, long-legged, long-tailed, chicken-like woodland birds. Eggs, 3-4.   p. 84

Turkeys (*Family* Phasianidae, *Subfamily* Meleagridinae) Very large long-legged birds, long broad tail. Head bare. Eggs, 10-12.   p. 84

Grouse (*Subfamily* Tetraoninae) Medium-sized birds with moderate to long tail. Nostrils and feet covered with feathers. Courtship displays often elaborate. Ground dwellers. Eggs, 7-12.   pp. 86-88

Quails, Partridges, and Pheasants (*Subfamily* Phasianinae) Small to large birds of fields or open country. Quails, the smallest, are worldwide. Eggs, 6-16. Partridges, from Europe, are larger. Eggs, 8-16. Pheasants, from Asia, are largest. Eggs, 7-15.   pp. 90-92

WILD TURKEY   *Meleágris gallopávo*
Gone from most of its original range, it has been widely reintroduced and is fairly common locally in open woodland or forest clearings. Similar to the familiar barnyard turkey, but slimmer and with rusty, not white, tip to the tail. Turkeys roost in trees at night. They fly strongly for short distances, but prefer to avoid danger by running. Their food is acorns, fruit, and seeds. The male, or gobbler, calls (gobbles) in the early morning to summon the hens of his harem.

PLAIN CHACHALACA   *Órtalis vétula*
Locally abundant in woodlands and thickets, preferring clearings in heavy growth. This large, long-tailed, arboreal species is quite unlike any other U.S. bird. Note the plain olive back and iridescent green tail. The patch of dull pinkish skin on the side of the throat becomes red on the male in spring. Outer edge of tail is tipped with white. Sexes similar. Call is loud repetition of *chachalaca*.

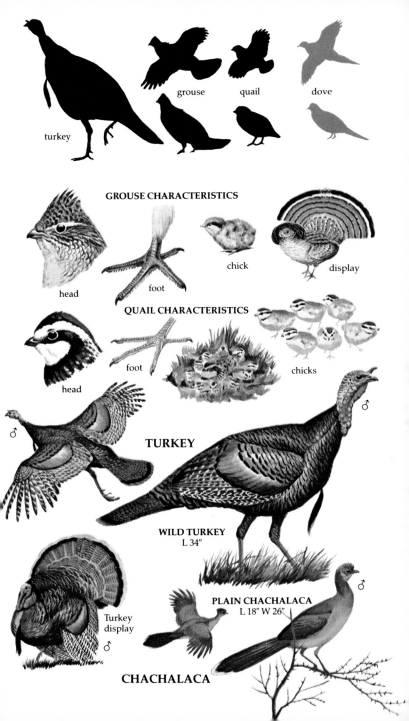

turkey

grouse

quail

dove

GROUSE CHARACTERISTICS

head

foot

chick

display

QUAIL CHARACTERISTICS

head

foot

chicks

♂

TURKEY

♂

WILD TURKEY
L 34″

Turkey
display

♂

PLAIN CHACHALACA
L 18″ W 26″

♂

CHACHALACA

BLUE GROUSE
Dendrágapus obscúrus

Common in deciduous woodlands in summer, in mountain thickets of fir in winter. The male is told by its plain gray plumage and the orange or yellow patch of skin above the eye. The female is a dark mottled brown; has a black tail with a pale gray terminal band. Birds in the northern Rockies lack the tailband. The male produces deep booming sounds from his inflated neck sacs, which are purple on interior birds and orange on coastal birds.

SPRUCE GROUSE
Dendrágapus canadénsis

A fairly common, very tame grouse of coniferous forests. The male is gray above, black below, with white spots on the sides. Bare skin above the eye is red. In the eastern race, the tail has a chestnut band. Western race has white spots on upper tail coverts. The mottled female is rustier than Blue Grouse, darker than Ruffed Grouse, with brown terminal band on blackish tail. Generally silent; hooting is extremely low-pitched.

RUFFED GROUSE
Bonása umbéllus

Usually fairly common, but the population is variable. A summer resident of clearings in open woods; winters in conifers. Two color phases occur, gray and red, differing mainly in the tones of the finely barred tail with its black terminal band. The male attracts females by a display pattern and by "drumming" the air with rapidly beating wings, producing an accelerating hollow roll.

SHARP-TAILED GROUSE
Tympanúchus phasianéllus

Locally common in prairies and brushland. Underparts are light. The narrow pointed tail is white-edged, distinguishing it in flight from female pheasant (p. 92) and prairie chicken (p. 88). The mottled body feathers produce an overall buffy appearance. During courting display male gives deep pigeon-like coos.

SAGE GROUSE
Centrocércus urophasiánus

Common in sagebrush country, summering in the foothills and wintering on the plains. Both sexes are recognized by their large size, black bellies, and long, pointed tails. Note also the white breast of the male and the black throat divided by a white band. Its principal food is sagebrush. During display male utters short, deep, bubbling notes. When flushed, often gives chicken-like clucking.

GROUSE

display

northern Rocky Mt. races

♂ Blue Grouse

♂ Spruce Grouse

♀

♂ display

♀ BLUE GROUSE
L 17″

♂

♀ SPRUCE GROUSE
L 13″

♂

gray phase ♂   red phase ♂

RUFFED GROUSE
L 14″

Sharp-tailed display

♂

♂ Sage Grouse

SHARP-TAILED GROUSE
L 15″

♂ display

♂

♀ SAGE GROUSE
L 22″

GREATER PRAIRIE-CHICKEN *Tympanúchus cúpido*

Uncommon and very local; in virgin grasslands and tall-grass prairies. May be told from other prairie birds by the short, rounded, blackish tail that contrasts with the brown body plumage. The males have long black tufts of feathers on the sides of the neck, and orange air sacs that are inflated during courtship. Female's tail is barred. Sharp-tailed Grouse (p. 86), which may occur in the same habitat, shows a pointed brown tail bordered with white. During display male makes a weird, deep, hollow sound.

LESSER PRAIRIE-CHICKEN
Tympanúchus pallidicínctus

Even less common than the Greater, and found more in arid regions, particularly short-grass prairie. It is smaller and paler, with reddish air sacs. Both species have court-ship, or booming, grounds where the males gather to display before the females. Courtship sound is higher in pitch than in the Greater Prairie-Chicken.

WILLOW PTARMIGAN *Lagópus lagópus*

Common in the Arctic but numbers vary greatly; winters in deep thickets or on windswept tundra not covered by snow. The summer male is more reddish than other ptar-migans. The female is similar in plumage to the smaller Rock Ptarmigan, but has a proportionately larger bill. Winter birds are all white, except for black tail, lacking the black lores of winter male Rock Ptarmigan. The principal food is willow leaves. Winters in small flocks.

ROCK PTARMIGAN *Lagópus mútus*

Common in mountain areas, usually above the tree line. In summer the male is lighter and more yellow than the larger Willow Ptarmigan, but females are virtually identi-cal except for size and bill. In winter both sexes are white, faintly tinged with pink; tail is black in both sexes, and the male has a black line through the eye. Found in pairs in the summer, in flocks in winter. Call, very low pitched and grating.

WHITE-TAILED PTARMIGAN *Lagópus leucúrus*

Locally common above timberline. Introduced in the High Sierra. This is the only ptarmigan with no black on the tail. Unwary in the wild, it runs from danger in pref-erence to flying. Its staple food is dwarf willow, although it also eats the needles of Alpine fir. Call is hen-like.

PRAIRIE-CHICKENS

GREATER PRAIRIE-CHICKEN L 14"

Sharp-tailed for comparison

Greater Prairie-Chicken

display ♂

LESSER PRAIRIE-CHICKEN L 13"

display ♂

PTARMIGANS

WILLOW PTARMIGAN L 13"

molting

summer ♀ ♂

winter

ROCK PTARMIGAN L 11"

molting

summer ♀ ♂ ♂

winter

WHITE-TAILED PTARMIGAN L 10"

molting

summer ♀ ♂

winter

SCALED QUAIL
Callipépla squamáta

Usually common, but population fluctuates from year to year. A bird of dry semi-desert country. Sexes are alike, gray-backed, scaled underneath, with a prominent cottony white crest that gives the birds a very pale appearance. Normally gregarious, usually found in flocks (of up to 100 birds). Seldom flies, preferring to run. Has a sharp, 2-syllable call.

CALIFORNIA QUAIL
Callipépla califórnica

Common in mixed woodlands and increasing in large city parks. Note the male's black face outlined in white, its bluish chest, and white marking on the gray flanks. Both sexes have scaling on the belly. The similar Gambel's Quail has a plain belly (with black spot in the male). Usually seen in flocks, feeding on the ground. Call of 3 slurred notes, the middle one highest and loudest, often given from low perch.

GAMBEL'S QUAIL
Callipépla gámbelii

This is a common quail of drier habitats than the California Quail, which it resembles. Ranges barely meet. Note the chestnut flanks, broadly streaked with white in both sexes. The black belly patch can also be used to separate the male from the California. The teardrop topknot, common to both species, distinguishes them from all other quails. Call is similar to California's.

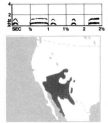

MOUNTAIN QUAIL
Oreórtyx píctus

This largest of North American quails is common in mountain regions in mixed woodlands and chaparral. The long, thin head plume is distinctive; the vertical white streaks on the flanks and the chestnut throat also are good field marks. Sexes are similar, but the female is duller than the male. Typically hard to flush. Call, a loud crowing note, or a soft *whook* like Northern Pygmy-Owl's (p. 180).

MONTEZUMA QUAIL
Cyrtónyx montezúmae

Rather common, but local on open woodland slopes under oaks or pines. The male is easily identified by the face pattern and the heavily spotted flanks. The dull brown female has enough traces of the male's face pattern to identify it. When approached, Montezuma Quail squats and hides rather than flying. Call is a gentle whistle, louder and more varied at dusk.

California Quail

WESTERN QUAILS

SCALED QUAIL L 8"

CALIFORNIA QUAIL L 8"

♂ ♀ ♂

GAMBEL'S QUAIL L 8½"

♂ ♂ ♀

MOUNTAIN QUAIL L 9"

MONTEZUMA QUAIL L 7"

♂ ♀ ♂

protective crouching

NORTHERN BOBWHITE *Colínus virginiánus*

Abundant in brush, abandoned fields, and open pine-lands, but avoids deep forests. A chunky reddish-brown quail with a gray tail. The male is identified by the white throat and eye line; in the female these areas are buffy. In winter found in flocks (coveys) of up to 30 birds. When disturbed, all burst into flight at once. Call is a whistled *bob-bob-white*, 4-6/min., sometimes given from a perch.

● **INTRODUCED GALLINACEOUS BIRDS** of many species have been released in the United States and Canada, but most have not become established. The four species below have succeeded in adapting to their new environment sufficiently to become common in several areas.

CHUKAR *Aléctoris chukár*

Locally common, this large European partridge prefers open, rocky, barren lands. Sexes are similar. Note cream-colored face with prominent black border. In flight (strong and direct), the reddish legs are visible. Eats grass shoots, seeds, grain, and insects. The male calls *chuck-ar*.

RING-NECKED PHEASANT *Phasiánus cólchicus*

Common in open woods and on farmland in brush, hedge-rows, and cornfields. Much larger than other gallinaceous birds except the turkey (p. 84). Both sexes have the long pointed tail and short rounded wings. Plumage variable, depending on origin of released stock. Female is told from the smaller Sharp-tailed Grouse (p. 86) by the much longer tail, large bill, and bare legs. Flight is strong, but only for short distances. Feeds mostly on waste grains, seeds, and berries. The loud, 2-syllable call is followed by a muffled rapid beating of wings.

GRAY PARTRIDGE *Pérdix pérdix*

Locally abundant on agricultural lands, especially those under irrigation. In flight the rusty tail is a good field mark. Larger than the Bobwhite, this partridge is much grayer, especially on the breast. Usually silent; call is a fast repetition of a 1-tone whistle.

BLACK FRANCOLIN *Francolínus francolínus*

Introduced in Calcasieu Parish, Louisiana. Male unmistakable. Female has prominent chestnut patch on nape. Call is a loud, grating, high-pitched *chik-chiree*.

BOBWHITE

NORTHERN BOBWHITE
L 8"

INTRODUCED GALLIFORMES

CHUKAR
L 10"

RING-NECKED PHEASANT
L 27"

BLACK FRANCOLIN
L 10"

GRAY PARTRIDGE
L 10"

HERONS AND THEIR ALLIES (*Order* Ciconiiformes) and **FLAMIN-GOS** (*Order* Phoenicopteriformes) are wading birds with long legs, neck, and bill. Most feed on aquatic animal life in shallow water. Some have long plumes, or aigrettes, in the breeding season. Wings are broad and rounded; tail is short. Eggs, 2-6.

FAMILIES OF HERON ALLIES AND FLAMINGOS

Herons and Bitterns (Ardeidàe) Bill straight. Flight slow, with head drawn back. Most nest in colonies. Calls, hoarse croaks.   pp. 94-98

Wood Stork (Ciconiidae) Bill heavy, decurved. Flight slow with neck outstretched. Head of adult bare.   p.100

Ibises and Spoonbills (Threskiornithidae) Bill thin and decurved or flat and spoon-shaped. East wingbeats, neck outstretched.   p.100

Flamingos (Phoenicopteridae) Legs and neck extremely long; bill stout, hooked. Flight ponderous, neck outstretched but drooping.   p.100

GREAT BLUE HERON   *Árdea heródias*
The Great Blue Heron's (p. 96) white phase is locally common in salt water in south Florida. Bill is yellow, legs yellowish. Does not flock.

GREAT EGRET   *Casmeródius álbus*
Common along streams, ponds, rice fields, salt- and fresh-water marshes, and mudflats. The plumage is white, bill yellow, legs and feet glossy black. White phase of Reddish Egret (p. 96) has flesh-colored, black-tipped bill and bluish legs. Larger than any other heron except the Great Blue. In flight, the Great Egret holds its neck in a more open S than do other white herons.

SNOWY EGRET   *Egrétta thúla*
Common, mostly in fresh- and salt-water marshes, but sometimes in ponds and rice fields. Plumage snow white, bill thin and black, with bare yellow skin at the base. Legs black, feet bright yellow in adult; legs and feet mostly pale green in immature. Immature Little Blue Heron (p. 96) has darker greenish legs and bluish bill. Snowy is slimmer and more active than other white herons. Flight is less abrupt than Cattle Egret's.

CATTLE EGRET   *Bubúlcus íbis*
An Old World species recently naturalized in North America; common and spreading. Seen in flocks in pastures, feeding on insects. The yellow or orange bill and the neck are shorter and thicker than in other herons. Note buffy-orange crest, breast, and shoulders in breeding plumage. Short legs are yellowish to pinkish in adults.

egret

ibis

Wood Stork

spoonbill

flamingo

WHITE HERONS

GREAT BLUE HERON
white phase
L 38" W 70"

Great Egret
open curve

Reddish Egret
for comparison

GREAT EGRET
L 32" W 55"

Snowy Egret
tight curve

white
phase

im. Little Blue
Heron for
comparison

SNOWY EGRET
L 20" W 38"

display

breeding

im.

CATTLE EGRET
L 17" W 37"

GREAT BLUE HERON
Árdea heródias

This largest North American heron is common on fresh as well as salt water. Head is largely white, underparts are dark. This pattern is reversed in the Louisiana Heron. When hunting, Great Blue Heron walks slowly through shallows or stands with head hunched on shoulders. A rare intermediate between this and the white phase (p. 94) occurs in Florida Bay. Called Würdemann's Heron, it is like a Great Blue but with a white head and neck. Alarm call of both is a series of about 4 hoarse squawks.

REDDISH EGRET
Egrétta ruféscens

An uncommon, dark heron of salt-water flats. Larger than the Louisiana Heron. The head and neck are quite shaggy. The bill usually is dark at the tip and flesh-colored at the base, a trait also distinguishing the rare white phase (p. 95). Very active when feeding—running, hopping, and flapping (canopy feeding) as it pursues fish.

LOUISIANA HERON
Egrétta trícolor

A common heron of salt-water shores. This dark heron with white underparts appears more slender-necked than other herons. An active feeder, though less so than the Reddish Egret. Often wades in deep water.

LITTLE BLUE HERON
Egrétta caerúlea

A common, small, dark heron of both fresh and salt water. Note the dark slaty-blue back and underparts, with a warm brown on the head and neck. The bill is bluish, with a black tip; the legs are bluish green. The Reddish Egret is larger, much paler, and thicker-necked. The more active Louisiana has white on the underparts and is not so stocky. The immature Little Blue is white with a dark-tipped bluish bill and greenish legs. Molting one-year birds (calico herons) are blotched blue and white.

GREEN HERON
Butorídes striátus

Common, locally abundant, in both fresh and salt water. Found more than other herons in small ponds and along wooded streams. Looks more blue than green. Told by its small size, dark underparts, and bright orange or yellow legs. Flight is rapid, with deep wingbeats. Appears all dark at a distance. The crest is not always visible. Neck is comparatively shorter than that of other herons. Call, a sharp, descending *kew*.

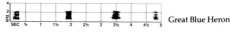

Great Blue Heron

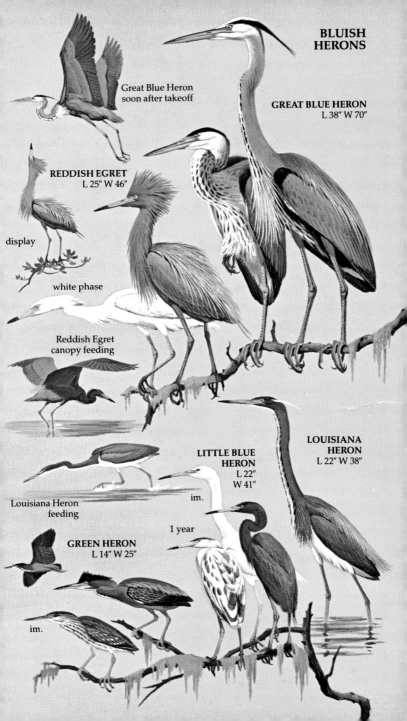

BLUISH HERONS

Great Blue Heron
soon after takeoff

GREAT BLUE HERON
L 38″ W 70″

REDDISH EGRET
L 25″ W 46″

display

white phase

Reddish Egret
canopy feeding

**LOUISIANA
HERON**
L 22″ W 38″

**LITTLE BLUE
HERON**
L 22″
W 41″

im.

Louisiana Heron
feeding

1 year

GREEN HERON
L 14″ W 25″

im.

98

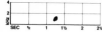

BLACK-CROWNED NIGHT-HERON
Nyctícorax nyctícorax

Night-herons are characterized by heavy bodies, short thick necks, and, in this species, short legs. A common heron of fresh-water swamps and tidal marshes. The adult is dark-backed and entirely white below. The Louisiana Heron (p. 96) has a white belly, but is a long slender bird. The heavily streaked immature can be confused only with the Yellow-crowned Night-Heron and American Bittern. Flies in loose flocks. Often inactive by day, roosting in trees. Fishes more at night. Call, a single *kwawk,* is most frequently heard at night.

YELLOW-CROWNED NIGHT-HERON
Nyctícorax violáceus

Much less common than the Black-crowned Night-Heron. Hunts at night, frequently also by day. Watch for distinct black and white face on otherwise gray adult. The immature is similar to immature Black-crowned, but has shorter, thicker bill, longer legs, and grayer plumage with smaller light spots on the back. In flight part of the tarsus extends beyond the tail. Call is slightly higher-pitched than Black-crowned's.

AMERICAN BITTERN
Botaúrus lentiginósus

Rather common but very elusive in the tall vegetation of fresh-water and brackish marshes. Most active at dusk and at night. Sometimes hides by freezing in position with head pointed upward. The best field mark for a sitting bird is the broad black whisker, which no other heron or bittern has. In flight the blackish flight feathers are diagnostic. Seldom calls when flushed. Does not flock. On the breeding ground it makes a hollow croaking or "pumping" sound, *oonck-a-tsoonck.*

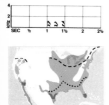

LEAST BITTERN
Ixobrýchus exílis

Common but very shy, usually remaining hidden in tall fresh-water grasses and sedges. This smallest heron is a weak flier. It will run or climb rather than take wing; seldom flies more than 100'. Both sexes have large wing patches of buff and chestnut that distinguish them immediately from dark-winged Green Heron (p. 96), which is a larger, chunkier bird. Hides by freezing. A rare dark phase is rich chestnut in color. Call, about 4 identical soft, low coos suggestive of Black-billed Cuckoo (p. 172).

NIGHT-HERONS

roosting

im.

BLACK-CROWNED NIGHT-HERON
L 20″ W 44″

Black-crowned Night-Heron

im.

ad.

YELLOW-CROWNED NIGHT-HERON
L 21″ W 44″

im.

Yellow-crowned Night-Heron

im.

bittern "freezing"

BITTERNS

im.

LEAST BITTERN
L 11″ W 17″

AMERICAN BITTERN
L 23″ W 45″

WOOD STORK
Myctéria americána

This only North American stork is locally common in southern swamps, marshes, and ponds. The bill is long and thick; adult's dark head is unfeathered. Immature has a paler head and neck; yellow bill. Flies with neck and legs extended; often soars. Wingbeats are slow, powerful, and audible. It feeds on fish, reptiles, and amphibians. Nests in colonies in trees. Call is of humming notes.

WHITE-FACED IBIS
Plégadis chihí

Uncommon. Breeds east to Mississippi. Told from Glossy Ibis, only in the breeding season, by the broad white line around the adult's eye and under chin. Immatures are identical to Glossy. Call of low quacks.

GLOSSY IBIS
Plégadis falcinéllus

Locally common. Feeds in small flocks in fresh or salt marshes. Adult is a uniform bronze-brown, appearing black at a distance. Immature resembles immature White Ibis but has a light neck and dark rump. The thin decurved bill, outstretched neck, rapid wingbeats, and alternately flapping and gliding flight distinguish it from herons. Flies in lines or V-formation.

WHITE IBIS
Eudócimus álbus

Locally abundant, but more confined to coastal locations than other ibises. Adult has red face and bill. The small black wing tips are usually hidden when at rest. Young birds show white rump when flying, and from below the dark neck contrasts with the white belly. Often seen in large flocks that fly in long lines or in V-formation. Calls are low and harsh grunts and growls. The **Scarlet Ibis** (*Eudócimus rúber*, L 22″ W 38″), perhaps just a red color phase, is a rare vagrant to southern Florida.

ROSEATE SPOONBILL
Ajáia ajája

Rare and local in shallow salt water. Bill, flattened at the tip, is unique. Adult is mostly pink; faint pink on immature intensifies with age. Flies with neck outstretched. Feeds on small marine life. Usually silent.

GREATER FLAMINGO
Phoenicópterus rúber

A rare straggler on mudflats of southern Florida; most are probably escapees. Neck and legs extremely long, bill thick and hooked, plumage from light pink to rose. Feeds on small marine life. Call, goose-like honks.

STORK, IBISES, SPOONBILL, AND FLAMINGO

WOOD STORK
L 35″ W 66″

im.

WHITE-FACED IBIS
L 19″ W 37″

GLOSSY IBIS
L 19″ W 37″

im.

Scarlet Ibis

WHITE IBIS
L 22″ W 38″

im.

GREATER FLAMINGO
L 42″ W 55″

½ scale

im.

ROSEATE SPOONBILL
L 28″ W 53″

■ **CRANES AND THEIR ALLIES** (*Order* Gruiformes) are a diversified group. All are wading birds with long legs, but other features such as size, body outline, bill shape, and neck length are variable.

FAMILIES OF CRANES AND THEIR ALLIES

Cranes (Gruidae) Tall, stately birds, with a heavy body and long legs. The long neck is extended in flight. Eggs, 2.   p.102

Limpkins (Aramidae) Medium-sized, with long legs and neck. Long, thin, slightly decurved bill. Eggs, 4 to 8.   p.102

Rails, Gallinules, and Coots (Rallidae) Rails and Gallinules: medium-sized to small, compact birds, with short neck, long legs, and long toes. Eggs, 6-15   pp. 104-106

Coots: duck-sized birds with lobed feet. The bill is short and thick. Eggs, about 12.   p.106

WHOOPING CRANE   *Grús americána*

Extremely rare; wild population totaled 78 in 1981. Breeds in northern bogs, winters in tidal coastal prairie. Note the adult's white head and body, bare red face and crown, and black primaries of all birds. Young are reddish-brown, lighter below. Black and white pattern of flying birds is more like that of Snow Goose (p. 44) than that of American White Pelican (p. 32) or Wood Stork (p. 100). Very long neck and white tail of Whooping Crane are diagnostic. Call, a vibrant trumpet note.

SANDHILL CRANE   *Grús canadénsis*

Locally common in prairies and fields, and occasionally in open pinelands and marshes. Both the gray adult and the brown immature can be recognized by their very large size and uniform coloration. Note the bare red cap of the adult. The flight is an alternation of gliding and flapping; the rapid upstroke of the wings is a good field mark. Often seen in large flocks except during the breeding season. Small rodents, frogs, and insects are its food. The voice is a low, loud, musical rattle.

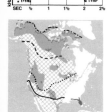

LIMPKIN   *Arámus guaraúna*

Locally common in wooded swamps; uncommon in marshes. The long slender bill, slightly decurved, will distinguish the Limpkin from the night-herons (p. 98). Each feather on the dark-brown body plumage has a large white crescent. The long neck is usually held erect and, like the cranes', is extended in flight. Active by day and night. Snails are its favorite food. Its call, a carrying *krr-oww*, is heard most often at night.

duck

coot

rail

ibis

egret

crane

rails and Limpkin in marsh

Whooping
Crane
dance

Purple Gallinule

coots take off

CRANES

SANDHILL CRANE
L 37″ W 80″

im.

im.

WHOOPING
CRANE
L 45″ W 90″

LIMPKIN
L 22″ W 42″

LIMPKIN

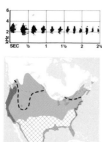

VIRGINIA RAIL
Rállus limícola

A common but elusive rail of fresh and brackish marshes. It is half the size of the King and Clapper Rails (p. 106), though similar in plumage except for the contrasting gray cheeks. Like other rails, it runs silently through the grass when pursued, seldom resorting to its weak, fluttering flight. When in the air on short flights its long legs dangle limply. The Virginia Rail is best identified by its metallic 2-syllable call, *kid-ick*, *kid-ick*, or *ticket-ticket*, or a descending Mallard-like series of quacks. It also has several less characteristic calls.

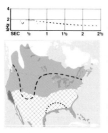

SORA
Porzána carolína

Most common of the rails, but seldom seen. It prefers fresh marshes, especially with dense vegetation, and rice fields. The best field mark is the short, sturdy chicken-like bill. The buffy immature lacks the black facial pattern of the adult, but is told from other small rails by the whitish undertail coverts. The Sora is easier to flush than other rails, but, like them, has a short weak flight. Call is a musical descending whinny or a whistled *ker-wee*.

CORN CRAKE
Créx créx

Accidental in fall on East Coast. A very rare European rail of hay and grain fields. Told by large rusty wing patch and buffy body. Rasping call is seldom heard.

YELLOW RAIL
Cotúrnicops noveboracénsis

A very small rail, rare and extremely shy. It inhabits fresh and salt marshes, also meadows and even grainfields. The yellowish plumage is interrupted by black striping on the back. The bill is small and yellow. In flight the best field mark is the white wing patch, but this bird can rarely be flushed. The voice, heard mostly at dusk, is clicking notes in alternating groups of 2 and 3, imitated by tapping two pebbles together.

BLACK RAIL
Laterállus jamaicénsis

This smallest rail is locally rather common, usually in salt marshes amid cordgrasses, rarely in fresh. The tiny size, the black coloration, and the white spots on the back identify it. The black bill of the adult is diagnostic. The chicks of all rails are black. Call, *kickee-doo*, the last note softer and much lower; heard late at night.

SMALL RAILS

VIRGINIA RAIL
L 7½" W 14"

im.

chick

SORA
L 6¾" W 12½"

im.

CORN CRAKE
L 9" W 20"

chick

im.

YELLOW RAIL
L 5½" W 11"

BLACK RAIL
L 4½" W 10"

chick

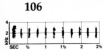

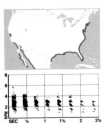

CLAPPER RAIL   *Rállus longiróstris*

An abundant, large, gray or gray-brown, salt-marsh rail, but local in the West. The neck is short, the bill long and slightly downturned. The very short tail is cocked upward. Immatures are dark above (see Virginia Rail, p. 104). Southern and western Clappers resemble King but are grayer at bend of wing and less strongly marked on belly. As in other rails, the body is compressed laterally. The voice is a series of loud unmusical ticks.

KING RAIL   *Rállus élegans*

This uncommon large rust-colored rail of fresh-water marshes occasionally occurs with the Clapper Rail in brackish marshes. Similar in plumage and habits but browner, and with stronger barring. The chicks are black with the entire bill pale white. Call is like Clapper's, but shorter and more musical and resonant.

COMMON MOORHEN   *Gallínula chlóropus*

Common in fresh-water marshes and along the edges of lakes. Its resemblance to ducks is countered by the bright red frontal plate of the head and the yellow-tipped chicken-like bill. Flanks are edged with white, wing is entirely dark. Feeds along edge of open water and, when disturbed, seeks cover in dense vegetation. Swims well and walks on lily pads. Call, hen-like clucks.

PURPLE GALLINULE   *Porphýrula martínica*

Less widespread and less common than the Common Moorhen, which it resembles closely in habits. The adult is unmistakable, with green back and purple head and underparts. The white plate on the front of the head marks this species. The immature is browner and paler than the immature Moorhen and lacks the white side stripe. Calls are similar to Common Moorhen's.

AMERICAN COOT   *Fúlica americána*

Common. In nesting season found on fresh water and in winter on both fresh and salt. The dark plumage contrasts with the stubby white bill and the white marking underneath the short tail. Feeds on shore, on the surface of the water or under it, diving with an upward jump before submerging. Swims buoyantly, nodding its head and paddling with its lobed toes. Flight is heavy, with trailing legs. Call, short rough croaks and cackles.

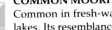

Common Moorhen

LARGE RAILS

CLAPPER RAIL
L 12″ W 20″

KING RAIL
L 14″ W 24″

GALLINULES

im.

COMMON MOORHEN
L 10½″ W 21″

im.

PURPLE GALLINULE
L 10½″ W 21″

chick

im.

AMERICAN COOT
L 12″ W 25″

■ **SHOREBIRDS, GULLS, AND ALCIDS** (*Order* Charadriiformes) form a diverse group of wading or swimming birds with seven families in North America. Most are white and gray or brown, with long pointed wings and long legs or webbed feet. Sexes are similar in most species. They are highly migratory. Most feed along shores, a few inland. Three of the five families of North American shorebirds (p. 109) are minor ones. Gulls (*Family* Laridae, *Subfamily* Larinae) and their relatives the terns (*Subfamily* Sterninae), skimmers (*Subfamily* Rynchopinae), and jaegers and skuas (*Subfamily* Stercorariinae) are short-legged, web-footed birds, more aquatic than all shorebirds except the phalaropes. The auks, murres, and puffins (*Family* Alcidae) are short-winged pelagic birds.

jaeger   gull   tern   alcid

BEHAVIOR OF SHOREBIRDS

Many of these birds, so varied in form and habits, have behavior traits that are characteristic either of shorebirds in general or of individual species.

1. Dowitcher probing in submerged sand or mud for worms and small mollusks.

2. Avocet skimming the surface of ponds for insects and their larvae.

3. Spotted Sandpiper tipping up tail. Often seen on rocks rather than sand.

4. Killdeer feigning wing injury to lead intruder away from its nest.

5. Oystercatchers bowing in courtship.

6. Willet showing wing stripe. Many shorebirds have a less conspicuous stripe.

7. Snipe "winnowing" in flight, making a whistling sound with its wings and tail.

8. Phalarope spinning in shallow water to stir up insect larvae.

9. Dunlin standing on one foot, a typical resting posture of shorebirds.

JACANAS (*Family* Jacanidae) are tropical birds with long legs and very long toes. They walk on lily pads, eat insect larvae. Eggs, 4.

OYSTERCATCHERS (*Family* Haematopodidae) are large chunky shorebirds with bright red bills and black heads. The long bill, which is compressed laterally, is used to open bivalves. Eggs, 2-3.

AVOCETS AND STILTS (*Family* Recurvirostridae) are medium-large slender-legged waders with long thin bills that are straight or curved upward. They feed on insects and small marine invertebrates. Eggs, usually 4.

PLOVERS AND LAPWINGS (*Family* Charadriidae) are small to medium-sized shorebirds, shorter-billed and shorter-necked than most sandpipers. The heads of most are strongly marked. Backs are plain or speckled. Food is small invertebrates. Eggs, 2-4.

SANDPIPERS AND PHALAROPES (*Family* Scolopacidae) are a large and varied group of shore and wading birds, some upland, some fresh-water; most seen along ocean shores on migration. Size ranges from 5" to 19". Plumage is mainly dull gray, buff, or brown, mottled or streaked. Many are identified by their tail, rump, and wing markings. Legs and bills are long and slender. Feed mainly on small invertebrates. Often seen in flocks. Sexes are similar except in the phalaropes, in which males are duller than females. Eggs, 3 to (usually) 4.

• **DARK-BACKED SHOREBIRDS** are grouped here for convenience because their plumage, silhouettes, and behavior are so different from those of other shorebirds. The heavy-bodied oystercatchers, the extremely long-legged avocet and stilt, and the long-toed jacana are in separate families; the round-winged, crested lapwing is a plover.

AMERICAN OYSTERCATCHER   *Haemátopus palliátus*
Uncommon but increasing; on coastal mudflats and sandy beaches, where it feeds on shellfish. Usually seen in very small flocks well apart from other shorebirds. Identified by its black and white plumage, large white wing stripe, and red bill. Call is a shrill, loud *kleep*.

AM. BLACK OYSTERCATCHER   *Haemátopus báchmani*
Uncommon. Prefers rocky shores. Note the black body, red bill, and pink legs. In courting, both American and Black males display by walking up to the female with bowed head. The flight is strong, and flocks fly in lines in V-formation. Calls are short peeps.

AMERICAN AVOCET   *Recurviróstra americána*
Rather common, breeding on the shores of marshes and lakes. Legs and neck are long and thin; the needle-like bill curves upward, strongly so on female. In flight the black bar on the white inner wing is an excellent field mark. The legs are blue-gray. Call, a loud *wheet*.

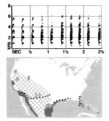

BLACK-NECKED STILT   *Himántopus mexicánus*
Common, breeding in both fresh- and salt-water habitats. Note the long thin legs and neck, and the thin straight bill. The plumage is black above, white below. In flight the wings are an unrelieved black; the red legs trail far behind the white tail. Call is a monotonous series of loud piping notes.

NORTHERN LAPWING   *Vanéllus vanéllus*
A Eurasian plover, casual in late fall on the Northeast coast. The crest is present in all plumages. The wings are broad and rounded at tip, face white, breast and back dark. Call is a high-pitched, sad *weep*.

NORTHERN JACANA   *Jacána spinósa*
Casual on ponds in southern Texas. Note long toes, long greenish legs, yellow flight feathers. Immature is white below. Very active; occasionally raises wings. Flight is rail-like, close to water. Call, a shrill whistle.

DARK-BACKED SHOREBIRDS

display   probing

AMERICAN OYSTERCATCHER
L 16″

AMERICAN BLACK OYSTERCATCHER
L 15″

summer

AMERICAN AVOCET
L 15″

winter

BLACK-NECKED STILT
L 13″

NORTHERN JACANA
L 7″

NORTHERN LAPWING
L 11″

⅔ scale

⅔ scale

● **PLOVERS** (*Family* Charadriidae) are medium-sized to small shore-birds. The short bill has a noticeable swelling near the tip. The neck is short; so is the tail, which is held horizontally, not drooping. The wings are pointed, almost narrow; flight is direct and fast. Plovers take several rapid steps, then pause. They forage for insects or small marine animals on shore or grasslands. Nests are on the ground. Typical plovers fall into two groups: the medium-sized unbanded plovers (this page) and the smaller ringed plovers (p. 114).

EURASIAN DOTTEREL *Charádrius morinéllus*
Rare breeder in western Alaska. Winters in Asia. Adult with its cinnamon underparts is unmistakable. Sexes similar. Male tends eggs and young. In fall could be mistaken for Lesser Golden-Plover, but the broad white eye stripes meet on the nape, and at close range the pale breast line is visible and diagnostic. Call is a soft trill.

MOUNTAIN PLOVER *Charádrius montánus*
Common, breeding in dry short-grass prairie and sage-brush; otherwise found in small flocks in cactus deserts or on high plains. The plumage is drab, and the white face pattern is lost in fall. The thin white wing stripe and the black tailband with the white border are the best field marks. Runs fast; seldom flies. When it does, it flies low, with downcurved wings. Call, a low drawling whistle.

LESSER GOLDEN-PLOVER *Pluviális domínica*
Common on the arctic tundra; winters in southern South America. Seen in spring in fields, pastures, and mudflats; in fall, most migrate offshore. The spring plumage is golden above and black below with dark rump and tail. In fall compare with Black-bellied Plover. Call is a clear, short, whistled *oodle-oo*. **Greater Golden-Plover** (*Pluviális apricária*, L 9½") is a rare visitor from Europe to Greenland, and accidental in Newfoundland. It is larger than Lesser and has white rather than gray axillars.

BLACK-BELLIED PLOVER *Pluviális squatárola*
A common plover that nests on the arctic tundra and winters along both coasts to central South America. It is larger than the Lesser Golden-Plover, from which it can always be told by the white rump and striking black axillars under the wing (gray in Lesser Golden). It is grayer above than the Lesser Golden and larger-billed. Does not migrate in large flocks, as the Lesser Golden does. Call is a plaintive, slurred whistle.

knot turnstone unbanded plover Spotted Sandpiper Dunlin banded plover

Lesser Golden-Plover

Semipalmated Plover for comparison

summer

winter

EURASIAN DOTTEREL
L 7"

winter

summer

MOUNTAIN PLOVER
L 7½"

winter

summer

LESSER GOLDEN-PLOVER
L 9"

winter

summer

BLACK-BELLIED PLOVER
L 9½"

winter

summer

UNBANDED PLOVERS

114

- **BANDED PLOVERS** *(Genus Charadrius)* are similar to the larger un-banded plovers (p. 112), but have one or two black neck bands.

PIPING PLOVER *Charádrius melódus*
Uncommon; on the drier portions of sandy beaches. Note the pale back, single (usually partial) neck band, yellow legs and feet. The bill is yellow with dark tip in spring, all dark in winter. Piping Plovers are seen singly or in small flocks. The call is 2-noted, soft and organ-like.

SNOWY PLOVER *Charádrius alexandrínus*
Locally common on sand flats and alkali ponds. Paler than the Piping Plover, with one incomplete dark band, dark bill and dark (sometimes pinkish) legs. At close range the bill appears to be longer and thinner than that of the Piping. Call is a low-pitched *chu-wee*.

SEMIPALMATED PLOVER *Charádrius semipalmátus*
Common on beaches and mudflats. Note the dark back, prominent white collar, white face markings, black and orange bill, and orange legs. In immature and adult winter plumage the band on the neck is brown and the legs yellow. Call, *chur-wée*. **Common Ringed Plover** *(Charádrius hiatícula,* L 6") breeds in Greenland and Baffin Island, winters in the Old World; rare migrant in western Alaska. It is very similar but lacks web on toes; call shorter, more abrupt.

WILSON'S PLOVER *Charádrius wilsónia*
Uncommon and rather local. Prefers sandy beaches and mudflats. Noticeably larger than Semipalmated Plover, with longer and broader eye stripe, heavier black bill, and wider neck band. The feet are dull pink. Female is much paler than male. Call, *wheet*. **Mongolian Plover** *(Charádrius mongólus,* L 6"), a rare visitor to western Alaska, has cinnamon breastband and strong facial markings in summer; gray breastband and pale facial markings in winter.

KILLDEER *Charádrius vocíferus*
Very common in fields and pastures, often far from water. Adult Killdeer has two neck bands, juvenile only one. The tail is longer than in other plovers. Note the orange on the upper tail and lower back. Seldom occurs in large flocks. Feigns injury near its nest to distract intruders. Repeats its name as a call.

BANDED PLOVERS

winter   summer

PIPING PLOVER
L 5½"

im.

♂
summer

SNOWY PLOVER
L 5¼"

winter   summer

SEMIPALMATED PLOVER
L 5¾"

MONGOLIAN PLOVER
6"

COMMON RINGED PLOVER
L 6"

♀

♂

WILSON'S PLOVER
L 6¼"

KILLDEER
L 8"

feigning

● **SANDPIPERS** (*Family* Scolopacidae) differ from plovers in having bills that are longer, more slender, and in several species distinctly curved. Necks tend to be longer than in plovers, and backs are cryptically patterned in most species by pale edging on feathers. In most species sexes are similar. In many, summer and winter plumages are different.

● **GODWITS** (*Genus Limosa*) are large, long-legged, reddish-brown or grayish shorebirds with long, slightly upturned bills. They are social in habits outside the breeding season.

MARBLED GODWIT   *Limósa fédoa*
Rather common in West, rare in East. Breeds on prairies, meadows, and pastures, and winters along the coasts. The brown plumage is mottled above and in breeding plumage is barred below. The very long bill turns up. Note the cinnamon wing linings, resembling those of Long-billed Curlew (p. 118). Call is a whistled *godwít*.

HUDSONIAN GODWIT   *Limósa haemástica*
Uncommon; in marshes, meadows, shores, and mud-flats. The bold black and white tail pattern separates it from all but the very rare Black-tailed Godwit. In flight, note the black axillars and sooty wing linings separating it from the Black-tailed Godwit. Call is like Marbled Godwit's, but higher pitched.

BLACK-TAILED GODWIT   *Limósa limósa*
Very rare spring and summer visitor to the Northeast and Alaska from the Old World, frequenting mudflats and marshes. Resembles Hudsonian Godwit, but has faintly marked whitish belly, flanks, and undertail coverts, and white wing linings. Bill is straighter than on other god-wits. Legs are black, not bluish, and in the breeding season the chin, neck, and upper breast are orange-rusty, not chestnut. Call is a loud *wicka* given three times.

BAR-TAILED GODWIT   *Limósa lappónica*
Nests in arctic Alaska, winters in western Pacific. Very rare visitor to East and West coasts, usually in fall. Found on mudflats and in marshes. Note barring on tail, no barring on underparts. In breeding plumage entire un-derparts are bright rusty. Western birds have barred rump; immatures can be told from Marbled Godwit by pale underparts, whitish wing linings, and short legs (only feet extend beyond tail). Call is a harsh, nasal *irrick*.

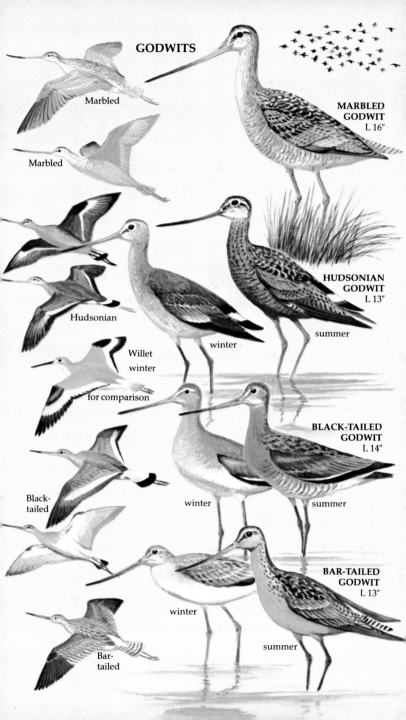

GODWITS

Marbled

Marbled

MARBLED GODWIT
L 16″

Hudsonian

HUDSONIAN GODWIT
L 13″

winter

summer

Willet
winter

for comparison

Black-tailed

winter

BLACK-TAILED GODWIT
L 14″

summer

Bar-tailed

winter

BAR-TAILED GODWIT
L 13″

summer

- **CURLEWS** (*Genus Numenius*) are large, long-legged, brownish shorebirds with long decurved bills. Sexes are alike. Gregarious outside the breeding season; they prefer marshes or grass to bare ground.

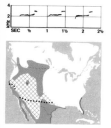

LONG-BILLED CURLEW   *Numénius americánus*
Rather common. Nests in meadows and pastures; outside breeding season also found in marshes, mudflats, and beaches. The very long bill (length varies greatly) is a good field mark. The cinnamon underwing linings clinch identification. Crown is unstreaked. Call, a plaintive *curlew* with rising inflection.

EURASIAN CURLEW   *Numénius arquáta*
Accidental in eastern North America. Told from Long-billed Curlew by shorter bill, very plain unstreaked head, conspicuous white rump, and unmarked white wing linings. Behavior and call similar to Long-billed's. Old World Whimbrel also has white rump.

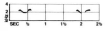

BRISTLE-THIGHED CURLEW   *Numénius tahitiénsis*
Rare local breeder in western Alaska; winters on central Pacific islands. Told from Whimbrel by contrast between bright-rusty rump and tail and somber brown back; note also the paler bill. Call, a plaintive whistle.

FAR EASTERN CURLEW   *Numénius madagascariénsis*
Vagrant in western Alaska. Told from Long-billed Curlew by heavy black barring on white wing linings.

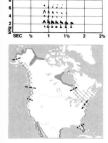

WHIMBREL   *Numénius phaéopus*
Common in marshes, mudflats, and shores. Smaller than Long-billed Curlew, with distinct striping on crown, shorter bill, and pale underparts. In good light the back appears grayer than Long-billed's; rump and tail are barred. Call, a short mellow whistle, rapidly repeated 6-7 times.

ESKIMO CURLEW   *Numénius boreális*
Nearly extinct; look for it in spring on Galveston Island, Texas, and in fall in the Northeast. Smaller than Whimbrel, with comparatively shorter, more slender bill, cinnamon wing linings, and less pronounced light central crown stripe. Call, a soft fluttering *tr-tr-tr*. **Little Curlew** (*Numénius minútus*, L 10") of Eurasia (no North American record) has buffy wing linings with black barring.

CURLEWS

EURASIAN CURLEW
L 19"

Long-billed
Curlews

**LONG-BILLED
CURLEW**
L 19"

**FAR EASTERN
CURLEW**
L 19½"

**BRISTLE-
THIGHED
CURLEW**
L 15"

European
Whimbrel

Whimbrels

WHIMBREL
L 14"

**ESKIMO
CURLEW**
L 11"

Eskimo
Curlews

- **MARSH SANDPIPERS** (*Genus Tringa*) are medium-sized long-legged birds that prefer marshes to tidal flats. Most have white rumps.

SPOTTED REDSHANK   *Tringa erythrópus*
Very rare vagrant to Alaska and East Coast. Black breeding plumage is unmistakable. Fall adults and young are uniform light gray with long, slender bill, and white rump extending far up back. Call, a musical whistle, *tew-it*.

COMMON GREENSHANK   *Tringa nebulária*
Vagrant to western Alaska. Told from Greater Yellowlegs by shorter and greenish legs, white rump extending up back, and call, *tu-tu-tu*, resembling Lesser Yellowlegs'.

MARSH SANDPIPER   *Tringa stagnátilis*
Accidental fall visitor to western Alaska. Slim wader with long needle-thin bill and white rump extending up back. In flight, long legs and feet project beyond tail.

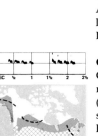

GREATER YELLOWLEGS   *Tringa melanoleúca*
Common on muskeg and tundra in summer and in marshes in winter. Noticeably slimmer than Willet (p. 122) and with thinner bill. Among the tall long-legged sandpipers, only the two yellowlegs have bright yellow legs. Greater is told from Lesser by size, long bill (barely upturned), and the sharp 3- to 5-note whistle.

LESSER YELLOWLEGS   *Tringa flávipes*
Fairly common (uncommon West). Similar to Greater Yellowlegs, but bill is much shorter and more slender. Call is a soft 1- to 3-note whistle that lacks the loud ringing quality of the Greater's. Often in loose flocks.

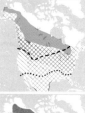

SOLITARY SANDPIPER   *Tringa solitária*
Common, usually solitary, along streams, lakes, swamps. Told from Spotted Sandpiper (p. 124), which frequents same habitats, by barred tail, longer darker legs, and in flight by plain dark wings. Dark rump separates it from Stilt Sandpiper (p. 122) and yellowlegs. At close range, white eye ring is diagnostic. Flight buoyant, almost swallow-like. Call like Spotted's, but higher. Sonagram below.

WOOD SANDPIPER   *Tringa glaréola*
Rare breeder in western Alaska; winters in Old World. Told from Solitary by white rump, eye stripe, and yellowish legs. Call, a high-pitched whistle, *chip-ip-ip*.

Lesser Yellowlegs   Solitary Sandpiper

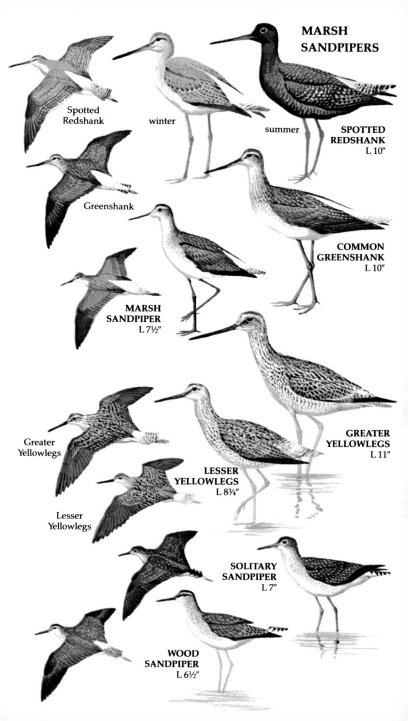

MARSH SANDPIPERS

Spotted Redshank

winter

summer

SPOTTED REDSHANK L 10"

Greenshank

COMMON GREENSHANK L 10"

MARSH SANDPIPER L 7½"

GREATER YELLOWLEGS L 11"

Greater Yellowlegs

LESSER YELLOWLEGS L 8¾"

Lesser Yellowlegs

SOLITARY SANDPIPER L 7"

WOOD SANDPIPER L 6½"

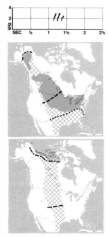

UPLAND SANDPIPER *Bartrámia longicáuda*

Local and uncommon in grass country. Has a distinctive silhouette—long neck, small head, short bill, and relatively long tail. The crown and outer wings are much darker than the rest of the plumage. Flies stiffly, like a Spotted Sandpiper (p. 124), and briefly holds its wings erect after it lands. Territorial call is a long slurred whistle; flight call shown above is also diagnostic.

BUFF-BREASTED SANDPIPER *Tryngítes subruficóllis*

Rare and local in short-grass prairies, golf courses, and airports. This buffy bird (paler below in fall) has the slender-necked profile of the Upland Sandpiper, but is much smaller. The white eye ring, broad buffy feather edgings on the back, and pale legs are good field marks. Wing linings in flight are white. When flushed, it twists and turns like a snipe. Call, a low trill.

RUFF (female, Reeve) *Philómachus púgnax*

A rare but regular spring and fall visitor from Eurasia. Female and autumn birds resemble Lesser Yellowlegs (p. 120), but are much browner, heavier bodied and shorter legged. The bill is thicker, drooped, and yellow at the base. Ruff is larger than Reeve. Legs are dull yellow. Plumage and leg color of adult male are extremely variable. Posture is erect. In flight the large white oval patches at the base of the tail are diagnostic in all plumages. Call, a low *tu-whit*.

STILT SANDPIPER *Calídris himántopus*

Uncommon; in fresh and salt marshes and mudflats. The rusty cheek and crown and the barred flanks are present only in breeding plumage. The long greenish legs, clear white rump, and dark trailing edges of wings are fall field marks. Often feeds with dowitchers (p. 124), but is more slender and has longer legs and a shorter bill. Call, a low *querp*, softer, hoarser than Lesser Yellowlegs'.

WILLET *Catoptróphorus semipalmátus*

Common; eastern birds breed in coastal marshes, western ones on lakes. Both winter in salt marshes. Best identified in flight by the prominent wing pattern (compare with oystercatcher, p. 110). Standing birds are very plain and plump, with bluish legs and thicker bill than yellowlegs'. Seen in small flocks or pairs. Call, *pill-will-willet*.

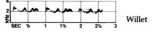

Willet

SANDPIPERS

UPLAND SANDPIPER L 10″

BUFF-BREASTED SANDPIPER L 6½″

RUFF L 10″ summer

Ruff
winter

Reeve

winter   winter

STILT SANDPIPER L 7¼″   summer

winter   summer

WILLET L 13½″

TEREK SANDPIPER — *Xénus cinéreus*

Spring and fall vagrant to western Alaska. Note long upturned bill, short, bright yellow legs, gray rump, and whitish trailing edge of wing. Habits suggest Spotted Sandpiper. Call is a fast repetition of flute-like notes.

COMMON SANDPIPER — *Actítis hypoléucos*

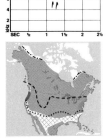

Rare migrant to western Alaska. Like winter Spotted but tail extends well beyond wing tips, wing bar is bolder and longer, bill is uniformly dark in spring, call higher.

SPOTTED SANDPIPER — *Actítis maculária*

Common breeder along fresh water, winters along southern coasts. Body is typically tilted forward, head held low. It bobs the tail up and down almost continuously. In flight the wings are held stiffly downward with shallow rapid beats. No breast spots in winter or on young. Usually seen singly. Call is a shrill 2- or 3-note piping.

GRAY-TAILED TATTLER — *Heteróscelus brévipes*

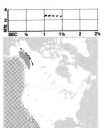

Rare but regular migrant in western Alaska. In spring told from Wandering Tattler by pure white undertail coverts and belly. In fall told by whitish forehead and sharp double-whistle, *too-weet*.

WANDERING TATTLER — *Heteróscelus incánus*

Uncommon. Nests along mountain streams and winters on rocky seashores and reefs. It is dark above and occasionally bobs its tail. The bill is rather long, the legs yellow. Call, 4-8 rapid plaintive notes.

SHORT-BILLED DOWITCHER — *Limnódromus gríseus*

Common, especially along coasts. Note the long bill, the tip of which is usually out of sight when the birds are feeding. The white rump patch extends farther up the back than on other American shorebirds. Legs are short, body chunky. Call, low mellow 3-note whistle, *tu-tu-tu*.

LONG-BILLED DOWITCHER — *Limnódromus scolopáceus*

This common western bird averages larger and longer billed than the Short-billed, prefers fresh water, and in summer plumage has rusty lower belly, barred (not spotted) flanks, and blacker bars on the white tail. Migrates later in fall and molts later into winter plumage than Short-billed; in winter plumage cannot be safely identified except by call, a single sharp *keek* or series of same.

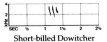

Short-billed Dowitcher

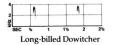

Long-billed Dowitcher

SANDPIPERS

TEREK SANDPIPER L 7½"

Common Sandpiper

COMMON SANDPIPER L 6½"

winter

SPOTTED SANDPIPER L 6¼"

summer

GRAY-TAILED TATTLER L 8"

winter

summer

WANDERING TATTLER L 8¾"

Short-billed Dowitcher

winter

Long-billed Dowitcher

SHORT-BILLED DOWITCHER L 9½"

winter

summer

summer

winter

LONG-BILLED DOWITCHER L 10"

● **PHALAROPES** are sandpipers that have lobed toes and swim readily. The neck and legs are rather long. Two species are pelagic. Females are larger and more colorful than males. Phalaropes spin in circles in shallow water to stir up food.

WILSON'S PHALAROPE   *Phaláropus trícolor*
Uncommon and the landlubber of the family; nests on prairie sloughs and ponds. The bill is very thin and much longer than the head. With its white rump and dark wings it looks like a short-legged yellowlegs (p. 120) or Stilt Sandpiper (p. 122) but its legs are much shorter. Call is a low, gallinule-like *chek*, softer than other phalaropes.

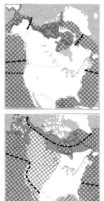

RED PHALAROPE   *Phaláropus fulicária*
An uncommon pelagic species most often seen during storms along the coast. The yellow bill (black in immature) is short and much stouter than in other phalaropes. In gray winter plumage the black eye line of phalaropes is characteristic. Common call is a loud *pik*.

RED-NECKED PHALAROPE   *Phaláropus lobátus*
Common on the breeding grounds and in flocks at sea; uncommon to rare inland. The slender bill is intermediate in length between those of the other two phalaropes. The legs are dark. Flying birds in winter plumage resemble Sanderlings (p. 130), but are darker-backed and slender-billed and have a black line through the eye. Its call is of low, short, scratchy notes; also a single *pik*.

● **WOODCOCK AND SNIPE** are primarily inland sandpipers of moist woodlands, marshes, and riverbanks. Neck and legs are short, and the bill is extemely long.

AMERICAN WOODCOCK   *Scólopax mínor*
Rather common, but nocturnal; lives in moist woodlands, swamps, and thickets. Stocky, with short legs, short neck, and very long bill. Permits close approach, then explodes with whistling wings. Call, a nasal *peent*.

COMMON SNIPE   *Gallinágo gallinágo*
Common in marshes and bogs and along riverbanks. The size and shape of dowitchers (p. 124), it is told by the browner, more streaked head and back, and in flight by the brown rump and orange tail. Flies in a rapid zigzag. Generally stays close to cover, while dowitchers prefer to feed in the open. Flight call, a low, rasping *kzrrt*.

American Woodcock

winnowing of Common Snipe

PHALAROPES, WOODCOCK, AND SNIPE

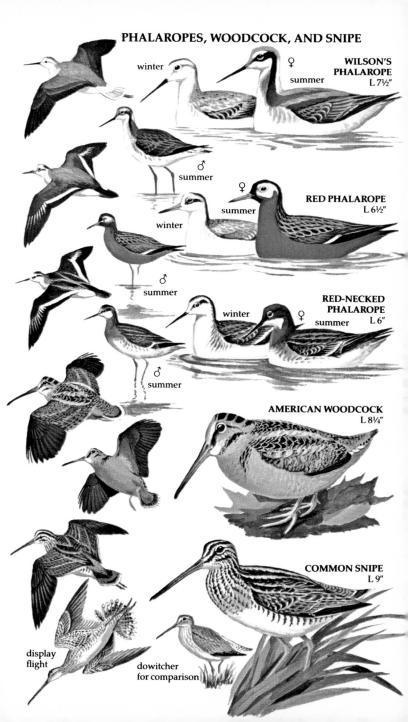

winter

♀ **WILSON'S PHALAROPE**
summer L 7½"

♂ summer

♀ summer **RED PHALAROPE**
winter L 6½"

♂ summer

winter ♀ **RED-NECKED PHALAROPE**
summer L 6"

♂ summer

AMERICAN WOODCOCK
L 8½"

COMMON SNIPE
L 9"

display flight

dowitcher for comparison

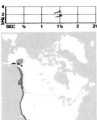

SURFBIRD   *Aphríza virgáta*

Common along rocky Pacific shorelines in winter; breeds in mountains above timberline. Dark and plump, with short yellow legs; told in flight by the black triangle at the tip of the white tail. Wandering Tattler (p. 124), found in the same habitat, has a dark rump and lacks the wing stripe. Call, a plaintive 3-note whistle.

RUDDY TURNSTONE   *Arenária intérpres*

Turnstones have slender pointed bills, slightly upturned at the tip. Ruddy is common along coasts, rare inland. It prefers rocky tidal shores, feeding in the seaweed. Note the head and breast pattern and short orange-red or yellow legs and in flight the striking black, brown, and white pattern of the wings, rump, and tail. Call, 1-8 fast, low, guttural, slurred whistles.

BLACK TURNSTONE   *Arenária melanocéphala*

Common on rocks along the Pacific Coast. All plumages appear darker and more uniform than in the Ruddy Turnstone, though the wing and back patterns are much the same. Note the white speckling on the side of the breast of the breeding adult. Immatures are grayer-headed than winter adult and have buffy edgings on back feathers. Legs variable, usually dark. Calls are slightly higher pitched than Ruddy Turnstone's.

PURPLE SANDPIPER   *Calídris marítima*

Common, but restricted to rocky coasts and jetties; winters farther north than other shorebirds. This darkest sandpiper on the East Coast has a thin yellow-based bill and yellow legs. Usually in small flocks, often with turnstones or Sanderlings (p. 130). Call, *wit* or *weet-wit*. This, the Rock Sandpiper, and the smaller species on pp. 130-132 are collectively known as peeps.

ROCK SANDPIPER   *Calídris ptilocnémis*

Common locally. Breeds on the tundra; winters along rocky shores with turnstones and Surfbirds. A plump bird with short neck and greenish legs. The dark breast patch (summer) is higher up than the black belly of the Dunlin (p. 130). In flight Rock shows a broad white wing stripe, but a dark tail; other western rock-inhabiting shorebirds have white on the tail except the dark-winged tattlers (p. 124). Call is flicker-like.

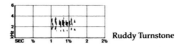

Ruddy Turnstone

SURFBIRD
L 8″

winter

summer

RUDDY TURNSTONE
L 7″

winter

summer

ROCK SHOREBIRDS

BLACK TURNSTONE
L 7″

winter

summer

PURPLE SANDPIPER
L 7½″

winter

summer

ROCK SANDPIPER
L 8″

Purple Sandpipers and turnstones

winter

summer

SHARP-TAILED SANDPIPER   *Calídris acumináta*

Rare fall migrant on the West Coast. Resembles Pectoral Sandpiper, but its breast is buffy, narrowly streaked at sides, undertail coverts have black streaks, crown is bright rufous, and there is no abrupt border between breast and belly. Call is a high-pitched 2-note whistle.

PECTORAL SANDPIPER   *Calídris melanótos*

Uncommon; in grassy marshes and wet fields. Note the abrupt border between the streaked breast and white underparts, erect stance, short bill, and greenish legs. When flushed, it flies zigzag like the Common Snipe; wings are uniformly dark. There is much size variation. Call, a low *prrrp*.

RED KNOT   *Calídris canútus*

A medium-sized, short-necked, stocky, locally common bird along sandy shores, rocks, and mudflats. The short bill and lack of a white streak up the back distinguish it from dowitchers. In spring the gray back and robin-like breast are distinctive. In flight, note the light rump and tail. Call is a low buzzy whistle, *tlu-tlu*.

CURLEW SANDPIPER   *Calídris ferrugínea*

A casual visitor on the East Coast. Resembles the Dunlin in winter, but legs, neck, and slender bill are longer and rump is white. Note the slim profile and erect posture. Call is a soft whistled *chirrup*.

DUNLIN   *Calídris alpína*

Common along coast in winter; less common inland. A stout short-necked shorebird with a long, slightly down-curved bill, heavy at base. In spring note the bright-rusty back and black belly. In winter it is plain gray above. Call is a rapid, low, grating trill.

SANDERLING   *Calídris álba*

Common along sandy beaches at the water's edge. Reddish in spring, very light gray in winter plumage. When with Least or Semipalmated Sandpipers, the larger size is apparent. At close range the lack of a hind toe is diagnostic. In flight note the broad white wing stripe and the black wrist. Flight call is a sharp, distinctive *plick*.

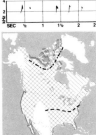

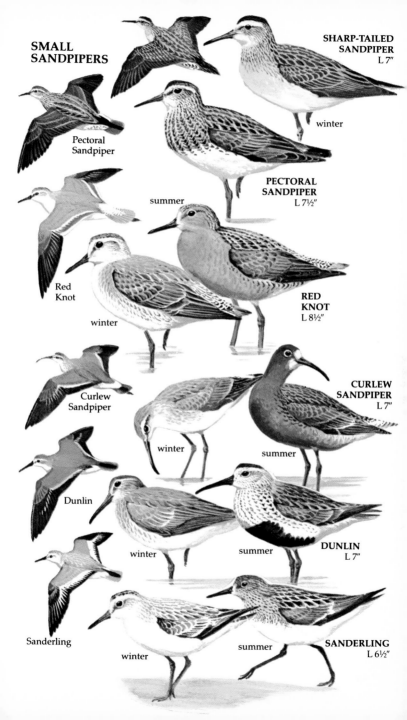

SMALL SANDPIPERS

Pectoral Sandpiper

SHARP-TAILED SANDPIPER L 7"

winter

summer

PECTORAL SANDPIPER L 7½"

Red Knot

winter

RED KNOT L 8½"

Curlew Sandpiper

CURLEW SANDPIPER L 7"

winter

summer

Dunlin

winter

summer

DUNLIN L 7"

Sanderling

winter

summer

SANDERLING L 6½"

WHITE-RUMPED SANDPIPER *Calídris fuscicóllis*
Uncommon; inland and along coast. Usually flocks with other peeps. The best field mark is the white rump. The only other short-legged sandpiper with a white rump is the rare Curlew Sandpiper (p. 130), which is larger and has a longer bill. Feeds by probing. Call, a high thin *jeet*.

BAIRD'S SANDPIPER *Calídris báirdii*
Uncommon; in drier short grassy marshes; sometimes found on shores and mudflats. Pale feather edgings give the back a scaly appearance, especially in fall. The body seems longer and slimmer than that of most peeps and is held more horizontal; the long wings extend well beyond the tail. The plumage is buffy even in fall. The legs are black to dark greenish. Rather tame. Picks rather than probes. Call, *kreep*.

LEAST SANDPIPER *Calídris minutílla*
Very common. Prefers salt marshes and muddy shores of rivers and estuaries. The bill is thin and short with slight droop at tip; head small; no other common small peep has yellow legs (greenish in some individuals). It feeds both by probing into the mud and by picking food from the surface. Browner and more streaked on the breast than other small sandpipers. Call, a high *breep*.

SEMIPALMATED SANDPIPER *Calídris pusílla*
Probably the most abundant shorebird; found on both fresh and salt water, often with Least and Western Sandpipers. Told from Least by black legs and grayer body with less streaking on the breast, from Western by shorter bill. Feeds by picking. Often seen in very large flocks with other peeps. Named for partial web at base of toes. Call is a short *krip*, lower pitched than Least's.

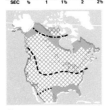

WESTERN SANDPIPER *Calídris maúri*
Common on sandbars and mudflats, where it probes in deeper water than the similar Semipalmated Sandpiper; sometimes submerges its head. Typical birds are told from Semipalmated by longer bill with a definite droop at the tip. In summer, back and crown are rusty; in fall the plumage is gray above, sometimes with a trace of rust on the scapulars (the feathers overlying the base of the wing). Many fall birds are inseparable. Call, *cheep*, is much higher pitched than Semipalmated's.

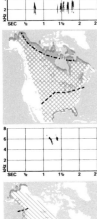

Baird's Sandpiper White-rumped Sandpiper

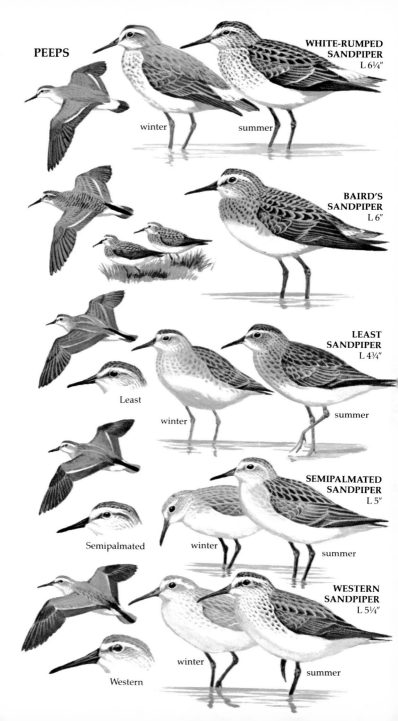

PEEPS

WHITE-RUMPED SANDPIPER
L 6¼"

winter   summer

BAIRD'S SANDPIPER
L 6"

LEAST SANDPIPER
L 4¾"

Least

winter   summer

SEMIPALMATED SANDPIPER
L 5"

Semipalmated   winter   summer

WESTERN SANDPIPER
L 5¼"

Western   winter   summer

● **ALASKAN PEEPS:** Very rare stragglers (May to September) to western Alaska from Eurasian breeding grounds.

GREAT KNOT   *Calídris tenuiróstris*
Resembles Red Knot (p. 130) but is much larger with longer, slimmer bill, drooping at tip. Upper parts are darker, white rump more distinct. Eye stripe is less pronounced. In summer the black breast and spotted flanks are diagnostic. In winter, underparts are more heavily spotted. Call, a low, 2-3 note whistle.

RUFOUS-NECKED STINT   *Calídris ruficóllis*
Resembles Western Sandpiper (p. 132) but in summer has russet upper breast, neck, and sides of head. In winter the broad white eye stripe, white forehead and white breast, blackish line through rump and tail, and un-webbed toes are distinctive. Call, a weak *chit*.

LITTLE STINT   *Calídris minúta*
Resembles Rufous-necked Stint but in summer has pale breast and neck with dark spots. The bill is thinner. The pattern on the back with two whitish V's suggests Least Sandpiper (p. 132), but the legs are dark. Call is a short, sharp *chik*, given about three times.

TEMMINCK'S STINT   *Calídris témminckii*
Resembles Semipalmated Sandpiper (p. 132) but has yellow-green legs and white (not gray) outer tail feathers. In winter upper parts are duller and more uniform than in other sandpipers. Call, a short high-pitched trill.

LONG-TOED STINT   *Calídris subminúta*
Black streaks make this the darkest-backed peep. Dark crown extends to bill. Legs yellowish. In summer, neck and upper breast are tinged rufous. Call, a purring *chrrrup*.

SPOONBILL SANDPIPER   *Eurynorhýnchus pygméus*
Resembles Rufous-necked Stint in all plumages, but has spatulate bill, and wing stripe is more prominent. In winter, paler than Rufous-necked, especially on head.

BROAD-BILLED SANDPIPER   *Limícola falcinéllus*
Plumage pattern snipe-like. Bill long with droop at tip. The short legs are dark greenish. Note the split eye stripe and blackish shoulder. Call, a deep trill, *crrrooit*.

ALASKAN PEEPS

GREAT KNOT L 10"

winter

summer

RUFOUS-NECKED STINT L 5¼"

winter

summer

LITTLE STINT L 4¾"

winter

summer

TEMMINCK'S STINT L 5"

winter

summer

LONG-TOED STINT L 5¼"

winter

summer

SPOONBILL SANDPIPER L 5"

winter

summer

BROAD-BILLED SANDPIPER L 5½"

WINTER PLUMAGE

Red Knot
p. 130

Rock Sandpiper
p. 128

Pectoral Sandpiper
p. 130

Baird's Sandpiper
p. 132

Least Sandpiper
p. 132

Semipalmated
Sandpiper
p. 132

Wilson's Phalarope
p. 126

Red Phalarope
p. 126

Red Knot—Chunky, gray with light rump; in flocks on beaches
Rock Sandpiper—Dark bird of West; small flocks on rocks
Pectoral Sandpiper—Rusty; heavily streaked breast; greenish legs
Baird's Sandpiper—Buffy, scaly back; long wings; black legs
Least Sandpiper—Very small, brown; short thin bill; yellow legs
Semipalmated Sandpiper—Very small, gray; sturdy bill; black legs
Wilson's Phalarope—Long thin bill; phalarope eye mark; gray
Red Phalarope—Small, gray; sturdy yellowish bill; eye mark; oceanic

Purple
Sandpiper
p. 128

Sanderling
p. 130

White-rumped
Sandpiper
p. 132

Curlew Sandpiper
p. 130

Western Sandpiper
p. 132

Dunlin
p. 130

Red-necked Phalarope
p. 126

Spotted
Sandpiper
p. 124

Purple Sandpiper—Small flocks on rocks in East; dark; yellow legs
Sanderling—Small flocks on beach; wide white wing stripe
White-rumped Sandpiper—Small, gray; white rump patch; dark tail
Curlew Sandpiper—Medium size; curved bill; white rump patch; rare
Western Sandpiper—Very small, brown; drooping bill; mostly coastal
Dunlin—Medium size; curved bill, dark rump; common, coastal
Red-necked Phalarope—Small, gray; short thin bill; eye mark
Spotted Sandpiper—Small, brownish; teeters; common inland

JAEGERS AND SKUAS (*Family* Laridae, *Subfamily* Stercorariinae) look like dark gulls with elongated central tail feathers, but their silhouette, flight, and feeding habits are different. Their slender wings are sharply bent at the wrist and their tails are frequently fanned as they suddenly change course. Wingbeats are powerful and rapid. Light bases of primaries distinguish these birds from gulls and terns. Jaegers and skuas are most often seen robbing other seabirds of fish. They seldom come ashore except to nest, and generally are silent. Dark phases are rare in East. Immatures lack the long tail feathers. Eggs, 2-3.

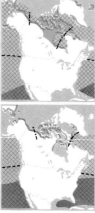

PARASITIC JAEGER
Stercorárius parasíticus

The most common jaeger, frequently seen pursuing terns. Adult is told from the larger, heavier Pomarine by the short, flat, pointed, central tail feathers; from the Long-tailed by tail length alone. Immature is browner than Long-tailed and has more white in the wing.

POMARINE JAEGER
Stercorárius pomarínus

The largest of the jaegers; nearly the size of Herring Gull (p. 144). The bill is proportionately larger than those of other jaegers. The flight is heavier and more steady. The long central tail feathers are broad and twisted. In the light phase the sides are barred and the female's breast band is more distinct than in other jaegers.

LONG-TAILED JAEGER
Stercorárius longicaúdus

Common on breeding grounds, rarely seen in migration. The smallest-bodied and slimmest of the jaegers. The adult's central tail feathers extend 5-8 inches behind the others. On nesting ground it often hovers. Dark phase is almost unknown. Light phase (adult and immature) is grayer than other jaegers', there is less white in the upper wing, and flight is more graceful and tern-like.

GREAT SKUA
Catharácta skúa

Rare but regular offshore visitor in Northeast. At a distance it looks like a dark short-tailed Herring Gull (p. 144), but can be told by the large white patches at the base of the primaries. More of a scavenger than the jaegers, it often soars with gulls.

SOUTH POLAR SKUA
Catharácta maccórmicki

Rare offshore summer visitor. Similar to Great Skua but slightly smaller and more uniformly dark brown to slaty gray without pale streaking. In spring most show a golden mane. Fall immatures are entirely dark brown.

Parasitic Jaeger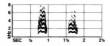

Long-tailed Jaeger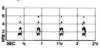

shearwater   falcon   gull   tern   jaeger

JAEGERS AND SKUAS

im.

PARASITIC JAEGER L 16″

light phase

dark phase

Parasitic

POMARINE JAEGER L 17″ W 48″

Pomarine chasing gull

LONG-TAILED JAEGER L 18″

Long-tailed hovering

GREAT SKUA L 17½″ W 59″

SOUTH POLAR SKUA L 16½″ W 55″

- **GULLS** (*Family* Laridae, *Subfamily* Larinae) are sturdy robust birds with webbed feet, long pointed wings, a stout hooked bill, and generally a square tail. They are primarily scavengers. Some species gather by thousands at garbage dumps and fish docks. They rarely dive from the air, but alight on the water to seize food. Flight is deliberate and powerful; some species soar frequently. Sexes are alike; immatures of the larger species take several years to acquire adult plumage. They nest in colonies. Eggs, 2-5. Immatures shown on pp. 150-151.

IVORY GULL *Pagóphila ebúrnea*

Rarely encountered outside the Arctic Ocean. In breeding season it is found along the coast, otherwise over open water in the Arctic. The Ivory Gull is much smaller than the other all-white gulls; it is easily told by the black legs and black bill (yellow-tipped in the adult). Its flight is more pigeon-like than that of other gulls.

GLAUCOUS GULL *Lárus hyperbóreus*

Uncommon south of Canada; is generally with Herring Gulls (p. 144) along the coast. Told from Iceland Gull by its size (larger than Herring Gull) and heavier bill and by its tail, which extends nearly to the wing tips when at rest. Immature can be told from all other "white-winged" gulls by more flesh color at base of bill. In all plumages of Glaucous and Iceland note in flight the translucent "windows" at base of primaries. Glaucous is predatory.

ICELAND GULL *Lárus glaucóides*

Uncommon along coast; rare on Great Lakes. Slightly smaller than Herring Gull (p. 144), Iceland has white wing tips in all plumages. Its folded wings protrude well beyond the tail. The head looks small for the body, and the bill seems still smaller. First- and second-year plumages also resemble those of Glaucous, but bill of Iceland has more extensive dark at tip and is much smaller. Feet of both species always flesh-colored. The western race (*L.g. kúmlieni*) has gray bar near wing tip.

GLAUCOUS-WINGED GULL *Lárus glaucéscens*

Abundant, especially in harbors and garbage dumps. In all plumages Glaucous-winged Gull lacks the paler primaries of the Glaucous and the dark wing tips of the other gulls with which it might be confused. Second-year plumage is lighter than first-year. Bill is black the first year, and has a flesh-colored base the second year. Flight, behavior, and call are like Herring's (p. 144).

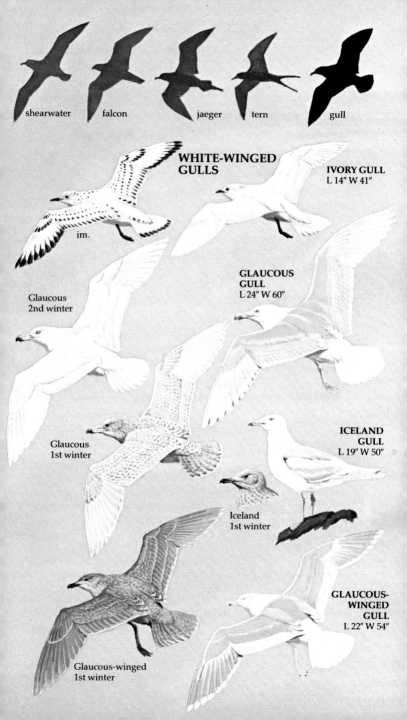

shearwater falcon jaeger tern gull

WHITE-WINGED GULLS

IVORY GULL
L 14″ W 41″

im.

GLAUCOUS GULL
L 24″ W 60″

Glaucous
2nd winter

Glaucous
1st winter

ICELAND GULL
L 19″ W 50″

Iceland
1st winter

Glaucous-winged
1st winter

GLAUCOUS-WINGED GULL
L 22″ W 54″

GREAT BLACK-BACKED GULL — *Lárus marínus*

Common and increasing in numbers and range. A predatory coastal species, rare inland. This and the Lesser are the only black-backed gulls in the East. Flies with slow wingbeats. Immature, which winters farther south than adult, can be confused only with Herring (p. 144) and Lesser Black-backed Gulls; note shape and lesser extent of black band on tail, contrast between light head and dark back, and heavy bill of Great Black-backed. Call, a low-pitched *kow-kow-kow*.

SLATY-BACKED GULL — *Lárus schistísagus*

Rare visitor (Feb.-Nov.) from eastern Asia to northwestern Alaska where no other black-backed gulls regularly occur. Narrow pale gray line separates wing tip from black mantle. The iris is yellow (pale gold in Western Gull). Immature closely resembles immature Herring Gull (p. 144), but has a heavier bill.

Western Gull

WESTERN GULL — *Lárus occidentális*

Common along the outer beaches, vagrant inland. Replaces the Great Black-backed Gull in the West. Smaller in size but almost identical in behavior and advanced plumages. Dark gray-brown first-winter birds resemble young Herring Gull (p. 144) but have heavy black bill and more prominent barring on rump and speckling on mantle. Feet are pink. Low-pitched call resembles Great Black-backed's. **Yellow-footed Gull** (*Lárus lívens*, L 21"), a Mexican species that wanders north to Salton Sea in summer, is recognized by its yellow legs and feet and more solid black back.

Yellow-footed Gull

LESSER BLACK-BACKED GULL — *Lárus fúscus*

Rare but regular winter visitor to the East Coast and Great Lakes from European breeding grounds. Adults told from Great Black-backed Gull by smaller size and yellow legs. The West European and most common subspecies (*L.f. graéllsii*) has lighter (slaty) back and mantle than the Great Black-backed, while the eastern and rarer subspecies (*L.f. fúscus*) is solid black on back and mantle. The dark area of the underwing is more extensive than in the Great Black-backed. Immature resembles immature Herring Gull (p. 144) and has pinkish legs, but outer wing is more uniformly dark brown, both above and below, and rump is paler than mantle and scapulars. Call is deeper and more nasal than Herring's.

**GREAT BLACK-
BACKED GULL**
L 24″ W 65″

2nd
winter

ad.

Great
Black-backed
1st winter

im.

**SLATY-BACKED
GULL**
L 22″ W 60″

ad.

1st
winter

2nd
winter

ad.

WESTERN GULL
L 21″ W 55″

ad.

1st
winter

2nd
winter

ad.

**LESSER
BLACK-BACKED
GULL**
L 18″ W 50″

144

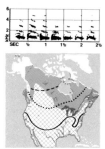

HERRING GULL *Lárus argentátus*

Abundant along the coasts, particularly in harbors and garbage dumps; common on lakes and rivers. Adults are told from the very similar California Gull and the Ring-billed Gull (p. 146) by larger size, heavier build, and pink legs. Eyelids are yellow in summer. First- and second-year Herrings are much darker-tailed than Ring-billed, and are darker-headed and smaller-billed than Great Black-backed (p. 142). First-year Herring is told from immature California by all-dark bill. Primaries are not as uniformly dark as in Lesser Black-backed (p. 142). Primarily a scavenger, the Herring also breaks mollusks by dropping them. Commonly seen high overhead, soaring like hawks. Call, loud, clear, and bugle-like.

THAYER'S GULL *Lárus tháyeri*

Common along Pacific Coast, very rare in Northeast in winter. Resembles Herring Gull closely but is slightly smaller with relatively smaller bill. The adult averages slightly darker gray on the mantle; black areas at wing tips are less extensive and paler and with larger white spots. Iris is brown rather than yellow and eyelids are purple in summer (yellow in Herring). The legs are deeper pinkish brown. Immatures are generally slightly paler than immature Herrings, but not as pale as immature Iceland or Glaucous-winged Gulls (p. 140). There is less contrast between the color of the mantle and the primaries. From below, the wing tips are whitish in both adult and immature, not dark as in Herring. The broad brown tailband is the darkest part of the immature in flight. Call is deeper than Herring's.

CALIFORNIA GULL *Lárus califórnicus*

Common along the Pacific Coast in winter and inland in the breeding season, nesting in large colonies on the prairies. Slightly smaller than the Herring Gull, but resembles it in all plumages. Adults have reddish eyelids in summer, as well as very yellow bill with red and black spots near tip of the lower mandible; the eyes are dark and the mantle is darker than on the Herring or Ring-billed (p. 146). The bill of the first-year bird is largely pinkish (not all black), and the legs begin to turn greenish by the second year (pink in Herring). Common call is a descending *kiarr*, repeated.

LARGE GRAY-BACKED GULLS

1st winter

2nd winter

ad.

HERRING GULL
L 20″ W 55″

Herring Gull

Herring Gull

Thayer's Gull

ad.

2nd winter

1st winter

THAYER'S GULL
L 20″ W 55″

ad.

1st winter

2nd winter

CALIFORNIA GULL
L 17″ W 52″

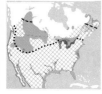

RING-BILLED GULL
Lárus delawarénsis

Common, especially inland. Complete black ring on yellow bill of adult is diagnostic. Adult has greenish-yellow legs. The other large eastern gulls have flesh-colored or black legs. Adult resembles California Gull (p. 144), which has a small red bill spot as well as a black one. Wing tip has larger dark area below than Herring Gull's. Immature is told from Herring and California by the narrow black tailband, from Mew by larger bill and whiter body. Calls are similar to Herring's (p. 144).

MEW GULL
Lárus cánus

Common on West Coast in winter, inland in breeding season. Adult is told from other gulls, except kittiwakes, by its unmarked, short, thin, yellow bill. Has less black in wing tips than Ring-billed and California (p. 144) Gulls. Immature resembles Ring-billed but tailband less distinct, small bill dark. Calls higher than Herring's (p. 144).

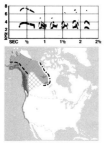

HEERMANN'S GULL
Lárus heérmanni

Common along West Coast except in spring, when confined to Mexican breeding islands. Rare inland; often found offshore. The darkest gull, it is the only species that is uniformly dark below. The adult's white head is mottled in winter. In flight the black tail and red bill of the adult are diagnostic, as are the narrow white terminal band and blackish underparts of the immature.

BLACK-LEGGED KITTIWAKE
Ríssa tridáctyla

Abundant on breeding cliffs, wintering well offshore. The adult is recognized by its sharply defined triangular black wing tips (no trace of white spot). The more commonly seen immature resembles several of the dark-headed gulls (p. 148), but is told by the combination of dark neck band, short black legs, and black wing tips, and very slightly forked tail. Often flies low over water.

RED-LEGGED KITTIWAKE
Ríssa brevíróstris

Common breeder on Pribilof Islands, winters to Aleutians. Bright red legs; shorter bill, darker underwing and mantle than Black-legged. Immature like adult, but has dark bill, nape line, and fore wing.

ROSS' GULL
Rhodostéthia rósea

Very rare breeder at Churchill, Manitoba; regular fall migrant at Pt. Barrow, Alaska. The only gull with a wedge-shaped tail. Adult is rosy at all seasons; no neck band in winter. Flight is pigeon-like.

SMALL
WHITE-HEADED
GULLS

im.

RING-BILLED
GULL
L 16" W 49"

im.

MEW
GULL
L 14" W 42"

im.

HEERMANN'S
GULL
L 15" W 45"

im.

winter

summer

BLACK-LEGGED
KITTIWAKE
L 13½" W 36"

RED-LEGGED
KITTIWAKE
L 15"

Ross' Gull

im.

ROSS' GULL
L 11" W 31"

LAUGHING GULL
Lárus atricílla

A very common coastal species; seldom found far from salt water, though it feeds on insects and earthworms in plowed fields. Adult is told from adult Franklin s Gull by solid dark wing tips. First-winter bird is very dark above; it is told from immature Franklin's by the dark breast, dark head, and complete tailband. One-year-old bird is like immature Franklin's. This is the largest and darkest of the black-headed gulls. Winter adult has a mottled head and darker bill. Calls, a variety of low chuckles.

FRANKLIN'S GULL
Lárus pipíxcan

The common gull of the prairies, wintering mostly south of U.S. Adult is told from adult Laughing Gull by the white spots on the primaries. Immature is told from Laughing by all-white outer tail feather. Feeds largely on insects, following the plow, hawking in the air, and fishing in ponds. Call is higher pitched than Laughing's.

BONAPARTE'S GULL
Lárus philadélphia

This small gull is common inland in the breeding season, on the coasts and larger lakes in winter. The flashy white wing tips are shared only by the rare Black-headed Gull. The black bill and the dark spot behind the eye are good field marks in winter. Flies buoyantly and tern-like, with the bill held down. Call, a low quacking.

SABINE'S GULL
Xéma sábini

Common on breeding grounds, elsewhere alone or in small flocks. Probably winters at sea. Casual in early fall and late spring along East Coast and inland. Note the forked tail and the bold pattern of triangles on the wings of both adult and young. Compare wing and tail pattern with immature kittiwake's (p. 146). Very tern-like in flight.

COMMON BLACK-HEADED GULL
Lárus ridibúndus

Rare but regular European straggler on East Coast; now breeding on Newfoundland. Usually with Bonaparte's. Similar but larger; bill larger and dark red. Primaries are conspicuously dark below. Call, *kwuririp.*

LITTLE GULL
Lárus minútus

European straggler and rare breeder. This smallest gull is tern-like in flight, but has rounded wings. Note dark underwing of adult and black tailband of immature. Hood more extensive than on Bonaparte's Gull, with which it usually flocks. Call, *kek-kek-kek.*

DARK-HEADED GULLS

2nd winter

winter

LAUGHING GULL L 13″ W 41″

im.

summer

winter

FRANKLIN'S GULL L 11″ W 35″

im.

summer

winter

BONAPARTE'S GULL L 11″ W 32″

im.

summer

winter

SABINE'S GULL L 11″ W 34″

im.

summer

winter

Black-headed

COMMON BLACK-HEADED GULL L 13″ W 38″

im.

summer

summer

LITTLE GULL

winter

im.

summer

L 9″ W 28″

IMMATURE GULLS are very difficult to identify. Only typical plumages are shown here. The time it takes to acquire adult plumage differs among species. In general, small gulls take two years, larger ones four. For example, Bonaparte's Gull acquires adult plumage the second winter, after partial molts in the fall and spring.

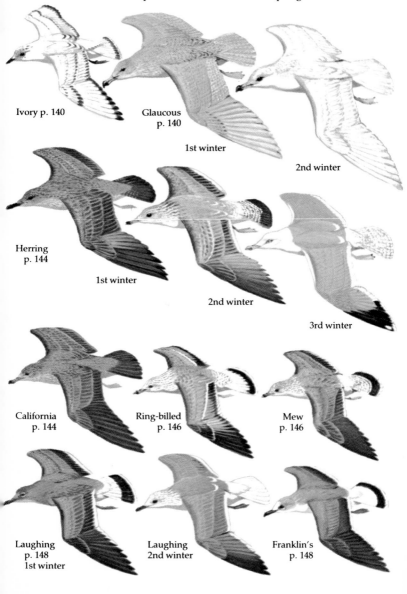

Ivory p. 140

Glaucous
p. 140

1st winter

2nd winter

Herring
p. 144

1st winter

2nd winter

3rd winter

California
p. 144

Ring-billed
p. 146

Mew
p. 146

Laughing
p. 148
1st winter

Laughing
2nd winter

Franklin's
p. 148

The larger Herring Gull acquires adult plumage in the fourth autumn, after two partial molts the first year and one complete and one partial each following year. This sequence of molt is important in understanding the intermediate plumages, not shown here.

Glaucous-winged
p. 140

1st winter

2nd winter

Great
Black-backed
p. 142

1st
winter

2nd
winter

3rd
winter

Little
p. 148

Heermann's
p. 146

Black-legged
Kittiwake
p. 146

Ross'
p. 146

Common
Black-headed
p. 148

Bonaparte's
p. 148

Sabine's
p. 148

●**TERNS** (*Family* Laridae, *Subfamily* Sterninae) are slender birds with long narrow wings, forked tails, and pointed bills. Flight is buoyant, with bill pointed downward as they search for small fish or insects. Dive from the air. Eggs, 1-4. Immatures shown on pp. 158-159.

LEAST TERN *Stérna antillárum*
Uncommon along eastern sandy beaches, rare inland. Note the rapid wingbeat, white forehead, yellow bill (spring), and yellow or yellowish (fall) legs. Immature has contrasting wing pattern. Call, a rapid series of paired notes.

ARCTIC TERN *Stérna paradisaéa*
Abundant, but migrates far offshore. Adult is told from Common Tern by the white streak below the black cap, the longer tail (extending to wing tips), short legs, short blood-red bill (no black tip), round head, short neck, and translucent spot near the wing tip. Immature has white upper wing coverts (gray on immature Common). Calls more nasal and rasping than Common's.

COMMON TERN *Stérna hirúndo*
Abundant coastally and over large inland lakes; the commonest U.S. tern. Flocks with Arctic, Roseate, or Forster's. Wing tips noticeably darker than in Roseate and Forster's, tail shorter, and bill bright red-orange (black tip varies in extent). Fall and immature head has pattern of Arctic's; also compare with Forster's. Upper wing coverts of immature are gray. Call, a harsh *kee-urr*.

ROSEATE TERN *Stérna doúgallii*
Locally common along Northeast coast. Paler above than Common and Arctic terns. Tail whiter, longer, more deeply forked, wing tips paler and bill black (red only at base). Note also its rapid, shallow wingbeat and distinctive calls: a soft *chivy* and a less frequent rasping *z-a-a-p*.

FORSTER'S TERN *Stérna fórsteri*
Common in fresh and salt marshes, rare on coastal beaches. Strongly resembles Common Tern, but primaries are lighter than rest of wing, tail is pale gray with white outer margin (reversed in the Common), bill and legs are more orange, and wing stroke is faster and more shallow. Winter birds are best told from the others on this page by the narrow black eye patch. Feeds on insects as well as fish. Call, a low toneless *zrurrr*.

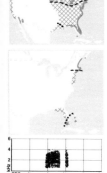

LIGHT-WINGED TERNS 1

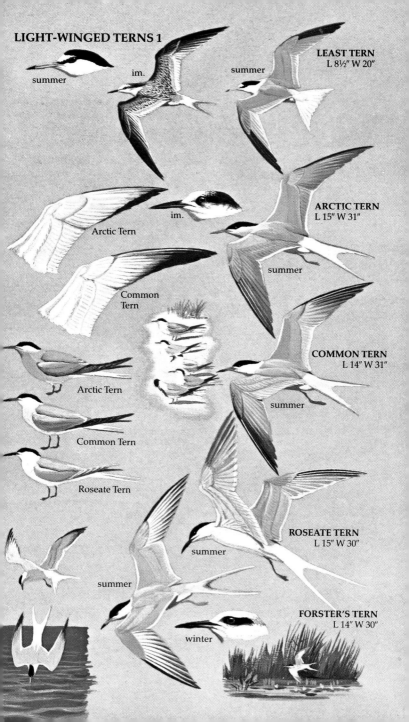

summer

im.

summer

LEAST TERN
L 8½″ W 20″

Arctic Tern

im.

Common
Tern

ARCTIC TERN
L 15″ W 31″

summer

Arctic Tern

Common Tern

Roseate Tern

COMMON TERN
L 14″ W 31″

summer

summer

ROSEATE TERN
L 15″ W 30″

summer

summer

winter

FORSTER'S TERN
L 14″ W 30″

SANDWICH TERN
Stérna sandvicénsis

Uncommon; on sandy beaches, often with Royal Terns. No other North American tern has a black bill tipped with yellow. Note also the long slender bill, the black legs, and the slight crest. Forehead of immature is mostly black, but adult has white on forehead and crown in winter. Fishes far offshore. Call, a loud grating *kirrik.*

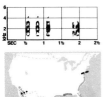

GULL-BILLED TERN
Stérna nilótica

Uncommon; over salt marshes. This whitest of North American terns is larger-bodied than the Common Tern. Recognized in all plumages by the short, thick, black, gull-like bill and the broad, very white wings. The tail is less forked than in most terns and the legs are black and long. The flight is more gull-like than other terns'. Rarely dives, but hawks for insects over marshes. The nasal 2- or 3-syllable call is characteristic.

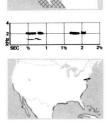

ELEGANT TERN
Stérna élegans

Regular visitor along southern California coast in fall from breeding grounds in Mexico. Similar to the larger Royal Tern, but has a slimmer bill and a longer crest. Bill of immature, blackish. Call, *karr-reek.*

ROYAL TERN
Stérna máxima

This large tern is quite common but is strictly limited to salt water. The Royal Tern has a crest in all plumages, can be told at a distance from the smaller terns by the thick orange bill and slower wingbeat. Told from Caspian by the white forehead (solid black cap is of very short duration in breeding season), orange bill, lighter wing tips from beneath, shorter legs (obvious when standing together), more deeply forked tail of adult in spring, and voice. It feeds almost entirely on fish. Usually fishes in inlets or offshore. Call, *chirrip.*

CASPIAN TERN
Stérna cáspia

Rather common both coastally and inland. The Caspian Tern closely resembles the Royal, but can always be told by its blood-red bill, loud raucous call, and other comparisons noted above. The wider wings give it a more gull-like appearance than most terns, and its behavior also is more gull-like. It alights on the water, occasionally soars, robs other seabirds, and eats eggs. Fish is its chief diet. Call, a very loud harsh *kraaa.*

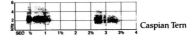

Caspian Tern

LIGHT-WINGED TERNS 2

im.

summer

SANDWICH TERN
L 15" W 34"

Sandwich Tern

Gull-billed Tern

summer

winter

GULL-BILLED TERN
L 13" W 35"

summer

ELEGANT TERN
L 17" W 43"

Elegant Tern winter

Royal Tern

Royal Tern winter

early summer

ROYAL TERN
L 18" W 43"

winter

summer

CASPIAN TERN
L 20" W 53"

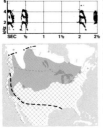

BLACK TERN
Chlidónias níger

Locally common breeder on lakes and fresh marshes. Adult is unmistakable. Fall birds are told from young Least Terns (p. 152) by very plain wings; underparts may be blotched with black. Black Terns dive little; eat mostly insects. Flight is erratic. Call is nasal. **White-winged Tern** (*Chlidónias leucópterus*, L 9"), casual Old World visitor, has white tail and fore wings, black back and wing linings, red legs; fall birds lack Black Tern's dark shoulder spot.

SOOTY TERN
Stérna fuscáta

Breeds abundantly on Dry Tortugas, Florida. Seen on Atlantic and Gulf coasts only during hurricanes. No other tern is jet black above. Immature is dark brown with white undertail coverts; its all-dark head and forked tail distinguish it from noddies. Does not dive; catches surface fish in flight. Call, a nasal *wide-a-wake*.

ALEUTIAN TERN
Stérna aleútica

Breeds very locally in coastal Alaska from Norton Sound to Yakutat. The pale Arctic (p. 152) is the only other tern in its U.S. range.

BRIDLED TERN
Stérna anaethétus

Pelagic; casual on East Coast during hurricanes. Compare face-neck-back-tail pattern with Sooty's. Note pale neck ring, pale underwing tips.

BROWN NODDY
Ánous stólidus

Common breeder at Dry Tortugas, Florida; accidental elsewhere in U.S. In all plumages, shows pattern opposite of other terns—dark body, white cap, and wedge-shaped rather than forked tail. Highly pelagic, feeds without diving. Call, soft low-pitched *k-a-a-a*.

BLACK NODDY
Ánous minútus

In U.S. seen only at Dry Tortugas, Florida, where it is rare but regular. Told from Brown by small size, black color, and slender bill.

● **SKIMMERS** (*Family* Laridae, *Subfamily* Rynchopinae) are the only birds with the lower mandible longer than the upper. They fly low over the water, the lower mandible cutting the surface. On contact with food, they quickly snap their head down and close the bill.

BLACK SKIMMER
Rýnchops níger

Locally common in flocks in coastal bays. The large red bill is distinctive. Young are brown above, speckled with white. Call is a loud, low-pitched, resonant *auw*.

| Sooty Tern | 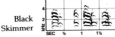 | Black Skimmer |  |

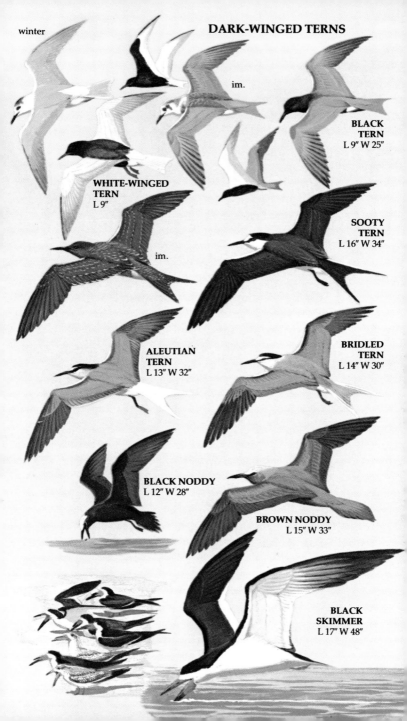

winter

DARK-WINGED TERNS

im.

BLACK TERN
L 9″ W 25″

WHITE-WINGED TERN
L 9″

SOOTY TERN
L 16″ W 34″

im.

ALEUTIAN TERN
L 13″ W 32″

BRIDLED TERN
L 14″ W 30″

BLACK NODDY
L 12″ W 28″

BROWN NODDY
L 15″ W 33″

BLACK SKIMMER
L 17″ W 48″

IMMATURE TERNS

Caspian Tern
p. 154

Royal Tern
p. 154

Elegant Tern
p. 154

Sandwich Tern
p. 154

Gull-billed Tern
p. 154

Sooty Tern
p. 156

Bridled Tern
p. 156

Black Tern
p. 156

White-winged Tern
p. 156

Common Terns
p. 152

Arctic Terns
p. 152

Roseate Terns
p. 152

Forster's Tern
p. 152

Least Tern
p. 152

● **ALCIDS** (Auks and relatives, *Family* Alcidae), black and white pelagic birds with short tails and rapid wingbeats, are usually silent. They come ashore only to breed. Swim underwater, using wings. Immatures are usually like adults. Eggs, 1-3.

RAZORBILL *Álca tórda*

Locally common, breeding on offshore cliffs. Winters at sea; sometimes is seen singly off rocky coasts. When swimming, its thick bill and tail are usually uptilted. In flight the back is more arched than in murres.

COMMON MURRE *Úria aálge*

Very common in large breeding colonies on cliffs. Winters at sea (East) or just offshore (West). Murres are told in all plumages from other alcids by the combination of long slender bills and white sides. The bill is longer than, but rarely half as thick as, the Thick-billed Murre's; at close range the narrow black streak back from the eye in winter plumage is diagnostic.

THICK-BILLED MURRE *Úria lómvia*

Strongly resembles Common Murre and is about equally common. Note the shorter thicker bill, evenly decurved above, sharply angled midway below, and the narrow white streak usually present at base of mouth. In winter there is no white above the black eye line.

DOVEKIE *Álle álle*

This smallest East Coast alcid is abundant at nesting sites in summer and locally common far offshore in the North Atlantic in winter. Appears along coast but rarely inland during Nov. storms. The short body, whirring wingbeats, and very small bill are distinctive.

BLACK GUILLEMOT *Cépphus grýlle*

Rare and local in winter within sight of land. Not as gregarious as other alcids nor as pelagic. The very large white wing patch of adult is diagnostic. In the immature the wing patch is usually mottled. Compare the adult with White-winged Scoter (p. 60). Wingbeats fast.

PIGEON GUILLEMOT *Cépphus colúmba*

Common. Resembles Black Guillemot in plumage and behavior. Usually distinguished from it by the black bars on the white wing patch, but immature Black Guillemot sometimes has black on the white wing patch.

loon   cormorant   scoter   Dovekie   murre

ALCIDS 1

winter

RAZORBILL
L 14"

summer

ringed phase

**COMMON
MURRE**
L 14"

summer

murre colony

winter

THICK-BILLED MURRE
L 14"

summer

winter

winter

DOVEKIE
L 6¾"

summer

Black
Guillemot

winter

BLACK GUILLEMOT
L 10½"

summer

winter

PIGEON GUILLEMOT
L 10½"

summer

ATLANTIC PUFFIN *Fratércula árctica*
Locally common in nesting colonies. Winters at sea. Outer layers of the bill are shed in late summer, so winter adults and especially the immatures have small bills (rectangular at base). Although the face is largely dark in winter, the characteristic facial pattern is still present. No other puffin occurs in North Atlantic.

HORNED PUFFIN *Fratércula corniculáta*
Common; similar to the Atlantic Puffin, but ranges do not overlap. The tiny erectile horn over the eye is seen only at close range. Winter puffins are told from other western alcids by the heavy rectangular (immature) or triangular (adult) bills and large chunky bodies.

TUFTED PUFFIN *Fratércula cirrháta*
Common, but very local in southern part of its range. The summer adult with its white face and jet-black body is unique. Winter birds can be told from the Horned Puffin by their dusky rather than pure white sides and at close range by the light line over the eye.

RHINOCEROS AUKLET *Cerorhínca monoceráta*
Auklets are small, short-billed, dark-backed, western alcids that nest in burrows or rock slides. Rhinoceros, the largest, is common along the Pacific Coast in winter. It is nearly puffin size but much more slender-billed. It is twice as large as the short-billed Cassin's (p. 164), the only other dark-breasted alcid within its range.

CRESTED AUKLET *Aéthia cristatélla*
Common resident in southwest Alaska (Aleutian, Pribilof, and Shumagin islands). Often nests under rocks with Parakeet Auklets (p. 164). The quail-like crest is shared only with the small rare Whiskered, which has 3, not 1, white facial plumes all year. The immature is separable from immature Whiskered and Cassin's (p. 164) only by direct comparison of size and face pattern at close range; the belly is sooty in Crested, whitish in Whiskered.

WHISKERED AUKLET *Aéthia pygmaéa*
Uncommon and local. Seldom wanders far from its limited range in the Aleutians (Kiska to Akutan). Adult always has the quail-like crest and three facial plumes. Compare immature with Cassin's (p. 164).

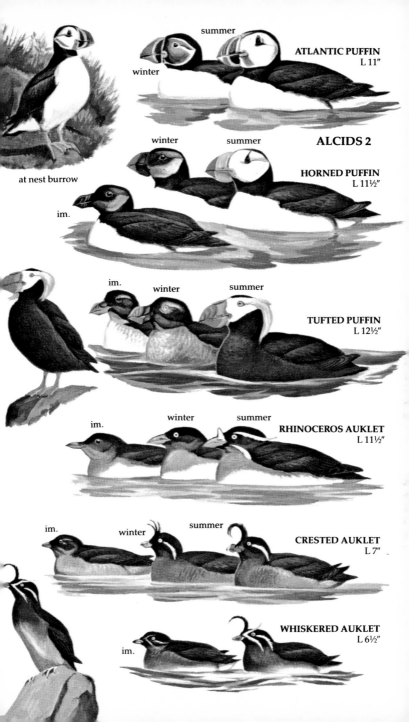

summer

winter

ATLANTIC PUFFIN
L 11"

ALCIDS 2

at nest burrow

winter   summer

HORNED PUFFIN
L 11½"

im.

im.   winter   summer

TUFTED PUFFIN
L 12½"

im.   winter   summer

RHINOCEROS AUKLET
L 11½"

im.   winter   summer

CRESTED AUKLET
L 7"

WHISKERED AUKLET
L 6½"

im.

164

CASSIN'S AUKLET   *Ptychorámphus aleúticus*
Common, especially offshore. This is the only small alcid
south of Alaska that is dark to the water line. Compare
with the much larger Rhinoceros Auklet and Tufted Puffin
(p. 162), both of which have much heavier bills.

LEAST AUKLET   *Aéthia pusílla*
Locally common resident in Bering Sea and Aleutians.
White throat patch is diagnostic. In winter plumage compare the head pattern and bill with those of the next two
species. These three are the only alcids with the white
scapulars. Neck is short; flight rapid.

MARBLED MURRELET   *Brachyrámphus marmorátus*
Murrelets are uniformly small alcids with short, generally
thin bills. Marbled Murrelet is told in summer by its plain
brown back and long slender bill. In winter it is the only
alcid south of Alaska with white scapulars.

KITTLITZ'S MURRELET   *Brachyrámphus brevirόstris*
Locally common breeder near glacial waters on west and
south coasts of Alaskan mainland (Cape Prince of Wales
to Glacier Bay). Winters in Asia. In summer, paler and
grayer-backed than other alcids. In winter entire face is
white. Bill half as long as Marbled's.

XANTUS' MURRELET   *Synthliborámphus hypoleúcus*
Uncommon. Looks like a miniature murre (p. 160), but
floats lower than shown, hiding white sides. In summer
note white underparts. In winter (same plumage) the
slender bill, all-dark back, and white underparts clinch
identification. **Craveri's Murrelet** (*S. cravéri*, L 8"), a rare
fall visitor north to Monterey, California, is similar but
has dark underwing coverts.

ANCIENT MURRELET   *Synthliborámphus antíquus*
Uncommon within sight of land, but stragglers occur far
inland. Note the pale bill, the contrast between black
throat and white neck and between black head and gray
back. The white plume is present in summer.

PARAKEET AUKLET   *Cyclorrhýnchus psittácula*
Fairly common offshore; seldom seen from land except
when nesting. The almost circular red bill is best field
mark, but bill of Rhinoceros (p. 162) can look reddish. Bill
of immature is dark. Winters s. to Oregon, far offshore.

Least Auklet

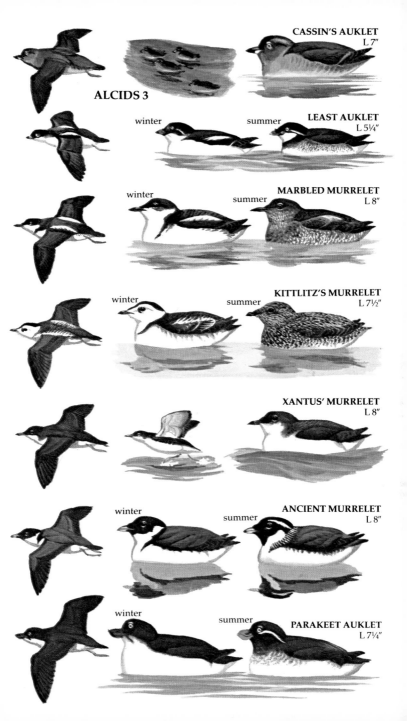

ALCIDS 3

CASSIN'S AUKLET
L 7"

LEAST AUKLET
L 5¼"
winter   summer

MARBLED MURRELET
L 8"
winter   summer

KITTLITZ'S MURRELET
L 7½"
winter   summer

XANTUS' MURRELET
L 8"

ANCIENT MURRELET
L 8"
winter   summer

PARAKEET AUKLET
L 7¼"
winter   summer

■ **PIGEONS AND DOVES** (*Order* Columbiformes, *Family* Columbidae) are small-headed, short-legged, swift-flying birds with pointed wings and fanned or tapered tails. Females are duller than males. All species coo; bob heads when walking. Eat grains, small seeds, acorns (Band-tailed Pigeon), and fruit. Nests are generally in trees; eggs, usually 2, are white except olive-buff for White-tipped Dove (p. 168).

BAND-TAILED PIGEON
Colúmba fasciáta

Locally common in western oak and pine woods, especially in summer. The large size and the broad gray tip on the fanned tail distinguish this bird from all others. Note the yellow bill and white neck band. Frequents water-holes and salt licks in large numbers. The call is a low-pitched, owl-like *coo-coo*.

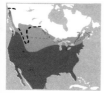

ROCK DOVE (domestic pigeon)
Colúmba lívia

This common introduced pigeon of farmyards and city parks has a white rump and (except in white birds) a dark terminal tailband. Wing tips collide on takeoff. Glides with wings raised at an angle. Nests on buildings.

WHITE-WINGED DOVE
Zenáida asiática

Locally abundant; our only dove with large white wing patches. In flight note the large, white corners of the tail. Nests in colonies in citrus groves, mesquite, and open woods. Call, a low *hhhooo-hoooo-hoo-hoooo*. Sonagram below.

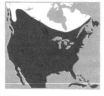

MOURNING DOVE
Zenáida macroúra

At all seasons the commonest native dove in suburbs and farmlands. Note the slim body and long tapered tail. Flight is swift and direct, without coasting; the whistling of the wings is diagnostic. Nests singly, feeds in flocks. Call, *ooah-ooo-oo-oo*, 4-6/min. Sonagram below.

WHITE-CROWNED PIGEON
Colúmba leucocéphala

Common in its limited range in the Florida Keys, where the only other doves are the Mourning Dove and Common Ground-Dove (p. 168). Adult's white crown contrasts sharply with dark body. Immature lacks white crown. Call is very low-pitched *co-woo* (about 5 times).

RED-BILLED PIGEON
Colúmba flavíróstris

Uncommon in summer (rare in midwinter); in woodlands and brush along the lower Rio Grande River (west to Falcon Reservoir) in southern Texas. A large all-dark bird, the size and shape of a Rock Dove; note its red bill. Call, *hoo-hoohoohoohooo*.

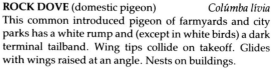

White-winged Dove

Mourning Dove

falcon

Killdeer

Mourning Dove

Rock Dove

cuckoo

BAND-
TAILED
PIGEON
L 13½"

Rock Doves
feeding

PIGEONS AND
LARGE DOVES

White-winged
Dove

ROCK DOVE
L 11"

WHITE-
WINGED
DOVE
L 10"

Mourning Dove
on nest

MOURNING
DOVE
L 10½"

WHITE-
CROWNED
PIGEON
L 11"

RED-
BILLED
PIGEON
L 11½"

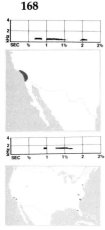

SPOTTED DOVE *Streptopélia chinénsis*
Introduced. Locally common resident in Los Angeles County, California; occurs from Santa Barbara to San Diego. Heavier-bodied than Mourning Dove (p. 166); its tail is rounded and more broadly tipped with white. No other dove has the "lace-neck" pattern, present only in the adult. Found in agricultural lands, parks, and suburbs. Call is a low, harsh whistle: *hoo-hoooo-hoo*.

RINGED TURTLE-DOVE *Streptopélia risória*
A common cage bird that has become resident in central downtown Los Angeles and locally from Miami to Baltimore. Told by its sandy plumage and black crescent on the back of its neck. Slimmer than brown Rock Dove (p. 166) and lacks white rump. Call, *hoo-hrrooo*.

RUDDY GROUND-DOVE *Columbína talpacóti*
Rare winter visitor to southern Texas. Rufous with gray crown. Female is less rufous, more gray, without scales.

COMMON GROUND-DOVE *Columbína passerína*
Common in brush and farmlands in the Far South. Wings flash bright rufous in flight. On the ground it looks like a miniature Mourning Dove (p. 166). Nests usually on ground. Call, a series of identical low soft whistles, each with a rising inflection: *hooah*, 40-60/min.

INCA DOVE *Columbína ínca*
A tiny-bodied, long-tailed dove resident in suburban areas, irrigated fields, and pastures in the arid Southwest. The body is distinctly gray, without a brownish cast; the rufous area in primaries may show only in flight. Scaly back is diagnostic when on the ground. In flight note the white margin to the long gray tail. Call is a monotonous repetition suggesting that of Common Ground-Dove, but the *coos* are in pairs, 25-30/min.

WHITE-TIPPED DOVE *Leptótila verreaúxi*
An uncommon resident of the lower Rio Grande Valley, Texas. Similar in size and shape to White-winged Dove (p. 166), but white is restricted to forehead, belly, and tip of the tail. Wings are uniform brown above with bright chestnut linings below. Feeds on the ground near brush or wooded areas. Call is 2 soft, very low-pitched *hoo*s, dropping in pitch at the end (like distant foghorn).

INTRODUCED AND SMALL DOVES

im.

SPOTTED DOVE L 11"

RINGED TURTLE-DOVE L 10"

♂

♀

RUDDY GROUND-DOVE L 5¾"

♂

♀

COMMON GROUND-DOVE L 5½"

♂

Common Ground-Doves

INCA DOVE L 6½"

WHITE-TIPPED DOVE L 10"

PARROTS (*Order* Psittaciformes, *Family* Psittacidae) are brightly colored tropical birds with short, heavy, strongly hooked beaks and short legs; 2 toes in front, 2 behind. All originate from escapees. Most lay 3-5 white eggs in a tree cavity.

BUDGERIGAR   *Melopsíttacus undulátus*
Abundant in the St. Petersburg, Fla., area; local elsewhere in s. Fla. and s. Calif. Note the small size, fine barring. From Australia.

GREEN PARAKEET   *Aratínga holóchlora*
Rare in s. Tex. and Fla.; recognized by yellow-green body, solid green wings. From Mexico. **Hispaniolan Parakeet** (*A. chloróptera*, L 11″), rare near Miami, is similar but has red underwing coverts contrasting with gold underwings and tail. From West Indies. (Not illustrated.)

ORANGE-FRONTED PARAKEET   *Aratínga caniculáris*
Casual in N. Mex., local s.e. Fla. to N.Y.; told by orange forehead, blue on wing, yellow underparts. From Mexico.

BLACK-HOODED CONURE   *Nandáyus nénday*
Rare in Loma Linda, Calif.; also several records from the Northeast. Told by its black head and red "pant legs." From South America.

MONK PARAKEET   *Myiopsítta mónachus*
Nearly became widely established in e. U.S.; builds huge colonial stick nests. Gray breast and hood are diagnostic. From South America.

CANARY-WINGED PARAKEET   *Brotógeris versicolúrus*
Well established in s.e. Fla. and in San Pedro, Calif.; local in Northeast. Recognized by yellow, white, blue, and green wing pattern. From South America. More local in s.e. Fla. is the **Orange-chinned Parakeet** (*B. juguláris*, L 5″), with its orange chin, yellow-lined green wings, and short tail. From South and Middle America. (Not illustrated.)

YELLOW-HEADED PARROT   *Amazóna ochrocéphala*
Presumably escaped; found occasionally from Fla. to s. Calif. Adult is recognized by all yellow head, large red wing patch, and red at base of short tail; young are all green. From Mexico.

RED-CROWNED PARROT   *Amazóna viridigénalis*
Rare in Los Angeles area and s. Tex., established in s.e. Fla. Has entire red cap, red wing patch, gold under its short tail. From Mexico.

ROSE-RINGED PARAKEET   *Psittácula krámeri*
Rare in s. Calif. and Miami areas; local in Northeast. Has green head, red bill, and pale greenish tail. From Asia.

BLOSSOM-HEADED PARAKEET   *Psittácula roseáta*
Rare and local in Northeast. Told by rose head, orange bill, and (on male) black neck band; young are all green with yellow bill. From Asia.

PARROTS

BUDGERIGAR
L 6"

MONK
PARAKEET
L 10"

GREEN
PARAKEET
L 10"

ORANGE-
FRONTED
PARAKEET
L 8"

CANARY-
WINGED
PARAKEET
L 7½"

BLACK-
HOODED
CONURE
L 10"

RED-
CROWNED
PARROT
L 10"

nest

ROSE-
RINGED
PARAKEET
L 14"

♂

♀

YELLOW-HEADED
PARROT   L 12"

BLOSSOM-
HEADED
PARAKEET
L 11"

■ **CUCKOOS, ANIS, AND ROADRUNNERS** (*Order* Cuculiformes, *Family* Cuculidae) are slender birds with rounded wings, curved upper mandibles, and long "graduated" tails, the outer tail feathers shortest. Sexes are alike. Cuckoos are sluggish birds of forest and brush; they eat hairy caterpillars. The coal-black anis resemble large grackles except for their weak flight, thick bills, and heavy tails. Roadrunners are large, crested ground birds of the arid Southwest. Eggs, 2-12.

MANGROVE CUCKOO   *Coccýzus mínor*
Rare and local resident in mangroves and hammocks of Florida Keys and southwest coast of Florida north to Tampa Bay. Usually outnumbered by Yellow-billed Cuckoos. Note the bright buffy underparts and black mask. Call is harsher and slower than Yellow-billed's.

YELLOW-BILLED CUCKOO   *Coccýzus americánus.*
The commonest nesting cuckoo south of the Missouri and Ohio rivers and the only one west of the Rockies. Told from Black-billed by large white spots contrasting with black undertail surface, also by the bright rufous flash in the open wing and by the yellow lower mandible. Found in woods and brush, especially during outbreaks of tent caterpillars. Song, guttural and toneless in comparison with Black-billed's, is never in series of 3 or 4.

BLACK-BILLED CUCKOO   *Coccýzus erythropthálmus*
Common in eastern North America. Tail spots are indistinct and the bill is all black. Has little or no rufous in spread wing. Bare skin around eye of adult is red. Like Yellow-billed Cuckoo, most common at caterpillar outbreaks. Typical song is 3 or 4 *coos*, 35-52 series/min.

SMOOTH-BILLED ANI   *Crotóphaga áni*
Local resident in southern Florida (Belleglade south into Keys). Feeds in small flocks on the ground in brush and farmland. Likely to be overlooked because of resemblance to grackles. **Groove-billed Ani** (*Crotóphaga sulciróstris*, L 14"), resident in southern Texas, has smoother bill-forehead profile; grooves on bill are visible at close range.

GREATER ROADRUNNER   *Geocóccyx californiánus*
Large, crested, terrestrial bird of arid Southwest. Wings are short and rounded. Runs rapidly, trailing its long white-tipped tail. Seldom flies. Eats lizards, snakes, insects. Song, dove-like, each note lower pitched.

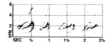

Smooth-billed Ani

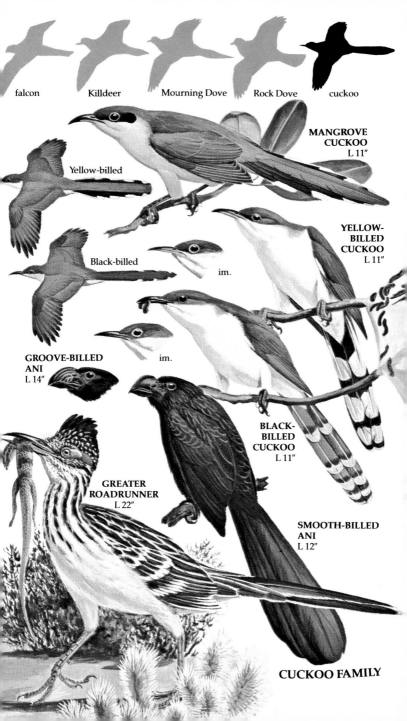

falcon   Killdeer   Mourning Dove   Rock Dove   cuckoo

MANGROVE
CUCKOO
L 11″

Yellow-billed

YELLOW-
BILLED
CUCKOO
L 11″

Black-billed

im.

GROOVE-BILLED
ANI
L 14″

im.

BLACK-
BILLED
CUCKOO
L 11″

GREATER
ROADRUNNER
L 22″

SMOOTH-BILLED
ANI
L 12″

CUCKOO FAMILY

■ **OWLS** (*Order* Strigiformes, *Families* Tytonidae—the Barn Owls—and Strigidae—all other owls), large-headed, short-necked birds of prey, are mostly nocturnal and best seen and more frequently heard at dusk. The large eyes are fixed in their sockets, so the entire head moves as owls shift their gaze. The flat, round or heart-shaped "facial disk" conceals the large external ear flaps. All owls on this page and some on p. 180 have erect ear tufts. All fly silently, hunting for rodents and other mammals. Females are like males, but larger; immatures resemble adults. Calls are distinctive hoots, wails, or whistles. Most small owls and some large ones are cavity nesters. Eggs, 2-8.

EASTERN SCREECH-OWL   *Ótus ásio*
This is the common small "eared" owl of towns, orchards, and small woodlots. Its plumage is bright rusty or gray. All other eastern "eared" owls are distinctly larger. Nests in cavities and even in flicker boxes. Song is quavering whistle (monotone or descending).

WESTERN SCREECH-OWL   *Ótus kénnicottii*
Similar to Eastern Screech-Owl but plumage is brown. Flammulated and Whiskered Screech-Owls (p. 180) are similar, but Western's facial disk is the same color as the head. Call, 4-10 short low-pitched whistles.

Western   Eastern

GREAT HORNED OWL   *Búbo virginiánus*
This common large "eared" owl is twice the size of the crows that often harass it. Color pattern is similar to the smaller slimmer Long-eared Owl's; Horned Owl's ear tufts are larger and farther apart; its belly is finely barred horizontally, whereas the Long-eared is more boldly streaked lengthwise. Call is typically 4 to 7 low hoots.

LONG-EARED OWL   *Ásio ótus*
Locally common in woods near open country. All similar species, especially the Great Horned Owl, are on this page. Looks large in flight because of its very long wings. Generally silent except near its nest, where it makes a variety of low hoots, whistles, and shrieks.

SHORT-EARED OWL   *Ásio flámmeus*
Locally common in open country over plains, sloughs, and marshes. The "ears" are hard to see. Note the black patch near bend of the underwing and the large buffy area on upper wing surface. Active before dark; flight is irregular. Wings are tilted upward like a harrier's (p. 70). Barks during breeding season; otherwise silent.

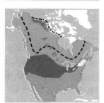

Great Horned Owl

Long-eared Owl

buteo

owl

nighthawk

crow

WIDESPREAD OWLS

EASTERN SCREECH-OWL
L 8″ W 22″

red phase

WESTERN SCREECH-OWL
L 8″ W 22″

Eastern gray phase

GREAT HORNED OWL
L 20″ W 55″

LONG-EARED OWL
L 13″ W 39″

Long-eared Owl

Short-eared Owl

SHORT-EARED OWL
L 13″ W 41″

BARN OWL *Týto álba*

This large light-colored uncommon owl is known by its heart-shaped face, small dark eyes, and long legs. All other owls except the Snowy are heavily marked below. It is strictly nocturnal; hunts rats and mice in farmyards, marshes, and fields. It has a peculiar habit of lowering its head and moving it back and forth. It nests in barns, abandoned buildings, and tree cavities. Does not hoot, but has a soft ascending wheezy cry. At the nest it gives a toneless hiss.

SNOWY OWL *Nýctea scandíaca*

A diurnal arctic owl that winters irregularly in the U.S. Most adult birds are almost pure white. Immatures, which are darker, go farther south than adults in winter. The large size, pale plumage, and lack of ear tufts are diagnostic. It perches near the ground in open country and often allows birders to approach closely. Feeds on lemmings and other rodents and hares. Silent south of its breeding grounds.

BARRED OWL *Stríx vária*

Common in southern swamps and river bottoms; less common, but widespread, in northern woods. Has dark eyes; the only other eastern owl with dark eyes is the unstreaked heart-faced Barn Owl. In flight the Barred Owl resembles the Great Horned (p. 174). Usually nests in cavities. Typically hoots 8 times; 4-7 series/min.

SPOTTED OWL *Stríx occidentális*

This rare western counterpart of the Barred Owl is identified by the horizontal barring of its underparts. The dark-eyed Flammulated Owl (p. 180) of the West is similar, but is much smaller and has short ear tufts. Common call of Spotted is suggestive of Barred Owl's, but consists of only 3 or 4 hoots.

GREAT GRAY OWL *Stríx nebulósa*

Rare and local at high elevations in north and central Sierra Nevada and Rockies, where it is found in pine and spruce forests. Common only in the Far North. Note the long tail and the prominent gray concentric circles on the facial disk. The only other large owl with yellow eyes and no ear tufts is the Snowy. Voice is a deep, booming series of *whoo*s, each lower in pitch.

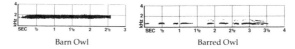

Barn Owl   Barred Owl

LARGE EARLESS OWLS

Barn Owls

BARN OWL
L 14″ W 44″

SNOWY OWL
L 20″ W 55″

ad.

im.
♀

BARRED OWL
L 17″ W 44″

SPOTTED OWL
L 16″ W 42″

GREAT GRAY OWL
L 22″ W 60″

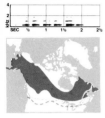

NORTHERN HAWK-OWL
Súrnia úlula

A tame diurnal owl of the muskegs of northern Canada, rarely moving south in winter into northern U.S. No other owls except the little pygmies (p. 180) have the long slender tail that gives this bird a falcon-like appearance. Told from Boreal and Northern Saw-whet Owls by the fine horizontal barring of its underparts. Perches in the open on treetops, where it raises its tail and slowly lowers it. Sometimes sits with its tail cocked up at an angle. Flight is straight and swift, usually very low, with alternate flapping and gliding. It also hovers, as does the American Kestrel (p. 80). Calls are series of whistles, 10-15 groups/min.

BURROWING OWL
Athéne cuniculária

A small long-legged diurnal owl of the plains, locally common, usually nesting in prairie dog "towns." The permanent residents in Florida inhabit prairies and airports. Frequently bobs up and down. Perches on the ground or on a fencepost. Hovers when hunting. Distinguished from all other owls except the Barn Owl (p. 176) by sandy color and long legs. Nests in burrows. Calls are a cackling alarm note and, at night, a 2-note *coo-c-o-o.*

BOREAL OWL
Aególius funéreus

A very tame, nocturnal, "earless" owl of coniferous forests in the Far North, irregular in northern U.S. in winter. Told from Saw-whet Owl by its light bill, black facial border, and chocolate streaking of its underparts. Told from Screech-Owls (p. 174) by the lack of ear tufts and from Northern Hawk-Owl by streaked underparts, short tail, and more erect posture. Only during the arctic summer does it feed by day. Call is a fast series of 7-8 whistles like the sound of water dripping; 12-15 groups/min.

NORTHERN SAW-WHET OWL
Aególius acádicus

The only tiny tuftless owl likely to be seen in the central and eastern states. Commoner than generally believed, but nocturnal and seldom seen unless found roosting in dense young evergreens or in thickets. In the West it overlaps the range of the Flammulated Owl (p. 180), which has dark eyes and ear tufts, and the Northern Pygmy-Owl (p. 180), which is slender and long-tailed with dark brown streaks on flanks. Common call is a long series of short whistles.

SMALL OWLS 1

NORTHERN HAWK-OWL
L 14″ W 33″

BURROWING OWL
L 8″ W 22″

Burrowing Owls
with prairie dogs

chickadees scolding
Northern Saw-whet Owl

BOREAL OWL
L 10″ W 24″

**NORTHERN
SAW-WHET OWL**
L 7″ W 17″

juv.

WHISKERED SCREECH-OWL · *Ótus trichópsis*

Common in Southwest canyons. Closely resembles the Western Screech-Owl (p. 174), whose range it overlaps; can be distinguished only at exceedingly close range. Watch for long whiskers and large white spots on scapulars. Generally found in dense oak or oak-pine woods. Distinctive call, 4 to 9 high-pitched *boos* slowing at the end, is best means of identification.

FLAMMULATED OWL · *Ótus flamméolus*

Rare and local. The only small owl with dark eyes. Like the Screech-Owls, it occurs in gray and rusty phases, but the facial disk of Flammulated is redder than the rest of its head. Only in southeast Arizona do Flammulated and Western and Whiskered Screech-Owls occur together. Prefers pine-oak woods. Call is a single or double low-pitched hoot, repeated for long periods, 40-60/min.

NORTHERN PYGMY-OWL · *Glaucídium gnóma*

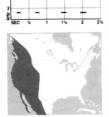

A small, common, tame, long-tailed owl of coniferous and deciduous woods. Partly diurnal. No other small "earless" owl has blackish-streaked flanks. Entire tail extends beyond the wing tips and is usually cocked at an angle. Flight is undulating like a shrike's (p. 260), with rapid wingbeats. Black patch at the side of its hind neck separates it from all owls but the rust-colored Ferruginous Pygmy-Owl. Song is an accelerating short series like Wrentit's (p. 232) followed by 2 or 3 singles.

ELF OWL · *Micrathéne whítneyi*

A nocturnal owl common in southwestern deserts. The underparts are buffy with indistinct streaking. No ear tufts. This tiny slim owl has a short tail that separates it from Northern and Ferruginous Pygmy-Owls. Best seen at dusk in saguaro deserts, as it roosts by day in holes in the giant cactus. Common call is a descending whistled *tu-tu-tu, tu-tu-tu-tu*.

FERRUGINOUS PYGMY-OWL · *Glaucídium brasiliánum*

This small, uncommon, rusty relative of the Northern Pygmy-Owl is typical of wooded river bottoms and saguaro deserts near the Mexican border. Told from Northern Pygmy-Owl by its plain rusty back, rusty streaks on the sides, and a tail faintly barred with black on rust. Call is a long series of single notes.

SMALL OWLS 2

WHISKERED SCREECH-OWL
L 6½" W 16"

Western Screech-Owl
for comparison

FLAMMULATED OWL
L 6" W 14"

NORTHERN PYGMY-OWL
L 6" W 15"

ELF OWL
L 5¼" W 15"

FERRUGINOUS PYGMY-OWL

L 6" W 15"

182

GOATSUCKERS (*Order* Caprimulgiformes, *Family* Caprimulgidae) are nocturnal insect eaters with large flat heads, small bills, enormous mouths, and distinctive white patches in wings or tail. Many are named for their call. Eggs (2) are usually laid on ground.

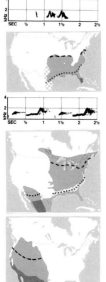

CHUCK-WILL'S-WIDOW *Caprimúlgus carolinénsis*
Common in Southeast pine woods. Told from nighthawks by lack of white in wing, from Whip-poor-will by much larger size, more buffy body, and by the call. Narrow throat band is buffy in female. Song, 25-40/min.

WHIP-POOR-WILL *Caprimúlgus vocíferus*
This common round-winged goatsucker is seen only at dusk unless flushed from nest or ground roost in woods. Its eyes glow red in a light beam. Prefers woods near fields. Female has buffy throat band, no white on tail. Song, 50-65/min. **Buff-collared Nightjar** (*Caprimúlgus rídgwayi*, L 8½"), of southeastern Arizona, is told from the Whip-poor-will by the buff collar across back of neck. Song, *co-co-co-co-cookachea*.

COMMON POORWILL *Phalaenóptilus núttallii*
This small relative replaces the Whip-poor-will in the West. White in tail of both sexes is quite limited; young have buffy collar. Song is repeated 30-40/min.

COMMON PAURAQUE *Nyctídromus albicóllis*
This large species of southern Texas brush country has white patches in its wings and tail. Call, 10-12/min.

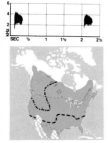

COMMON NIGHTHAWK *Chordeíles mínor*
Nighthawks differ from other goatsuckers in their long pointed wings, slightly forked tails, and white wing patches. They become active before dark, flying above treetops and houses. They sit lengthwise on limbs, diagonally on wires. In cities it nests on flat-topped buildings. In courtship dive, the wings produce a peculiar musical hum. Call is a nasal *peent* like woodcock's, 25-35/min.

ANTILLEAN NIGHTHAWK *Chordeíles gúndlachii*
Breeds on Florida keys. Told by *pit-a-pit* call.

LESSER NIGHTHAWK *Chordeíles acutipénnis*
Told from Common Nighthawk by its smaller size, position of white in wings, browner color, habit of flying very low, and low trilling call. Young in late summer are buffy.

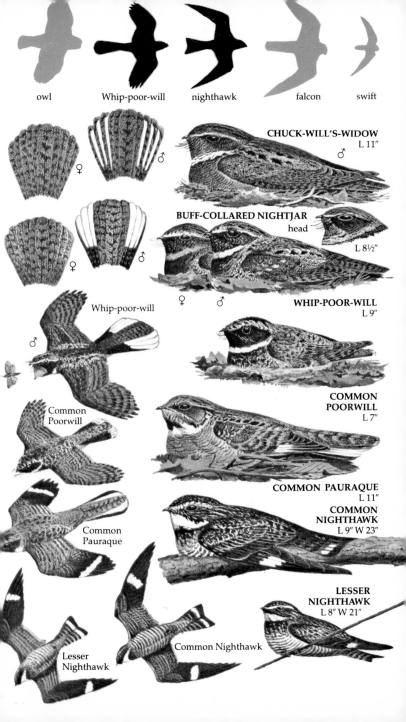

owl Whip-poor-will nighthawk falcon swift

♀ ♂

♀ ♂

CHUCK-WILL'S-WIDOW
♂
L 11″

BUFF-COLLARED NIGHTJAR
head
L 8½″

♀ ♂

WHIP-POOR-WILL
L 9″

Whip-poor-will
♂

Common
Poorwill

**COMMON
POORWILL**
L 7″

COMMON PAURAQUE
L 11″

Common
Pauraque

**COMMON
NIGHTHAWK**
L 9″ W 23″

**LESSER
NIGHTHAWK**
L 8″ W 21″

Lesser
Nighthawk

Common Nighthawk

184

■ **SWIFTS** (*Order* Apodiformes, *Family* Apodidae), like goatsuckers, feed almost exclusively on flying insects caught on the wing with their wide mouths. Swifts fly continuously all day except in heavy rain. Their wings, built for speed, are long, stiff, slender, and slightly decurved. In contrast to swallows, with which they are often found, swifts appear to beat their wings alternately. Sexes are alike. Swifts nest on cliffs, in chimneys, and in hollow trees. Eggs are white, 3-6 (1 by Black Swift).

BLACK SWIFT
Cypseloídes níger

This uncommon swift has solid black underparts and a slightly forked tail. When seen with Vaux's Swift, its larger size is obvious. The adult male Purple Martin (p. 220) is similar, but has broad wings bent at the wrist. The Black Swift's wrist is so close to the body that the wing angle is barely visible. Cruises many miles from its high-altitude and coastal nesting cliffs. Unlike Vaux's and Chimney Swifts, is seldom heard away from the nest.

CHIMNEY SWIFT
Chaetúra pelágica

Normally the only swift east of the Missouri and Mississippi rivers. Common, usually in flocks of flittering dark birds. Tail is stiff, slightly rounded, and never forked or fanned; bristles that support the tail when clinging to a vertical surface are not visible in the field. Noisy chatter of chipping notes generally discloses Chimney Swifts overhead. During migration they roost by the hundreds in tall chimneys, entering in a huge funnel formation at dusk. Call, rapid short chips.

VAUX'S SWIFT
Chaetúra vaúxi

Replaces Chimney Swift west of Rockies. Told from swallows by typical body shape, from White-throated Swift by slightly rounded tail and uniformly pale underparts. Smaller, browner, and paler below than the very similar Chimney Swift. It nests in hollow trees in dense forests; rarely in chimneys. Voice is like Chimney's.

WHITE-THROATED SWIFT
Aeronaútes saxátalis

Common. Only North American swift with bold black and white pattern. Most likely to be confused with Violet-green Swallow (p. 220), with which it associates. Violet-green also has white flank patches, visible from above and below, but its entire underparts are white. White-throated is found near cliffs and canyons. Call, shrill twitter.

falcon

nighthawk

swift

swallow

SWIFTS

BLACK SWIFT
L 7″

CHIMNEY SWIFT
L 5″ W 12½″

VAUX'S SWIFT
L 4½″

White-throated Swift

WHITE-THROATED SWIFT
L 6½″ W 14″

Violet-green Swallow
for comparison

● **HUMMINGBIRDS** (*Order* Apodiformes, *Family* Trochilidae) are the smallest of North American birds, all with long slender bills adapted for reaching deep into tubular flowers. Wingbeat is so rapid it produces a humming sound. All species feed while hovering and can also fly backward. Throat feathers look black when light does not reflect the brilliant iridescent colors. Young birds resemble females; some are difficult to identify. All are fearless and pugnacious. Males have a "pendulum" courting flight, with distinctive patterns for some species. Migrate by day, flying low. Eggs, 2, are small, white.

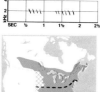

RUBY-THROATED HUMMINGBIRD
Archílochus cólubris

Common. Only hummingbird east of Great Plains except Rufous (p. 188), which is rare in Gulf and South Atlantic states in late fall and winter. Only the adult male has the bright red throat. Often detected by rapid, squeaky, chipping made in flight or by the hum of the wings. Found near tubular flowers in gardens or woods.

BROAD-TAILED HUMMINGBIRD
Selásphorus platycércus

This is the common breeding hummer of the Rockies. Adult male is readily told from Ruby-throated by its distinctive shrill metallic wing whistling. First-year male does not whistle; look for wider rounded tail and rose-colored throat. No other western hummer has a green crown and tail and a solid red throat. Females are similar to several other hummers. Calliope is much smaller, with wings extending beyond the tail. Broad-tailed female cannot safely be separated from Rufous and Allen's (p. 188).

CALLIOPE HUMMINGBIRD
Stéllula callíope

Smallest U.S. hummer; uncommon in western mountains. Male is only hummer whose colored throat feathers form streaks against a white background. The red feathers can be distended. Female is much smaller than Broad-tailed; smaller, slimmer, and shorter-tailed than Rufous and Allen's (p. 188), with less rufous on sides and tail.

ANNA'S HUMMINGBIRD
Calýpte ánna

Common resident west of Sierras. Forehead and throat red. Female's green tail broadly tipped with white; throat usually has a few red feathers. Female is larger and stouter than Black-chinned (p. 188), and grayer breasted; larger and darker below than Costa's (p. 188). Male is only California hummer with a real song (from perch).

flight display

HUMMINGBIRDS 1

RUBY-THROATED HUMMINGBIRD
L 3″

♀ im. ♂ ♂

♂ Broad-tailed

♂

BROAD-TAILED HUMMINGBIRD
L 3¾″

♀

♀

Broad-tailed Hummingbird

♀

distended bib

♂ ♂

CALLIOPE HUMMINGBIRD
L 2¾″

Calliope Hummingbird flight display

♂ ♂

♀

ANNA'S HUMMINGBIRD
L 3½″

BLACK-CHINNED HUMMINGBIRD
Archílochus alexándri

Common in western mountains, this is our only hummer with a truly black throat; throats of other species may look black in poor light. White below the purple stripe confirms this species. Often captures insects flycatcher-fashion. Female has no rufous on sides and tail and is not safely separable from Costa's. Female Anna's (p. 187), which is restricted to California and southern Arizona, is larger and plumper. Call, a slurred *thew*.

COSTA'S HUMMINGBIRD
Calýpte cóstae

Common in Southwest deserts. Male is unmistakable with violet cap and throat, the latter with long side feathers. Female is not safely told from Black-chinned. Female Anna's (p. 187) is larger and slightly darker below and often has red flecks on throat. Immature Calliope and other species commonly found in Costa's range have rufous sides and tail base. Call is rapid ticking.

RUFOUS HUMMINGBIRD
Selásphorus rúfus

Abundant migrant in West; the common breeding hummer of western Oregon, Washington, and western Canada. Adult male has unmistakable solid rufous back. Female and immature are similar to Allen's, the larger Broad-tailed, and smaller Calliope (folded wings of Calliope extend beyond tail). Female Allen's is separable only at very close range by its narrow outer tail feather. In normal flight the male produces a subdued humming, but his aerial display is a rapid dive to within inches of female, accompanied by a loud whine.

ALLEN'S HUMMINGBIRD
Selásphorus sásin

Common only in coastal California. The male is our only red-throated hummer with a solid rufous tail and a green cap and back. The female and immature are so similar to Rufous they can be told only in breeding season when Rufous is absent. Even the call notes of the two species are the same: a sharp *bzee*. The courtship pendulum flight of the male (a 25′ arc) is followed by a dive from about 100′.

CUBAN EMERALD
Chlorostílbon ricórdii

Casual, all seasons, on Florida east coast and Keys. Male is told by bright green underparts and black forked tail, female by forked tail and dingy underparts.

♀

♂

**BLACK-CHINNED
HUMMINGBIRD**
L 3″

Costa's
display
flight

♂

bib
extended

♂

**COSTA'S
HUMMINGBIRD**
L 3″

♀

**RUFOUS
HUMMINGBIRD**
L 3½″

♂

im. ♂

Rufous
display
flight

**ALLEN'S
HUMMINGBIRD**
L 3″

♂

♂

♀

**CUBAN
EMERALD**
L 4″

♀

- **SOUTHWEST HUMMINGBIRDS** include species found in summer along U.S.-Mexican border. Those that breed in U.S. are mapped below. Four species have bright red or orange bills with black tips.

LUCIFER HUMMINGBIRD *Calothórax lúcifer*
Male is only violet-throated hummingbird with green crown; tail deeply forked. Female is the only one with a buff throat and decurved bill. Very rare breeder in Chisos Mountains, Texas, and s.e. Arizona.

MAGNIFICENT HUMMINGBIRD *Eúgenes fúlgens*
Male is told by its large size, green throat, and violet-blue crown; female is recognized by its large size, dark bill, and narrow grayish tail edging. Breeds from southeastern Arizona mountains to Chisos Mountains, Texas.

BLUE-THROATED HUMMINGBIRD
Lampórnis cleménciae
Recognized by its large size, the very broad white tip to its long black tail, and double white line on the face. Blue throat of male is obvious at close range.

VIOLET-CROWNED HUMMINGBIRD
Amazília vióliceps
No other North American hummingbird has violet crown and white throat. Female and immature have lighter and greener crowns. Breeds in Guadalupe Canyon, Chiricahua Mountains, Arizona; recorded in Huachucas.

BUFF-BELLIED HUMMINGBIRD *Amazília yucatanénsis*
Bright orange bill, large size, and green throat separate this species from other Texas hummers. Sexes are alike. Breeds and in small numbers winters in the lower Rio Grande Valley, in wood margins and thickets.

BROAD-BILLED HUMMINGBIRD
Cynánthus latiróstris
Male is told by its dark body, long orange bill, and forked tail; female by its orange bill and sooty underparts. Compare carefully with the paler-breasted White-eared. Breeds from south central Arizona and southwest New Mexico southward, rarely in western Texas.

WHITE-EARED HUMMINGBIRD *Hylocháris leucótis*
Only small hummingbird with long "ear" stripe. Male may appear all dark, like Broad-billed, but tail is square-tipped. Note green flanks, spotted throat of female. Casual in s.e. Arizona mountains in summer.

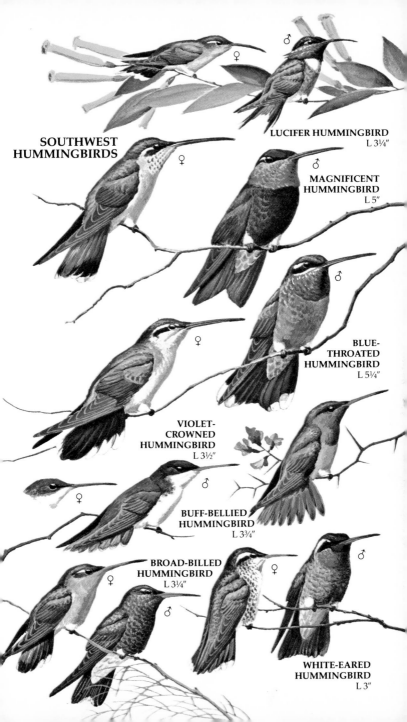

SOUTHWEST HUMMINGBIRDS

LUCIFER HUMMINGBIRD
L 3¼″

MAGNIFICENT HUMMINGBIRD
L 5″

BLUE-THROATED HUMMINGBIRD
L 5¼″

VIOLET-CROWNED HUMMINGBIRD
L 3½″

BUFF-BELLIED HUMMINGBIRD
L 3¾″

BROAD-BILLED HUMMINGBIRD
L 3¼″

WHITE-EARED HUMMINGBIRD
L 3″

■ **TROGONS** (*Order* Trogoniformes, *Family* Trogonidae) are short-billed, long-tailed, tropical fruit eaters represented in extreme southwestern U.S. by one regular breeder and one accidental species. Habit of sitting still makes them hard to find despite brilliant coloration. Posture is erect, tail hanging straight down. Nest in cavities. Eggs 2-4.

ELEGANT TROGON
Trógon élegans

Rare summer resident in mountains of southeast Arizona; casual in lower Rio Grande Valley, Texas. Iridescent male is unmistakable; all plumages have black band at tip of long square-cut tail, rose on belly, and yellow bill. Call, 4-6 low croaks. **Eared Trogon** (*Euptilótis neoxénus*, L 11"), accidental in Chiricahua Mountains, Arizona, has black bill, no barring on white undertail, no white chest band.

■ **KINGFISHERS** (*Order* Coraciiformes, *Family* Alcedinidae) are large-headed, short-tailed birds that dive for fish, which they catch with their long sharp beaks. They perch motionless in the open, over water. Their legs are very short. Usually lay 3-8 white eggs in a deep burrow in a steep bank.

RINGED KINGFISHER
Céryle torquáta

Rare permanent resident along Rio Grande River, Texas, especially below Falcon Dam. Told from Belted Kingfisher in all plumages by much larger size and bright rusty belly. Female has a broad blue neck band set off from the rusty breast by a white ring. Both sexes have the shaggy crest. Calls, a harsh *keerek* and a rattle louder than that of the Belted Kingfisher.

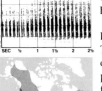

BELTED KINGFISHER
Céryle álcyon

The most common kingfisher in North America and the only one north of Texas and Arizona. Seen singly or in pairs along streams and ponds. Except for terns, kingfishers are the only small birds that dive headlong from air into water. Recognized in flight by its deep, irregular wingbeats, its big-headed appearance, and its loud rattling call. Often hovers before diving.

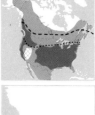

GREEN KINGFISHER
Chlorocéryle americána

Rare in southeast Arizona and lower Rio Grande Valley. Its small size, green back, and lack of a crest distinguish it immediately from the other kingfishers. Rattle is higher-pitched and less harsh than Belted Kingfisher's. Female has greenish breast bands; male has a rusty one.

TROGONS, KINGFISHERS

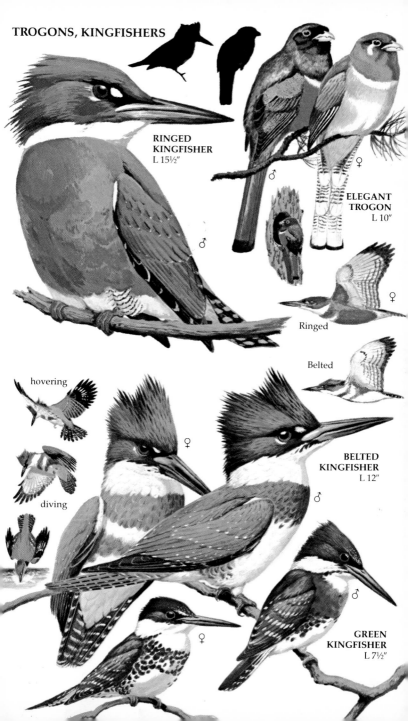

RINGED KINGFISHER L 15½″ ♂

ELEGANT TROGON L 10″ ♂ ♀

Ringed ♀

Belted

hovering

diving

♀

BELTED KINGFISHER L 12″ ♂

GREEN KINGFISHER L 7½″ ♂

♀

194

WOODPECKERS (*Order* Piciformes, *Family* Picidae) have a strong bill, sharply pointed for chipping and digging into tree trunks or branches for wood-boring insects. The stiff tail is used as a prop. Most species "drum" on resonant limbs, poles, or drainpipes. Flight is usually undulating, with wings folded against the body after each series of flaps. Nest is in a cavity chiseled deep into a large branch or trunk. Eggs, 4-8, are white.

Yellow-shafted races

Red-shafted races

Gilded races

Pileated Woodpecker

COMMON FLICKER — *Coláptes aurátus*

Common in open country near large trees. Flickers are jay-sized woodpeckers with brown back, no white on wings, and a black breast crescent. In flight note white rump, yellow or salmon under wings and tail. Often seen on the ground eating ants and displaying. Call is a loud repeated *flick* or *flicker*; series repeated 2-7/min. Also a shrill descending *kee-oo*.

Three populations, formerly recognized as distinct species, are separable in the field by their plumage. The northern and eastern Yellow-shafted races are recognized by the red nape and gray cap, the black moustaches (absent only in the adult female), and the golden undersurface of the wings and tail. The Red-shafted races, which occupy most of the West, are told by the salmon wing and tail linings, and by the brown cap, gray face, and red moustaches that they have in common with the Gilded races of the Southwest. The Gilded races have golden wing and tail linings like the Yellow-shafted races, but their ranges do not overlap. Red-shafted birds hybridize with both Yellow-shafted and Gilded birds, producing intermediate plumages.

PILEATED WOODPECKER — *Dryócopus pileátus*

Uncommon; a wary bird of extensive deciduous or mixed forests. Solid black back distinguishes it from other large birds except crows and some hawks. It is conspicuously crested in all plumages. Flight is strong with irregular flaps of wings. Drumming is distinctive: loud, slow, softer at end. Call is a series, never single.

IVORY-BILLED WOODPECKER
Campéphilus principális

On verge of extinction. Last reported in deep forests of southeast Texas, central Louisiana, northwest Florida, and South Carolina. Extensive white on wing, folded and in flight, and white bill are diagnostic. Male has red crest, female black. Call is a high-pitched single note.

Pileated Woodpecker

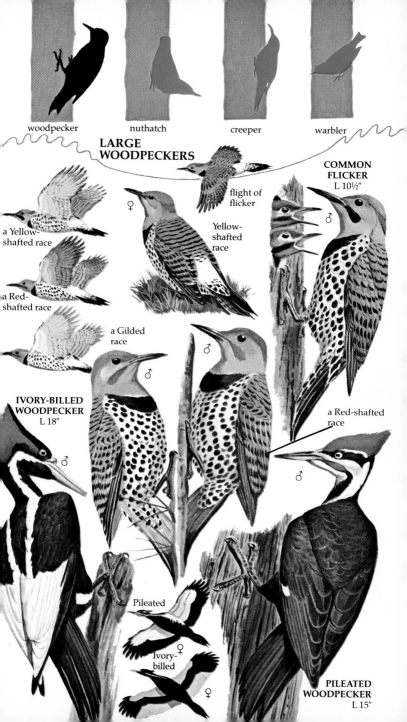

woodpecker

nuthatch

creeper

warbler

LARGE WOODPECKERS

flight of flicker

COMMON FLICKER
L 10½″

♂

a Yellow-shafted race

♀

Yellow-shafted race

a Red-shafted race

a Gilded race

♂

♂

IVORY-BILLED WOODPECKER
L 18″

♂

a Red-shafted race

♂

Pileated

Ivory-billed

♀

♀

PILEATED WOODPECKER
L 15″

- **LADDER-BACKED WOODPECKERS** fall into two groups: medium-sized birds with light rumps, colored or pale napes, and white wing patches that show in flight; and small birds with dark rumps, black napes, and spotted sides. All are non-migratory. Juvenile is like adult, but juvenile heads are browner in *Melanérpes*.

RED-BELLIED WOODPECKER   *Melanérpes carolínus*
Common in southeastern woodlands. Red-headed Woodpecker (p. 198) is same size and has a similar call, but note the ladder back and red cap and hind neck (not head) of the Red-bellied. Immature has brown head. May occur with Red-cockaded in longleaf pine woods. Calls are low, short, and hoarse; also a rattle.

GOLDEN-FRONTED WOODPECKER
Melanérpes aúrifrons
Common in deciduous woodlands. Note the large gold spot on hind neck (duller in immature) and yellow above bill in adult. Voice is like Red-bellied's.

GILA WOODPECKER   *Melanérpes uropygiális*
Common around giant cactus. Note that only the male has a red cap. White wing patches, as in Red-bellied, tell it from all ladder-backed woodpeckers in its range. Compare with immature sapsuckers (p. 198).

LADDER-BACKED WOODPECKER   *Picoídes scaláris*
Fairly common in deciduous woods and mesquite, less common in cactus. Note distinct black and white on side of head. Told from Gila and Golden-fronted Woodpeckers by dark rump, finely spotted sides, and lack of white wing patch in flight. Call is like a hoarse Downy's (p. 200).

RED-COCKADED WOODPECKER   *Picoídes boreális*
Rare and local in longleaf pine woods. Told from Red-bellied by solid black nape and cap; from Hairy and Downy (p. 200) by ladder back and large white cheek patches. Nest hole, in pine trunk, is recognized by oozing gum.

NUTTALL'S WOODPECKER   *Picoídes núttallii*
Common, especially in live oaks and chaparral west of the Sierras. Face is blacker than Ladder-backed Woodpecker's. See also Williamson's Sapsucker (p. 198) and Downy and Hairy Woodpeckers (p. 200). Call is like Ladder-back's but rapidly doubled, an abrupt *pa-teek*.

LADDER-BACKED WOODPECKERS

RED-BELLIED
WOODPECKER
L 8½"

♀

♂

Red-bellied

GILA
WOOD-
PECKER
L 8¼"

♂

♀

♀

♂

GOLDEN-
FRONTED
WOODPECKER
L 8½"

LADDER-BACKED
WOODPECKER
L 7"

♀

♂

♂

NUTTALL'S
WOODPECKER
L 6¾"

♂

♀

RED-
COCKADED
WOODPECKER
L 7¼"

198

RED-HEADED WOODPECKER
Melanérpes erythrocéphalus

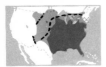

Uncommon in much of its range; prefers open deciduous woods. Adult head is entirely red. Large white wing area separates it from other species. The similar Red-breasted Sapsucker (below) has a narrow white wing stripe. Often perches in the open. Call is a raucous *kwrrk*.

ACORN WOODPECKER   *Melanérpes formicívorus*
Common, especially in oaks, and gregarious. Its black chin, white rump, and small but conspicuous white wing patch separate it from all other dark-backed woodpeckers except sapsuckers. Call is a series of raucous laughs.

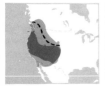

LEWIS' WOODPECKER   *Melanérpes léwis*
Locally common in large trees in open country. Red face and light collar and underparts contrast with the rest of its dark-greenish plumage. The rump is black. Flight is slow, with even, crow-like flapping. Gregarious. Catches flying insects. Call is of soft short notes.

WHITE-HEADED WOODPECKER   *Picoídes albolarvátus*
Locally common in pines and firs. The only white-headed woodpecker. Also note white wing patch at rest and in flight. May alight sideways or upside down. Calls are hoarse, often doubled.

YELLOW-BELLIED SAPSUCKER   *Sphyrápicus várius*
Common (but quiet, retiring, and easily overlooked) in woods and orchards. The narrow longitudinal wing stripe and finely mottled back are diagnostic. Sapsuckers tap in distinctive rhythms (2 or 3 series/min.), but do not drum. They drill parallel rows of small holes in live trees, then return to feed on sap and small insects. Calls are weak.

Red-   Yellow-
breasted   bellied

RED-BREASTED SAPSUCKER   *Sphyrápicus rúber*
Told from other sapsuckers by red head and breast. Birds w. of Cascades on combined map are Red-breasted.

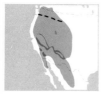

WILLIAMSON'S SAPSUCKER   *Sphyrápicus thyroídeus*
Uncommon; in pine forests, at higher elevations in summer. Sexes are entirely different. Male has two white stripes on solid black head and a solid black breast. Female has a more uniformly brown head and more black on the breast than female Yellow-bellied Sapsucker. It is also more distinctly marked on the back.

Yellow-bellied Sapsucker

Red-headed

Acorn

Lewis'

White-headed

Yellow-bellied

Yellow-bellied

Williamson's

ACORN WOODPECKER
L 8"

RED-HEADED WOODPECKER

im.

L 7½"

WHITE-HEADED WOODPECKER
L 7¾"

juv.

LEWIS' WOODPECKER
L 9"

YELLOW-BELLIED SAPSUCKER
L 7¾"

♂

WILLIAMSON'S SAPSUCKER
L 8¼"

♀

♂

im.

♀

RED-BREASTED SAPSUCKER

L 7¼"

STRICKLAND'S WOODPECKER   *Picoídes strícklandi*
Fairly common resident in its limited range on pine-oak slopes, 4,500-7,000'. No other brown-backed woodpecker has a dark rump, unbarred back, or white on the face. Female lacks red on the back of the neck. Call, *beep,* similar to Downy's, but longer and louder.

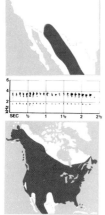

HAIRY WOODPECKER   *Picoídes villósus*
Fairly common, especially in mature deciduous or mixed woods. Recognized by its medium size, the vertical white stripe on the back, and its long bill. Sexes are similar, but the female does not have a red patch on the back of its head. Easily confused with Downy Woodpecker, which is smaller and has a much smaller bill, and Three-toed, which has barred sides and a much narrower white eye stripe. Call is a loud *peek,* also a loud kingfisher-like rattle.

DOWNY WOODPECKER   *Picoídes pubéscens*
Commonest eastern woodpecker; also common in parts of West. Seen in suburbs, orchards, shade trees, and woods. Looks like a miniature Hairy Woodpecker; is best told by its short slender bill and by its calls. Barred outer tail feathers when visible are diagnostic (they are rarely unbarred like Hairy's). May be mistaken for a sapsucker, whose white stripe is on the wing, not the back. Call, *pik,* is much softer than Hairy's; rattle call descends in pitch toward end.

BLACK-BACKED WOODPECKER   *Picoídes árctus*
Uncommon even in its preferred habitat—dead conifers, from which it peels bark. Note barred sides and black back. In East, only this and the much larger Pileated (p. 194) have solid black backs. In West only Lewis' and White-headed (p. 198) have black back and rump. Only the male has yellow crown. Call, a sharp *pik.*

THREE-TOED WOODPECKER   *Picoídes tridáctylus*
Locally common in western coniferous forests; rare in the East. Note the black wings, rump, and tail, the barred sides and back, and the yellow cap. No other woodpecker except the Black-backed (and, very rarely, the Hairy) has a yellow crown. Female has barred sides, no crown patch. Calls are similar to preceding species.

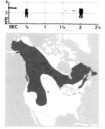

STRICKLAND'S WOODPECKER
L 7¼"

Hairy ♀

juv.
Downy

HAIRY WOODPECKER
L 7½"
♂

♀

DOWNY WOODPECKER
L 5¾"
♂

♀

♂

BLACK-BACKED WOODPECKER
L 8"
♀

THREE-TOED WOODPECKER
L 7½"

■ **PERCHING BIRDS** (*Order* Passeriformes) are medium to small land birds. All have feet well adapted for perching: 3 toes in front and 1 long one behind. Most are fine singers. Bill shape, feather colors, and habits are most useful for family identification. Most insectivorous species and some fruit and seed eaters are highly migratory.

1. **FLYCATCHERS** have broad flat bills; plumage mostly olive or gray; catch flying insects with a loud snap of the beak. p. 204

2. **LARKS** walk; they are generally in flocks in large open fields, never in trees. p. 218

3. **SWALLOWS** have long pointed wings, often notched or forked tails. They catch insects in flight; most nest in colonies. p. 218

4. **JAYS AND CROWS** are large, noisy, omnivorous birds, mostly blue or green (jays and magpies) or all black (crows); gregarious. p. 222

5. **CHICKADEES AND TITMICE** are small friendly long-tailed birds, mostly gray, white, and black; stubby bill; in small flocks. p. 228

6. **WRENTITS** are long-tailed dark brown birds of dense thickets; West Coast only. p. 232

7. **BULBULS** have long tails and crests. p. 232

8. **DIPPERS** are plump gray birds of western mountain streams; short tails. p. 232

9. **NUTHATCHES** are slender-billed short-tailed birds that crawl over trunks and branches, often in small flocks. p. 234

10. **CREEPERS** creep up tree trunks, then fly to base of another; use tail as prop. p. 234

11. **WRENS** are brown, generally solitary, with finely barred tails cocked upward, and slender bills; loud songs, scolding rattles. p. 236

12. **MOCKINGBIRDS AND THRASHERS** are long-tailed brush-loving birds, either brown or gray, with loud repetitious songs. p. 240

13. THRUSHES, medium-sized birds, typically are brown with spotted breasts; bills shaped like robin's; eat worms, fruit; fine singers. p. 244

14. GNATCATCHERS AND KINGLETS are tiny, very active gray or olive birds with eye ring or line over eye; body unstreaked. p. 252

15. PIPITS walk; slender-billed, sparrow-like birds; in flocks in large fields. p. 256

16. WAXWINGS are crested flocking birds with yellow fringe at tip of tail. p. 258

17. PHAINOPEPLAS are slender, crested birds of Southwest deserts; black or dark gray. p. 258

18. SHRIKES have heavy hooked bill, black mask, black wing with white patch. p. 260

19. STARLINGS look like short-tailed blackbirds; noisy, in large flocks. p. 260

20. VIREOS glean insects from leaves of deciduous trees and brush with their slightly hooked bills; plain olive backs. p. 262

21. WARBLERS are mostly brightly colored insect eaters of woods and brush; slender bills; very active; many have white tail spots and wing bars. p. 268

22. OLD WORLD SPARROWS are represented in N.A. by two introduced species. p. 296

23. BLACKBIRDS AND ORIOLES represent a large family of robin-sized birds, some all black, others with bright orange or yellow. p. 296

24. TANAGERS are brilliant arboreal robin-sized insect and fruit eaters; heavy bills; unstreaked plumage; most with no wing bars. p. 306

25. GROSBEAKS, FINCHES, AND SPARROWS have heavy conical seed-cracking bills. Mostly brown, red, yellow, or blue, seldom olive. p. 308

● **TYRANT FLYCATCHERS** (*Family* Tyrannidae) are large-headed, broad-billed, short-legged birds that perch on bare branches or wires, waiting for flying insects. Many of the small species flip their tails. Sexes similar (except becard and Vermilion); young are only slightly different. Most nest in trees or shrubs. Eggs, 2-6.

ROSE-THROATED BECARD   *Pachyrámphus aglaíae*
Rare and local along U.S.–Mexican border in Arizona, New Mexico, and Texas. Male has distinctive rose throat; female and young are brown with broad buffy neck band and black crown. This is the only North American representative of the large neotropical subfamily of becards. These large-headed treetop birds with large beaks often hover. Nests are bulky. Eggs, 3-6. Call is a thin sputtering whistle.

SCISSOR-TAILED FLYCATCHER   *Tyránnus forficátus*
Common in open country. Note long streaming tail of adult. Young similar to the Western Kingbird (p. 206), but have pink sides and a whiter tail. Calls suggest Western Kingbird's. **Fork-tailed Flycatcher** (*Tyránnus savána*, L 15") is similar, with long streaming tail, but underparts are white and crown is black. Immature is brownish. A casual visitor in eastern U.S.

GREAT KISKADEE   *Pitángus sulphurátus*
Locally common in lower Rio Grande Valley. Easily recognized by its bold black and white face pattern. In flight notice the rufous wings. Named for its call.

VERMILION FLYCATCHER   *Pyrocéphalus rubínus*
Common near streams in arid Southwest. Decidedly smaller than cardinal and tanagers, it is readily recognized by its small bill and flycatching habit. Male is unmistakable. Finely streaked sides and strawberry wash on flanks identify the female. Say's Phoebe (p. 210) has longer tail and no streaks. Song, rapid, high, sputtering.

SULPHUR-BELLIED FLYCATCHER
                              Myiodynástes luteivéntris
Fairly common locally in canyons at 5,000-7,500'. Noisy, but hard to see high in foliage. Only North American flycatcher with bold streaking below. Call resembles Western Flycatcher's (p. 214), but is much louder.

bluebird
shrike
flycatcher
vireo
warbler
sparrow

FLASHY FLYCATCHERS

Rose-throated Becard
♀
♂

ROSE-THROATED BECARD
L 5½″

im.

SCISSOR-TAILED FLYCATCHER
L 13″

FORK-TAILED FLYCATCHER
♂
L 15″

Great Kiskadee

VERMILION FLYCATCHER ♂
L 5″

♀

GREAT KISKADEE
L 9″

SULPHUR-BELLIED FLYCATCHER
L 6¾″

● **KINGBIRDS** are aggressive, open-country flycatchers with almost horizontal posture. Crown patches are generally concealed.

EASTERN KINGBIRD *Tyránnus tyránnus*
Common east of the Great Plains. No other songbird has a complete, broad, white terminal band on the tail (see shrikes, p. 260). Waxwings (p. 258), which often act like flycatchers, have a yellow tailband. Call is emphatic, rasping; 13-15/min. (at dawn).

WESTERN KINGBIRD *Tyránnus verticális*
Common about farms and along streams where scattered trees provide nesting sites. White outer tail feather when visible will identify this species. If white is lacking (as in some immatures) or not visible, Western Kingbird can be confused with Cassin's, which has small, more definite white throat patch and dark head. Black tail separates Western from *Myiarchus* flycatchers (p. 208). Calls, very different from Eastern's, are less rasping.

CASSIN'S KINGBIRD *Tyránnus vocíferans*
Fairly common, but less widespread than Western Kingbird; prefers higher land near brushy or wooded areas. Heavier than Western and less active. Tail is narrowly tipped with gray or white and lacks white outer tail feathers. Call is like Couch's, but is lower pitched.

TROPICAL KINGBIRD *Tyránnus melanchólicus*
Common in chaparral near Mexican border. Fall vagrant along California coast. The breast, as well as the belly, is bright yellow; back is olive. There is no white on the pale notched tail. Call is a series of high-pitched *kittik* notes. **Couch's Kingbird** (*Tyránnus coúchii*, L 7″) is nearly identical to Tropical, but call is a loud *chi-queer*.

Tropical   Couch's

GRAY KINGBIRD *Tyránnus dominicénsis*
Common on utility wires in Florida Keys; local elsewhere near the coast. Note huge bill, pale upper parts, and lack of white on the notched tail. Call, *pe-cheerrry*.

THICK-BILLED KINGBIRD *Tyránnus crassiróstris*
Rare; in southern Arizona and New Mexico. Brownish upper parts and pale underparts suggest *Myiarchus* flycatchers (p. 208), but facial mask, white throat, dark tail, lack of wing bars, and actions identify this as a kingbird. Note the heavy bill. Immatures are entirely yellow below.

Gray Kingbird

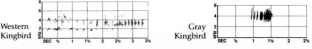

Western Kingbird   Gray Kingbird

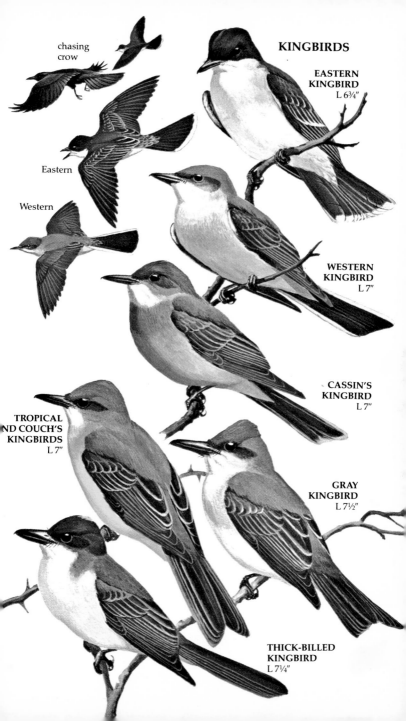

chasing crow

Eastern

Western

KINGBIRDS

EASTERN KINGBIRD
L 6¾"

WESTERN KINGBIRD
L 7"

CASSIN'S KINGBIRD
L 7"

TROPICAL ND COUCH'S KINGBIRDS
L 7"

GRAY KINGBIRD
L 7½"

THICK-BILLED KINGBIRD
L 7¼"

208

- **MYIARCHUS FLYCATCHERS** are large, with olive head and back, yellowish belly, brighter in immatures, and (except in Dusky-capped) bright rusty tail; all have wing bars. Their posture is more erect than kingbirds', and they are more inclined to perch in the shade. All nest in cavities in trees and posts; also in bird or newspaper boxes.

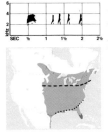

GREAT CRESTED FLYCATCHER *Myiárchus crinítus*
Common in deciduous and mixed woods. This is the only *Myiarchus* to be expected east of the Rockies and central Texas. Identified as a flycatcher by its broad bill, large head, and flycatching habits. No other eastern flycatcher has a long rust tail. Note similarity to Western Kingbird (p. 206), which is rare but regular along the Atlantic Coast in Sept. and Oct. Western Kingbird perches in the open and has a black tail with white outer feathers. Call is a harsh ascending *wheep*, 30-45/min.

BROWN-CRESTED FLYCATCHER
Myiárchus tyránnulus
Fairly common in deciduous woods and desert saguaros in the Southwest. Larger and yellower below, with a longer brighter tail, than the similar Ash-throated and Dusky-capped Flycatchers. Migrants in southern Texas can be distinguished from the Great Crested Flycatcher by their heavy solid black bill and much paler throat and breast. Call, a loud *ke-woow*.

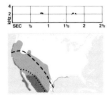

ASH-THROATED FLYCATCHER *Myiárchus cineráscens*
Common in western deciduous woods, mesquite, and saguaros. Palest of the *Myiarchus* group, it is decidedly smaller than Great Crested and Brown-crested and more slender-billed. White throat is a good field mark. Ash-throated is only *Myiarchus* north of s. Nevada and s.w. New Mexico. Call, *pee-reer;* also short sharp notes with quality of Western Kingbird (p. 206).

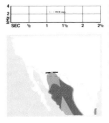

DUSKY-CAPPED FLYCATCHER *Myiárchus tubercúlifer*
Fairly common, especially below 6,000' in scrub-oak thickets. Adult shows little if any rusty color in the tail. Barely larger than the phoebe (p. 210), it is not likely to be confused with Brown-crested Flycatcher and lacks throat contrast of Ash-throated. Unlike other birds on this page, it often picks insects from foliage while hovering. The other *Myiarchus* flycatchers eat flying insects almost exclusively. Call is a long, mournful, slightly descending whistle; imitating sound will often bring the bird into view.

MYIARCHUS FLYCATCHERS

nesting in mailbox

GREAT CRESTED FLYCATCHER
L 7"

BROWN-CRESTED FLYCATCHER
L 7¼"

ASH-THROATED FLYCATCHER
L 6½"

DUSKY-CAPPED FLYCATCHER
L 5¾"

210

● **PHOEBES** are medium-sized flycatchers that differ from the others in their habit of leisurely jerking their longish tail downward. Phoebes do not have an eye ring. Adults lack conspicuous wing bars, but young may have quite conspicuous ones. Typically they are found near water, although all species, especially Say's, occur and even nest far from water. Also, unlike other flycatchers, phoebes nest under overhanging cliffs or banks, under bridges and eaves, or inside farm buildings. Quite tame and easily seen as they perch in the open, usually less than 20' off the ground. Eggs, 4-5, are usually plain white.

EASTERN PHOEBE
Sayórnis phoébe

Common near farm buildings and bridges. The dark head, solid black bill, and tail-wagging habit provide the best identification in all plumages. Although adult phoebes lack wing bars, immatures have conspicuous buffy ones and can be mistaken for pewees (p. 216); pewees as well as the small *Empidonax* flycatchers (p. 212) always have wing bars and usually a pale lower mandible. Head of Eastern Phoebe is darker than back; head of pewee is same shade as back. Phoebes do not whistle, but say *fee-be* and *fee-blee*, 20-40 times/min.

BLACK PHOEBE
Sayórnis nígricans

Common about western farmyards and along streams, generally below 6,000'. This is our only black-breasted flycatcher, and also the only flycatcher with a sharp color break between breast and belly. Its color pattern suggests a junco (p. 334), but the erect posture, tail-wagging, and flycatching habits do not. As in other phoebes, the head is darker than the body. A solitary species; usually perches in shady places. Food is almost entirely flying insects. Song is high thin *ti-wee, ti-wee*; alternate calls descend gradually at the end, 20-30 pairs/min.

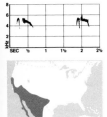

SAY'S PHOEBE
Sayórnis sáya

Common on the plains in the vicinity of ranch buildings, bluffs, and cliffs; prefers dry sunny locations more than the other phoebes. From the front it is recognized by the rusty belly and undertail coverts, from behind by the contrast between the pale back and the black tail, which it frequently wags. The female Vermilion Flycatcher (p. 204) is much the same color, but is decidedly smaller, with a white throat and finely streaked sides. Say's song is a slurred *chu-weer* (30-40/min.) and *pippety-chee*. Call, a single descending whistle.

Eastern Phoebe

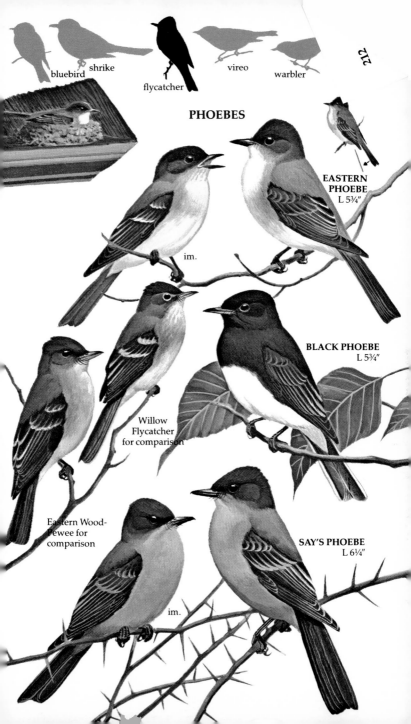

bluebird shrike

flycatcher

vireo

warbler

PHOEBES

EASTERN PHOEBE
L 5¾"

im.

BLACK PHOEBE
L 5¾"

Willow
Flycatcher
for comparison

Eastern Wood-
Pewee for
comparison

SAY'S PHOEBE
L 6¼"

im.

- **THE GENUS EMPIDONAX** contains small short-tailed flycatchers with eye rings and wing bars. Wing bars of immature are more buffy than adults'. With experience most species can be identified on the breeding ground when habitat and song provide clues. Most species also have distinctive chips. Most flip their tails rapidly up then down.

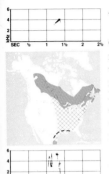

YELLOW-BELLIED FLYCATCHER

Empídonax flavivéntris

Common on its breeding ground in spruce-fir forests, but rarely seen on migration. The only eastern *Empidonax* with a yellow throat. Acadian Flycatcher has yellow on flanks, especially in the immature, but its throat is white. No other eastern *Empidonax* has a whistled song—an ascending *per-wee* suggestive of Semipalmated Plover's (p. 114); also a single leisurely *che-bunk* similar to the oft-repeated *che-bek'* of the Least Flycatcher.

ACADIAN FLYCATCHER

Empídonax viréscens

Common in moist woodlands, especially deciduous floodplain forests, where it usually stays below the canopy. During migration, Acadian and Yellow-bellied Flycatchers can be seen in the same habitat; Acadian can be told by its white throat. Acadian is larger and heavier billed than Least, slightly greener above than Willow, but not safely distinguishable except by its calls. Song is an explosive *peet-suh*, 2-4 times/min.

WILLOW FLYCATCHER

Empídonax traíllii

Common on brushy slopes. Browner-backed than the two species above and the western species (p. 214). Larger than Least Flycatcher, with more contrast between throat and breast. Eye ring faint. Song, *fitz'bew,* a whistle superimposed on a buzz; 16-28/min. See Alder, below.

ALDER FLYCATCHER

Empídonax alnórum

Common, primarily in alder swamps. Plumage not separable from Willow Flycatcher's. Some overlap in breeding range. Song, *fee-bee'o,* similar in quality to Willow's, but accented on second of 3 syllables; 12-24/min.

LEAST FLYCATCHER

Empídonax mínimus

Common in scrub growth, wood margins, and unsprayed orchards. This smallest eastern *Empidonax* has less contrast between throat and side of breast than Alder and Willow, and little or no greenish on back. Told by its song, a dry *che-bek'*, repeated 50-70/min.

Willow 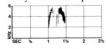 Least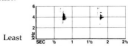

EASTERN EMPIDONAX FLYCATCHERS

**YELLOW-BELLIED
FLYCATCHER**
L 4½″

im.

tail wag

**ACADIAN
FLYCATCHER**
L 4¾″

**WILLOW
AND ALDER
FLYCATCHERS**
L 4¾″

**LEAST
FLYCATCHER**
L 4½″

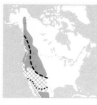

HAMMOND'S FLYCATCHER   *Empídonax hámmondii*

Common in firs, spruces, and pines; nests up to 11,000'. Likes solid coniferous forest. Flicks wings and tail constantly. Often impossible to tell from Dusky Flycatcher by sight or songs. Note olive-brown back, gray breast, and pale yellow belly. Song very low-pitched, often of 3 parts: *seput*, a burry *pzrrrt*, and *treeip*. Call, a sharp *pic.*

DUSKY FLYCATCHER   *Empídonax oberhólseri*

Common on brushy slopes below 2,000' in Washington, but at 7,000-9,000' in New Mexico. Similar to Hammond's, but has less contrast between breast and belly; tail is slightly longer, back is grayer, underparts less yellow. Few tail or wing flicks. Song is low pitched, no particular sequence: *cheepit, chuwee, cheepit, pseet.* Call, a soft *whit.*

GRAY FLYCATCHER   *Empídonax wríghtii*

Fairly common in sagebrush and junipers of the Great Basin. Slightly larger than Hammond's Flycatcher, with distinctly grayer crown, back, and underparts than Hammond's and Dusky's. Basal two-thirds of lower mandible is pink; little or no yellow on underparts. Only *Empidonax* to pump tail *down* first. Song is typically of 2 elements: a vigorous rapid low *churweeoo*, and a faint higher *cheeip.*

WESTERN FLYCATCHER   *Empídonax difficilis*

Common in moist deciduous or coniferous woods or on mixed slopes with tall trees, where it seeks an inconspicuous perch. The only western *Empidonax* with a yellow throat. Much yellower below than Hammond's, Dusky, Willow, or Alder Flycatchers (pp. 213, 215). Song is very high: *pchip, ee, pcheewee*; call, *whee-see.*

BUFF-BREASTED FLYCATCHER   *Empídonax fúlvifrons*

Rare and local on steep canyon slopes with scattered tall pines, small oaks, and shrubby undergrowth, 5,000-8,500'. May be recognized by its small size and bright buff-colored breast, flanks, and belly.

NORTHERN BEARDLESS-TYRANNULET
Camptóstoma imbérbe

Rare; in dense low deciduous growth, 0-4,000'. Told from kinglets (p. 252) by buffy wing bars and by lack of bold eye ring. A leaf-gleaner; behavior and call notes resemble Verdin's (p. 232). Told from *Empidonax* by tiny bill, dusky throat and breast. Call, shrill descending *pier pier pier.*

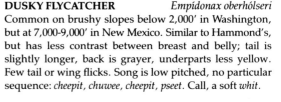

Dusky   Gray

WESTERN EMPIDONAX FLYCATCHERS

HAMMOND'S FLYCATCHER L 4½″

im.

GRAY FLYCATCHER L 4¾″

DUSKY FLYCATCHER L 4¾″

WESTERN FLYCATCHER L 5″

NORTHERN BEARDLESS-TYRANNULET L 3½″

BUFF-BREASTED FLYCATCHER L 4″

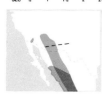

GREATER PEWEE
Contópus pértinax

Fairly common at 7,000-10,000' on steep pine-oak slopes. This large tropical pewee is separated from other pewees and the *Empidonax* species (p. 212) by its lack of wing bars and its larger size. Its large head and large bill resemble the Olive-sided Flycatcher's, which, however, always has a vertical white streak separating the olive sides. Note that Greater has a grayer cast on the sides and breast and a yellow lower mandible. A slight crest gives it a different head shape from other pewees'. It differs also in giving short jerks of its tail. Call is a sad, whistled *ho-say mari-a*.

EASTERN WOOD-PEWEE
Contópus vírens

Common in deciduous and mixed woods. Told from Eastern Phoebe (p. 210) by light lower mandible, prominent wing bars, and the lack of contrast between head and back. Told from all *Empidonax* species (p. 212) by lack of eye ring (see Willow, p. 212), shorter legs, more deeply notched tail, and longer wings (extending nearly halfway down the tail). Pewees usually do not wag their tails. Immature Eastern Phoebes have buffy wing bars in fall, but their breasts are lemon yellow. Song is a plaintive, whistled *pee-oo-wee*, *pee-oo* (6-11/min.). Twilight song (25-33/min.) also includes a third call, *pee-widdi*.

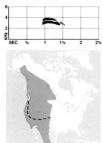

WESTERN WOOD-PEWEE
Contópus sordídulus

Common in deciduous and coniferous woods and in tall trees along streams. Seldom separable in the field from Eastern Wood-Pewee except by song. The western species tends to be darker on the sides, breast, lower mandible, and underwing surface. The nasal song (9-12/min.), a descending burry call, is entirely different from Eastern Wood-Pewee's and is occasionally given even during fall migration.

song   call

OLIVE-SIDED FLYCATCHER
Contópus boreális

Fairly common in northern coniferous woods, locally in aspens, birch, maple, and eucalyptus. Resembles Eastern Phoebe (p. 210), but the head and bill are much larger and the tail is shorter. The white throat and breast streak contrast with the dark olive sides. White tufts under wings often protrude. Habitually returns to the same perch at the top of a dead snag. Song is a loud melodious whistle, *whip-three-beers*, 6-10/min.; call, *pip-pip-pip*.

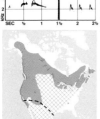

Eastern Wood-Pewee

OLIVE-SIDED FLYCATCHERS

GREATER PEWEE
L 6″

im.

im.

EASTERN WOOD-PEWEE
L 5¼″

WESTERN WOOD-PEWEE
L 5¼″

im.

OLIVE-SIDED FLYCATCHER
L 6¼″

● **LARKS** (*Family* Alaudidae), slender-billed birds of large fields with sparse or low vegetation, usually walk; seldom alight in trees or shrubs. If flushed, they return to the ground. They sing in flight, high above the ground; outside the breeding season are seen in loose flocks. Eat insects and small seeds. Nest on the ground; eggs, 3-5.

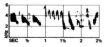

EURASIAN SKYLARK
Alaúda arvénsis

Casual in western Aleutians; introduced on Vancouver Island, B.C. Told from sparrows by slender bill, from pipits by shorter tail and heavier build, from Horned Lark by streaked breast. Long aerial song, sweet liquid notes.

HORNED LARK
Eremóphila alpéstris

Common in large fields, at the shore, and in other open places. Recognize adults by the black breast mark and facial design; immature shows these marks less distinctly. In normal flight, low and slightly undulating, notice the black tail feathers. Feeds in winter in freshly manured fields. Song, weak, high pitched, is repeated many times (9-13/min.) in a single flight high overhead. Winter call, faint tinkling notes.

● **SWALLOWS** (*Family* Hirundinidae) have long pointed wings, and most species have notched or deeply forked tails. All are strong, elegant fliers. Legs and bills are short, but mouths are wide for capturing flying insects. Commonly perch on wires. Often seen in large mixed flocks. Most nest in colonies. Eggs, 4-7, are white or spotted.

BARN SWALLOW
Hirúndo rústica

Common near farms, where it builds a mud nest on timbers of barns and other buildings. The only common swallow with a deeply forked tail; others with rusty underparts have orange rumps. Song, long and twittering.

CLIFF SWALLOW
Hirúndo pyrrhonóta

Locally common. Note the orange rump, square tail, broad martin-like wings, and buffy forehead. Soars more than other swallows. The bulb-shaped nests are built under eaves or in the shelter of cliffs, dams, or bridges. Call is a single melodious note. Sonagram below.

CAVE SWALLOW
Hirúndo fúlva

Very local in summer in Carlsbad Caverns area, New Mexico, and in south-central Texas. Told from Cliff Swallow by buffy throat, translucent wings. Nests in caves and culverts.

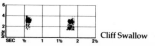

Cliff Swallow

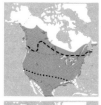

Killdeer nighthawk swift lark Barn Swallow Cliff Swallow

LARKS

im.

Horned Lark

EURASIAN SKYLARK
L 6¼"

HORNED LARK
L 6½"

prairie race

northern race

SWALLOWS 1

im.

BARN SWALLOW
L 6"

CLIFF SWALLOW
L 5"

CAVE SWALLOW
head
L 4¾"

Cliff Swallow at nest

220

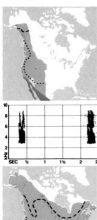

VIOLET-GREEN SWALLOW *Tachycinéta thalassína*

Common in mountains and locally in towns. Best told by large white flank patches, which nearly meet over the tail. Adult is confused only with the Tree Swallow or White-throated Swift (p. 184). Violet-green Swallow flaps more rapidly than Tree, glides less, has translucent wings and a shorter tail. Young are brown above and have a less conspicuous eye patch. Song is a rapid twitter.

TREE SWALLOW *Tachycinéta bícolor*

Common nester in tree cavities or nest boxes, especially near water. It is the only green-backed swallow regularly seen in the East. Brown-backed young may be confused in fall and winter with Rough-winged or Bank Swallows, but white of flanks extends slightly above tail, throat is always white, and breast band is not clean-cut. Flocks of thousands gather along the Atlantic Coast in fall. In cold weather they eat bayberries. Song is of separate liquid notes. **Bahama Swallow** (*T. cyaneovíridis*, L 5½″), casual in Florida, is similar but with tail deeply forked like Barn (p. 218). (See upper right bird, on wire.)

BANK SWALLOW *Ripária ripária*

Locally common near steep riverbanks and gravel pits. Told from all other swallows by narrow brown breast band contrasting with white throat. Nests in colonies, burrowing into banks. Call is a low unmusical buzz.

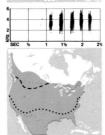

NORTHERN ROUGH-WINGED SWALLOW
  Stelgidópteryx serripénnis

Fairly common, especially near water. Brown back and brown throat and breast separate it from all but the much larger martins, which show a purplish tinge on the back and head. Nests, usually single, are in burrows in banks or in small drainpipes at highway bridges. Call is like Bank Swallow's, but separable with practice.

PURPLE MARTIN *Prógne súbis*

Locally common where proper multicelled nesting boxes or gourds are provided. No other North American swallow is dark all over. Females, young, and first-year males are light-bellied and could be confused with smaller swallows. Watch for purple iridescence on head and top of wings. Note the broad wings and more soaring flight of martins. Song and calls are a distinctive, low-pitched, liquid, rolling twitter.

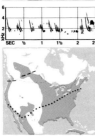

Bank Swallow

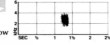

Violet-green

Barn

Cliff

Violet-green

Tree

Bank

Rough-wing

Purple Martin

Bahama

im.

SWALLOWS 2

VIOLET-GREEN SWALLOW
L 4¾″

im.

TREE SWALLOW
L 5″

NORTHERN ROUGH-WINGED SWALLOW
L 4¾″

BANK SWALLOW
L 4¾″

♂

PURPLE MARTIN
L 7″

♀

1st year

♂

martin house

222

● **JAYS, MAGPIES, AND CROWS** (*Family* Corvidae) are medium to large, gregarious, omnivorous birds with heavy bills. Wings of jays and magpies are short and rounded, reaching only to the base of the long rounded tail. Wings of crows and ravens are long and rounded, extending nearly to the tail tip. Sexes are similar. Often scolded and chased by smaller birds in nesting season. Songs are poor, mostly raucous. Eggs, 3-6 (magpies, 5-9), are colored and speckled.

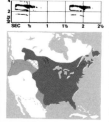

BLUE JAY *Cyanocítta cristáta*
Common in oak and pine woods. The only eastern jay except in central Florida and Far North, and the only blue-winged jay with white on wings and tail. Conspicuously crested in all plumages. Migrates by day in loose flocks of 5-50. Common call is a loud *jay, jay,* 10-20 pairs/min.

STELLER'S JAY *Cyanocítta stélleri*
The common crested jay in and west of the Rockies; prefers coniferous forests. Dark crest is always present. Calls are low pitched, raucous, and varied, often in series of 3. Like the Blue Jay, Steller's imitates hawks expertly.

SCRUB JAY *Aphelócoma coeruléscens*
Locally common, especially in scrub oaks, where it skillfully remains out of sight. This crestless jay is best told by its white throat, outlined in blue. The sharp contrast between blue crown and olive-gray back also separates it from the other jays. Flights are short, ending with a sweeping glide. Calls, similar to Steller's, are higher and often in ones or twos.

GRAY-BREASTED JAY *Aphelócoma ultramarína*
Common in oak and oak-pine forest, 2,000-8,000'. Looks like a faded Scrub Jay with a dark mask and uniformly gray throat and breast. Calls, less raucous than other jays', are slurred upward; frequently repeated.

PINYON JAY *Gymnorhínus cyanocéphalus*
Short-tailed, crow-like in flight and habits; common in arid regions. Nests in pinyon pines and junipers; is often seen on the ground around sagebrush. In winter huge flocks wander erratically to farmlands. Told from other jays by its uniform steel-blue color and short tail. Compare with Mountain Bluebird (p. 250). Has a high mewing call in flight; when perched, a *queh queh queh.*

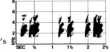

Steller's

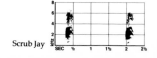

Scrub Jay

kingfisher jay cardinal magpie crow grackle shrike

BLUE JAY
L 10"

BLUE JAYS

Scrub Jay

STELLER'S JAY
L 11"

SCRUB JAY
L 10"

**GRAY-BREASTED
JAY**
L 10¾"

PINYON JAY
L 9"

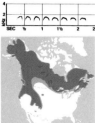

GRAY JAY

Perisóreus canadénsis

Locally common in northern coniferous woods; becomes tame at lumber camps. Adult is recognized by black and white pattern of head and nape; lacks black and white wing and tail pattern of Clark's Nutcracker. A Blue Jay (p. 222) flying overhead, with its blue feathers appearing gray against the sky, may be mistaken for a Gray Jay. The dusky juvenile is told by its short rounded wings, long rounded tail, and lack of a crest. Call is a whistled *wheeoo;* also many other jay-like sounds.

GREEN JAY

Cyanocórax ýncas

Locally common resident in woods along lower Rio Grande west to Laredo, Texas. Normally the only jay in that area, it is unmistakable, with brilliant green body and golden outer tail feathers. Has various jay-like calls, especially a long call followed by 3 short ones, 10-14/min.

BROWN JAY

Cyanocórax mório

Rare, shy, and local along lower Rio Grande. Told by large size, plain brown plumage; immature has yellow bill.

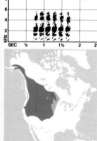

BLACK-BILLED MAGPIE

Píca píca

Common in open country near heavy brush or occasional trees that support its huge nest. Long streaming tail and white wing patches characterize magpies. No other North American land birds except Scissor-tailed and Fork-tailed Flycatchers (p. 204) have tails longer than the body. Ranges of this and Yellow-billed Magpie do not overlap. Black-billed Magpie wanders erratically in winter. Call is an ascending whine or a rapid series of loud harsh cries.

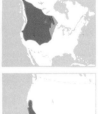

YELLOW-BILLED MAGPIE

Píca núttalli

Common in farming areas of California valleys and nearby hills. Easily recognized in all plumages by its typical magpie form and its bright yellow bill. Calls are similar to those of Black-billed Magpie.

CLARK'S NUTCRACKER

Nucífraga columbiána

Locally common in conifers near timberline. Flashy white wing and tail patches and the even gray body suggest a stub-tailed mockingbird (p. 240), but mockingbirds are not found at high elevations. Long sharply pointed bill and white face confirm the identification. Flight and general body form are crow-like. It wanders irregularly to low country. Call is a drawn-out grating *kr-a-a-a.*

Clark's

juv.

GRAY JAY
L 10"

GREEN JAY
L 9¾"

YELLOW-BILLED MAGPIE
L 16"

Black-billed

Yellow-billed

BROWN JAY
L 14"

BLACK-BILLED MAGPIE
L 18"

CLARK'S NUTCRACKER
L 11"

AVENS AND CROWS are large flocking birds told by solid black plumage, cawing or croaking calls, and fondness for open country. They post a sentinel while feeding and walk rather than hop. Fly in long lines to and from their communal roosts.

COMMON RAVEN
Córvus córax

Common in the Far North and in the West, especially near heavy timber. Local in the Appalachians. It can be mistaken only for a hawk or for other birds on this page. The heavy bill and the wedge shape of the tail are diagnostic. It flaps less and soars more than crows and is more of a carrion feeder. Call, a low hoarse croak.

CHIHUAHUAN RAVEN
Córvus cryptoleúcus

Common in arid open farmland near the Mexican border. The white neck is seldom visible, so in the narrow zone of overlap with the American Crow one must rely on the voice. Note that this raven glides more in flight and has a slightly wedge-shaped tail. The raven-like croak is higher pitched than Common Raven's.

AMERICAN CROW
Córvus brachyrhýnchos

Well known, easily recognized, and abundant in the East and locally in the West except in arid regions. Told from a distant hawk by its frequent steady flapping. Seldom glides more than 2 or 3 seconds except in strong updrafts or when descending. Barely smaller than Red-shouldered Hawk (p. 74). Call is a distinctive *caw*.

NORTHWESTERN CROW
Córvus caurínus

Common near tidewater. Slightly smaller than American Crow; can generally be recognized by voice, which typically is lower pitched and a bit hoarser. Feeds sometimes in croplands, but more easily recognized when scavenging along shorelines; most northwest Washington birds are hybrids.

FISH CROW
Córvus ossífragus

Locally common. Scavenges on shore; inland feeds with American Crows. It is slightly smaller and thinner-billed. Identified best by its voice, a short nasal *car*, which may be confused with the *caw* of a young American Crow; also a more distinctive *cuh-cuh*. **Mexican Crow** (*Córvus imparátus*, L 14¼") visits the Brownsville, Texas, dump in flocks in fall and winter. Told by voice, a frog-like *gurrr*.

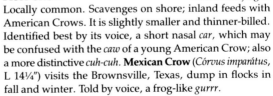

American Crow

kingfisher jay cardinal magpie crow grackle shrike

RAVENS, CROWS

COMMON RAVEN
L 21″

CHIHUAHUAN RAVEN
L 17½″

white neck
exposed

crows chasing
Red-tailed Hawk

**AMERICAN
CROW**
L 17″

kingbirds
attacking crow

FISH CROW
L 15″

**NORTHWESTERN
CROW**
L 14½″

228

● **CHICKADEES** (*Family* Paridae, part) are black-bibbed, dark-capped acrobats, tame and friendly. Only in the mountains of the Northwest do more than two species occur together. Sexes are similar and young are like adults. Chickadees nest in cavities in trees and nest boxes, and most are easily attracted to feeding stations. Eggs, 5-8.

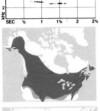

BLACK-CAPPED CHICKADEE   *Párus atricapíllus*
This common black-capped species is told from the Carolina, whose range it may invade in winter, by its rustier sides, white feather edges on wing, and whiter cheek patches. It is tamer than Carolina. Whistled song is easily imitated; second note is 1 full tone lower, 16-23/min.

CAROLINA CHICKADEE   *Párus carolinénsis*
Fairly common. Smaller than Black-capped Chickadee, sides paler. Has narrow gray edging on wing feathers, smaller neat bib, shorter tail. Non-migratory. Calls are faster than corresponding calls of Black-capped; whistled song is an octave higher, of 4 or 5 notes, 8-12/min.

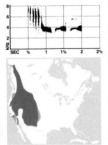

MOUNTAIN CHICKADEE   *Párus gámbeli*
Common in conifers. The only chickadee with a white eye stripe (missing during late summer molt); see Bridled Titmouse (p. 230). Nests in mountains, may wander to valleys in winter. Call hoarser, song nearly same as Black-capped's, 8-10/min.

MEXICAN CHICKADEE   *Párus sclâteri*
Note the large black throat patch and gray sides. This is the only chickadee found in its limited range in southern Arizona and New Mexico. Call is low and rasping.

BOREAL CHICKADEE   *Párus hudsónicus*
Fairly common in northern coniferous forests. Only chickadee with brown cap, back, and sides. No whistled song; *chick-a-dee* call is slow and hoarse.

CHESTNUT-BACKED CHICKADEE   *Párus ruféscens*
Common in Pacific lowlands, local in mountains; prefers conifers. Note the bright chestnut back and sides, sooty cap. Has no whistled song; calls are hoarse, rapid.

SIBERIAN TIT   *Párus cínctus*
Larger and paler than Boreal and lacks brown sides. Found in spruce, aspen, and willow at edge of Alaskan and west Canadian tundra. Call resembles Boreal's.

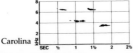

Carolina

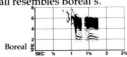

Boreal

chickadee

titmouse

nuthatch

creeper

wren

CHICKADEES

CAROLINA CHICKADEE L 4¼″

BLACK-CAPPED CHICKADEE L 4½″

MOUNTAIN CHICKADEE L 4¼″

MEXICAN CHICKADEE L 4¼″

BOREAL CHICKADEE L 4¼″

CHESTNUT-BACKED CHICKADEE L 4¼″

SIBERIAN TIT L 4¾″

- **TITMICE** (*Family* Paridae, part) are crested birds that act like chicka-dees, but are larger. Only the Bridled Titmouse has a bib. Other birds with conspicuous crests are larger, crests usually longer. Sexes are similar. Often flock with chickadees, warblers, and kinglets except in nesting season. Do not migrate. Nest in natural cavities, occasionally in nest boxes; 5-8 eggs.

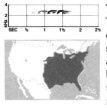

TUFTED TITMOUSE
Párus bícolor

This largest North American titmouse is common in deciduous woodlands of the Southeast, especially along streams. Told from chickadees (with which it usually associates) by the crest, the larger size, and the lack of a black bib. Usually found in flocks of 3-8 birds. No other titmouse occurs east of Texas. Visits feeding stations near woods. Whistled song is 2 notes (or one slurred one) repeated 2 to 4 times, 14-22/min. Other calls are chickadee-like but distinctive. The Black-crested race (formerly considered a separate species) is easily recog-nized. It is common in deciduous woodlands, scrub oaks, and shade trees in Texas and northeastern Mexico. Adults with the black crest are unmistakable. Young Black-cresteds are told from typical Tufteds by the whit-ish rather than gray forehead, and from Plain Titmice by the rusty tinge on the flanks. Songs and calls of the Black-crested race are like those of other Tufted Titmice.

PLAIN TITMOUSE
Párus inornátus

This is the common plain gray titmouse of the West. Its range overlaps only with the Bridled Titmouse. It is told from all chickadees by its white throat. Prefers oaks, also pinyon-juniper. The Plain Titmouse repeats a whistled 2-note song, accented on the first note (its form similar to Tufted Titmouse's). Unlike other titmice, it also has a *chick-a-dee-dee* call that sounds much more like the call of a chickadee than of a titmouse.

BRIDLED TITMOUSE
Párus wollwéberi

This distinctively marked titmouse is common in stands of scrub oak and junipers in the Southwest mountains at elevations of 5,000-7,000' (occasionally to 8,500'). It can be confused only with the uncrested Mountain Chicka-dee (p. 228), whose range it overlaps. Young Bridled Titmice always show enough face pattern to separate them from other titmice and chickadees.

chickadee   titmouse   nuthatch   creeper   wren

juv.

TITMICE

TUFTED TITMOUSE
L 5½″

juv.

Black-crested race
L 5″

juv.

PLAIN TITMOUSE
L 5″

juv.

BRIDLED TITMOUSE
L 4½″

Mountain Chickadee for comparison

● **VERDINS** (*Family* Remizidae) **AND BUSHTITS** (*Family* Aegithalidae) are small, slim, long-tailed birds that resemble chickadees in habits.

VERDIN
Auríparus fláviceps

Common in mesquite and other desert scrub. Note yellow head and throat, gray body, and chestnut shoulders. Juveniles resemble young Bushtits until late Aug., but are told by their shorter tails and high thin whistles.

BUSHTIT
Psaltríparus mínimus

Abundant in large flocks in scrub, open woodlands, and suburbs. Told by its nondescript plumage, lack of wing bars, long tail, and short bill. Call, high, thin, fussing notes. Rocky Mt. race has gray cap and brown lores. The rare Black-eared morph is found above 5,000′ in the mountains of southern New Mexico and western Texas. Male has the black face. Female and immature are told from typical Bushtits by the whiter throat, darker flanks, and grayer face.

● **WRENTITS** (*Family* Muscicapidae, part) are small, non-migratory, wren-like birds. Weak fliers, they prefer to hop through vegetation.

WRENTIT
Chamaéa fascíata

Common in dense chaparral, but usually stays out of sight. Told from wrens by the pale yellow eye, longer unbarred tail, and short bill. Song is a loud clear monotone, which in the male ends in a trill.

● **BULBULS** (*Family* Pycnonotidae) are Old World birds with a patch of hair-like feathers on the nape. They lay 2-5 eggs.

RED-WHISKERED BULBUL
Pycnonótus jocósus

Locally common. Liberated August, 1960, in south Miami (Kendall), Florida. Told by black crest and red ear patch and undertail coverts. Sexes similar.

● **DIPPERS** (*Family* Cinclidae), with their strong legs and special oil glands, are uniquely adapted to a watery habitat. Solitary birds, they build large moss nests near running water; lay 3-6 eggs.

AMERICAN DIPPER
Cínclus mexicánus

Fairly common along the larger, rapid mountain streams. Told by sooty plumage, short cocked tail, white eyelids. Bobs up and down. Walks under water. Flight low and direct. Song long, melodious, with trills and repetitions.

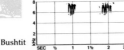

Bushtit

Wrentit

TITS, WRENTIT, DIPPER, BULBUL

VERDIN
L 3½″
♂

juv.
♀

BUSHTIT
L 3½″

Rocky Mt. race

♀

♂

Black-eared
morph

WRENTIT
L 5¼″

**AMERICAN
DIPPER**
L 5¾″

**RED-
WHISKERED
BULBUL**
L 7″

● **NUTHATCHES** (*Family* Sittidae) are large-headed, short-tailed, short-legged, tree-climbing birds that glean insects from the bark of trunks and limbs. Acrobatic, equally at home climbing up, around, or down a trunk head first. Often flock with chickadees and titmice. Wings extend nearly to tip of tail. Sexes differ only slightly. Those that migrate do so by day. Flight is jerky. Lay 4-9 eggs in cavities.

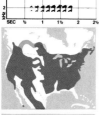

WHITE-BREASTED NUTHATCH — *Sítta carolinénsis*
Common in deciduous woodlands. Except for the white throat, resembles chickadee in plumage, though not in shape and actions. Note the white face and solid black cap of male (gray in female). Call, a low *yank-yank*. Song, 5-15 low rapid notes, given 6-15/min.

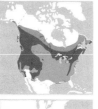

RED-BREASTED NUTHATCH — *Sítta canadénsis*
Common in conifers within its wide range. This is our only nuthatch with white stripe above and black stripe through the eye. Migrates irregularly, often in alternate years. The call is more nasal and less loud than the White-breasted's.

BROWN-HEADED NUTHATCH — *Sítta pusílla*
Occurs in large flocks with chickadees and warblers. This small nuthatch is the only eastern one with a brown cap. Feeds along outer branches and cones of southern pines. Its calls are soft and twittering, with no resemblance to the calls of other eastern nuthatches.

PYGMY NUTHATCH — *Sítta pygmaéa*
Western counterpart of Brown-headed Nuthatch, which it resembles in plumage and habits. Pygmy's cap is grayer. Partial to pines, especially Yellow Pines, at 3,500-10,000'; leaves high elevations in winter. Calls are similar to Brown-headed's.

● **CREEPERS** (*Family* Certhiidae) are short-legged, small, brown-backed birds that creep spirally up tree trunks searching for insects. Bill is decurved. Solitary. Lay 6-7 eggs in oval nest behind loose bark.

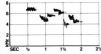

BROWN CREEPER — *Cérthia americána*
A common but inconspicuous small woodland bird. The stiff points on its long tail feathers are used as props as it works up and around a trunk. Song is high, faint, rarely heard outside its breeding grounds, 6-12/min. Call is a single very high note.

Red-breasted

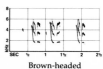

Brown-headed

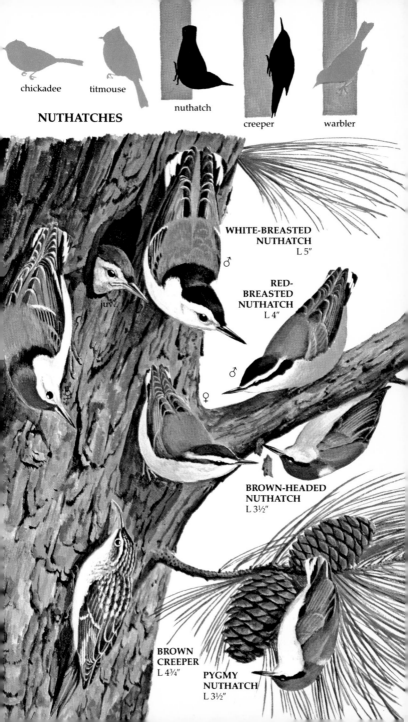

chickadee

titmouse

nuthatch

creeper

warbler

NUTHATCHES

WHITE-BREASTED
NUTHATCH
L 5″ ♂

RED-
BREASTED
NUTHATCH
L 4″

juv.

♂

♀

BROWN-HEADED
NUTHATCH
L 3½″

BROWN
CREEPER
L 4¾″

PYGMY
NUTHATCH
L 3½″

● **WRENS** (*Family* Troglodytidae) are small, restless, brownish birds with finely barred, narrow, rounded tails that are usually cocked upward. Females and immatures resemble males. With their long slender bills they feed mainly on insects. Eggs, 4-9, are laid in a cavity or globular nest, usually within 12' of the ground. Wrens have loud songs and dry scolding rattles.

HOUSE WREN *Troglódytes aédon*
Common in shrubbery and brush. The plainest wren and the commonest one in the East. Told from Marsh and Sedge Wrens (p. 238) by its unstreaked back, from other wrens by the indistinct eye stripe and lack of a dark belly. It is aggressive, driving other birds from nest boxes. Also nests in natural cavities. The Brown-throated race, *T. a. brunneicóllis,* is an uncommon resident at 7,000-8,000' in southeast Arizona mountains. Note its buffy eye stripe, buffy throat and breast. Song is loud and bubbling.

WINTER WREN *Troglódytes troglódytes*
Uncommon; in brush piles or thick undergrowth in moist forests. A very short tail, bobbing action, and dark brown barring on the belly separate this bird from the larger House Wren, which it barely overlaps in breeding range and migration dates. Note the inconspicuous eye stripe. Song is a rapid succession of very high clear notes and trills; it lasts about 5 sec. and is repeated 4-6/min. Low double call note, *tick-tick,* is distinctive. Sonagram, p. 14.

BEWICK'S WREN *Thryómanes béwickii*
Common and widespread in the West; decreasing and becoming rare and local in the Appalachians. Found in farmyards, brush, and fencerows. Distinguished from other wrens by its eye stripe, white underparts, and unstreaked brown back. Note also the characteristic sideways jerking of its long white-fringed tail. The song is higher and thinner than House Wren's, 2-5 notes followed by a trill, 6-12/min.

CAROLINA WREN *Thryóthorus ludoviciánus*
Common in thick underbrush in Southeast except after severe winters. This largest eastern wren is identified by its broad white eye stripe, rufous back, and bright buffy underparts. Prefers moist areas. Song consists of very loud triplets repeated 4-6 times, 8-13/min.

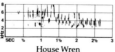

House Wren

chickadee titmouse nuthatch creeper wren

WRENS 1

HOUSE WREN
L 4¼″

WINTER WREN
L 3¼″

Brown-throated race
of House Wren

**BEWICK'S
WREN**
L 4½″

CAROLINA WREN
L 4¾″

CACTUS WREN   *Campylorhýnchus brunneicapíllus*
This common giant wren of the deserts is recognized by its broad white eye stripe and densely spotted breast. The tail is barred and white-tipped, usually not cocked upward. Flies low over the ground. Sage Thrasher (p. 240) is similar but has no white on its back. Generally found below 4,000' among thorny shrubs or large cacti. The song, one of the most familiar sounds of the desert, is an unmusical monotone of low-pitched notes.

ROCK WREN   *Salpínctes obsolétus*
Fairly common in rocky barrens. Best recognized by the light buffy tips on all but the central tail feathers, contrasting with the black subterminal band. Its buffy rump also contrasts with its gray back. No other wren, including the rather similar Bewick's (p. 236), has light streaking on the breast. Bobs as it walks. Song is a remarkable variety of trills, 8-20/min.

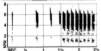

CANYON WREN   *Cathérpes mexicánus*
Fairly common in canyons. A clear white throat and breast contrasting with its chestnut-brown belly distinguish this bird at a distance from other cliff-dwelling canyon species. The Rock Wren, similar in size, is grayer and has a much lighter belly. The song is of loud clear descending whistles, slowing at the end.

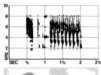

MARSH WREN   *Cistóthorus palústris*
Abundant in its limited habitat. Marsh and Sedge Wrens are quickly told from other small wrens by their streaked backs. This species also has a solid rusty cap and a distinct white line over the eye. It is seldom found far from cattails, rushes, sedges, or tall marsh grasses. Song is 1-3 musical rattles on different pitches, often preceded by a faint nighthawk-like buzz, 10-16/min.

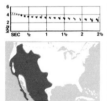

SEDGE WREN   *Cistóthorus platénsis*
Scarce and local in sedge meadows. Streaked crown and back, buffy underparts, short slim bill, cocked tail, and obscure buffy stripe over the eye identify this shy wren. It may even sing in hay fields during migration. An irregular migrant, it may arrive in some nesting areas as late as Aug. Song is soft, almost insect-like: about 3 introductory chips followed by an unmusical trill, 5-15/min.

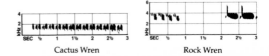

Cactus Wren   Rock Wren

WRENS 2

CACTUS
WREN
L 6½″

ROCK
WREN
L 4¾″

CANYON WREN
L 4½″

MARSH WREN
L 4″

SEDGE WREN
L 3¾″

● **MOCKINGBIRDS AND THRASHERS** (*Family* Mimidae) are long-tailed, short-winged, slender-billed birds that sing loudly from conspicuous perches. Mockingbirds are known for their excellent imitations. Thrashers repeat phrases fewer times, mimic less. All prefer brushy habitats, wood margins, or residential areas. Eggs, 3-6.

NORTHERN MOCKINGBIRD · *Mímus polyglóttos*

Common and conspicuous throughout southern U.S. At a distance it is best told in flight; white wing patches show clearly, and wingbeats are slow enough to be counted (see shrikes, p. 260). At rest the slender bill and white on wings and tail will clinch identification. Flicks tail from side to side. An expert mimic; it repeats most song phrases many times. Sings both while perched and in flight, and more at night than do other mimids.

GRAY CATBIRD · *Dumetélla carolinénsis*

Common near dense cover. No other bird is plain dark gray with rusty undertail coverts. Note the distinct black cap. Gray Catbird, named for its mewing call, often flicks its long tail. Song is of squeaky quality, with little or no repetition; it is a poor imitator.

BROWN THRASHER · *Toxóstoma rúfum*

Common. The only thrasher east of the Rockies and central Texas. It is heavily streaked below and rich rufous brown above. Most often confused with Wood Thrush (p. 248), which has shorter tail and dark eyes. Most phrases of the song are given twice rather than once (catbird) or many times (mockingbird), 25-42/min.

LONG-BILLED THRASHER · *Toxóstoma longiróstre*

Absence of rufous on head and back separates this common resident of southern Texas from the Brown Thrasher in the limited area of range overlap. Bill is longer and blacker. Song more like catbird's than Brown Thrasher's.

SAGE THRASHER · *Oreoscóptes montánus*

A common short-tailed thrasher of sagebrush habitats. Note the short bill, yellow eye, and white corners on the tail. No streaked thrush nests in the arid country where it occurs, but in winter compare it with other thrashers. Song, given from conspicuous perch or in flight, resembles Brown Thrasher's, but is more melodious and lacks the pauses between phrases.

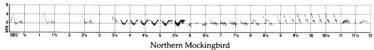

Northern Mockingbird

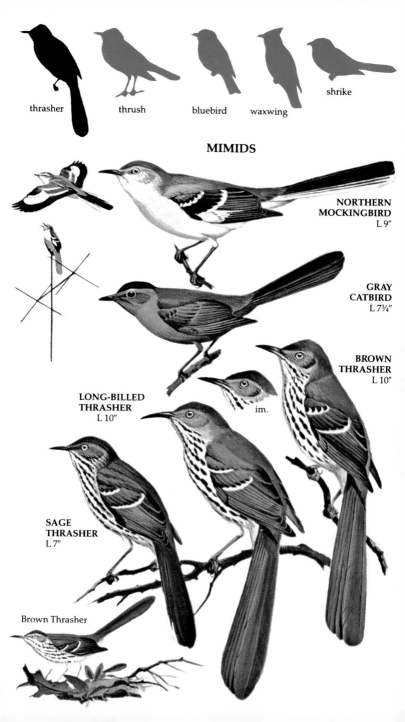

thrasher thrush bluebird waxwing shrike

MIMIDS

NORTHERN MOCKINGBIRD
L 9"

GRAY CATBIRD
L 7¾"

BROWN THRASHER
L 10"

LONG-BILLED THRASHER
L 10"

im.

SAGE THRASHER
L 7"

Brown Thrasher

- **UNSTREAKED THRASHERS** require extreme caution in identification, especially in Arizona, where three or four species may occur together at water holes. These comparatively plain-breasted thrashers of the Southwest are similar in appearance and song. They feed mostly on the ground, nest in mesquite or cacti. Only Bendire's migrates.

BENDIRE'S THRASHER
Toxóstoma béndirei

The best field mark of this small thrasher is the short bill, which is nearly straight. Also note the indistinct breast streaks and the lemon-yellow eye. Often nests in cacti. Song is more varied than those of most thrashers, and phrases are not separated.

CURVE-BILLED THRASHER
Toxóstoma curviróstre

Common in sparse desert brush. Told from Bendire's by the orange or red-orange eye of adult and by the tail, which is blacker than the back. Juvenile has yellow eye and straighter bill, much like Bendire's. The other thrashers in its range have plain breasts. Song is less varied than those of other thrashers, and phrases are not separated; call, a loud whistled *whit-wheet,* is more distinctive.

CALIFORNIA THRASHER
Toxóstoma redivívum

Common in chaparral and other brushy habitats. Note the eye stripe and dark brown body, pale rusty below. Only Le Conte's and Crissal overlap any part of this bird's U.S. range. The California flies less and runs more than other thrashers. When feeding on the ground, this species and the next two hold their tail more erect than the two above. Digs with curved beak rather than scratching with its feet. Song includes a great variety of phrases, many repeated; also is a good imitator. Sonagram below.

LE CONTE'S THRASHER
Toxóstoma lecóntei

Common in saltbush and very open cactus deserts. The dark bill, black eye line, and dark tail contrasting with the pale gray body distinguish it from the darker California and Crissal Thrashers. Song is irregular; phrases not repeated as much as by other thrashers.

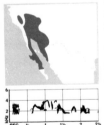

CRISSAL THRASHER
Toxóstoma dorsále

In fertile valleys and densely vegetated canyons. The only other thrasher with rusty undertail coverts, the California, has a buffy eye stripe. Flies little. Call, *pitchoórip.*

California Thrasher

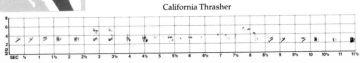

UNSTREAKED THRASHERS

CURVE-BILLED THRASHER
L 10″

BENDIRE'S THRASHER
L 8¼″

CALIFORNIA THRASHER
L 10″

LE CONTE'S THRASHER
L 9¼″

CRISSAL THRASHER
L 10½″

● **THRUSHES, SOLITAIRES, AND BLUEBIRDS** (*Family* Muscicapidae, *Subfamily* Turdinae)·are a varied group of fine singers. All young have spotted breasts. All except bluebirds and solitaires are often seen standing or running on the ground. Typical thrushes migrate at night; robins and bluebirds migrate in flocks by day. Bluebirds nest in cavities or bird boxes; other thrushes build nests in crotches of trees or shrubs. The 3-6 eggs are usually greenish-blue, plain, or lightly spotted.

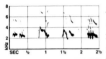

AMERICAN ROBIN   *Túrdus migratórius*
A common well-known bird often seen on lawns searching for insects and earthworms. In cold weather prefers moist woods or fruit-bearing trees. Adult is orange-breasted (head of female is paler than male's); breast of juvenile is spotted. Builds a nest of grass and mud in orchard trees or shrubs or on buildings. Song is a series of 6-10 whistled phrases of 3 or 4 notes, 5-20/min.

FIELDFARE   *Túrdus piláris*
Casual (Alaska to Delaware) from Eurasia. Chestnut back and wings separate gray rump from gray head and nape. Breast dull reddish brown, heavily streaked. Wing linings white. Call, loud, nasal *shahk, shahk.*

REDWING   *Túrdus ilíacus*
Casual in Greenland and New York from northern Europe. Found in deciduous woods, gardens, fields. Note prominent white eye stripe, streaked underparts, reddish flank, and chestnut wing lining. Call, a high *zee-up.*

RUFOUS-BACKED ROBIN   *Túrdus rufopalliátus*
Casual in fruit-bearing deciduous trees in southern Arizona and southern Texas. Resembles Fieldfare in upper coloring, American Robin in lower. No eye stripe. Juvenile has underparts boldly spotted with black. Call, *meoo.*

CLAY-COLORED ROBIN   *Túrdus gráyi*
Casual, all seasons, in woodland and edge habitats in southern Texas. Very plain, dull robin with uniform tawny olive breast, buffy olive belly. Calls, *whee-oo-weet* and a low pitched *pup-up-up.*

EURASIAN BLACKBIRD   *Túrdus mérula*
Accidental in Greenland and Quebec. This common European replacement of the American Robin is recognized by its uniform dark color (black in male, brown in female), yellow bill, and robin-like behavior, and calls.

American Robin   bluebird   waxwing   shrike   starling

ROBIN-LIKE THRUSHES

juv.

♂

AMERICAN ROBIN
L 8½"

FIELDFARE
L 8½"

Fieldfare

REDWING
L 7¼"

RUFOUS-BACKED ROBIN
L 8"

CLAY-COLORED ROBIN
L 8"

♀

EURASIAN BLACKBIRD
L 8½"

EYE-BROWED THRUSH   *Túrdus obscúrus*
Rare spring migrant in western Aleutians. Casual elsewhere in western and northern Alaska. Note white eye stripe, pale, plain olive-brown body. Male's white chin contrasts with gray hood. Call, harsh *seee*.

DUSKY THRUSH   *Túrdus naúmanni eunómus*
Casual in western and northern Alaska in spring. Prominent white eye stripe and heavy black speckling on breast, flanks, and back of male are diagnostic. Black breast markings often form one or two bands, contrasting with white throat. Note white half collar; also rusty areas on rump and both wing surfaces. Call similar to Fieldfare's (p. 244).

VARIED THRUSH   *Ixóreus naévius*
Common in moist coniferous woods in the Northwest. The only similar species are the robins (p. 244), which it resembles in appearance and habits. Note the orange wing bars and eye stripe and the black (male) or gray (female) breastband. Song is an un-robin-like series of long musical notes on different pitches, each note loudest in the middle. Call, a descending whistled hum.

TOWNSEND'S SOLITAIRE   *Myadéstes tównsendi*
Uncommon; in coniferous forests in summer, woods or brush in winter. Like an erect, short-billed mockingbird (p. 240), but with a white eye ring, notched tail, and darker gray breast. Unlike typical thrushes, it flycatches from a conspicuous perch in the open and nests on the ground. At a distance it resembles a robin. Song is a loud long warble. Call, a single piping note.

SIBERIAN RUBYTHROAT   *Luscínia callíope*
Rare spring and fall migrant in western Aleutians. Male is unmistakable. Female is similar to Bluethroat but tail is plain, necklace lacking. Song suggests Gray Catbird.

BLUETHROAT   *Luscínia svécica*
Rare breeder in upland and foothill areas of northwestern and northern Alaska; winters in Asia. Throat of male is unique. On female, note bright rusty patches at base of tail, white eye stripe, black necklace. Tail is often jerked and spread. Song is high gentle warbling suggesting Winter Wren (p. 236).

NORTHERN WHEATEAR   *Oenánthe oenánthe*
Common from northern Alaska to Greenland, rare elsewhere; most winter in Africa. Note the long wings, short tail, thin bill, white rump, black face mask, flashy tail pattern, and upright posture.

Varied Thrush

WESTERN AND ALASKAN THRUSHES

♀

♂

EYE-BROWED
THRUSH
L 6¾″

Dusky Thrush

DUSKY
THRUSH
L 7¾″

♀

VARIED
THRUSH
L 8″

♂

juv.

TOWNSEND'S
SOLITAIRE
L 6¾″

BLUETHROAT
L 4¾″

♂

winter

SIBERIAN
RUBYTHROAT
L 5″

♂

summer

NORTHERN
WHEATEAR
L 5¼″

Wheatear
female and
winter

● **SPOTTED-BREASTED THRUSHES** are typically slightly smaller than robins. Their dark eyes, shorter tails, and spotted breasts distinguish them from thrashers. They prefer the forest understory; eat insects and berries. All are fine singers.

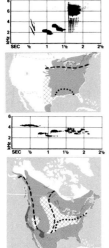

WOOD THRUSH   *Hylocíchla mustelína*

The common nesting thrush in eastern deciduous forests and suburbs. Told from Brown Thrasher (p. 240) by round breast spots, dark eyes, and short tail; from other thrushes by the large breast spots and rusty head. Song is a series of loud flute-like phrases, each followed by a softer guttural trill, 11-19/min.

HERMIT THRUSH   *Cátharus guttátus*

Common and widespread in northern woodlands. Our only thrush with the habit of slowly raising its tail several times a minute. Note contrast of rusty tail and olive-brown back. Nearly all spotted-breasted thrushes seen in U.S. in winter are of this species. Song (seldom heard except on breeding ground) is a single high flute-like note followed by a rapid series of rising and falling notes, this pattern repeated in other pitches, 9-16/min.

SWAINSON'S THRUSH   *Cátharus ustulátus*

The best field marks for this common thrush are the buffy face and eye ring; compare carefully with the other thrushes on this page. Breeds like Gray-cheeked Thrush in evergreen forests. Song is a rolling series of rapid flute-like notes, rising up the scale, 8-14/min.

GRAY-CHEEKED THRUSH   *Cátharus mínimus*

Fairly common. Told from Swainson's Thrush by its gray face and absence of a distinct eye ring, from Veery by back color, and from Hermit by olive tail, which is the same color as the back. Song is like Veery's but softer, more nasal, and with a rising inflection at the end.

VEERY   *Cátharus fuscéscens*

Common. Typical plumage is entirely rusty above. Compare with Wood Thrush and Hermit Thrush. Spots on breast are less distinct and more restricted than in the other thrushes. Summers in deciduous forests; prefers wetter habitats than other thrushes. Nests on or very near the ground. The loud song is a rolling series of rapid flute-like notes, dropping down the scale, 8-14/min.

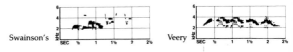

Swainson's   Veery

SPOTTED-BREASTED THRUSHES

juv.

WOOD THRUSH
L 7"

HERMIT THRUSH
L 6"

SWAINSON'S THRUSH
L 6¼"

GRAY-CHEEKED THRUSH
L 6¼"

dark race
im.

VEERY
L 6"

rusty race

● **BLUEBIRDS** are found in orchards, farmyards, roadsides, and open woodlands, often in family groups or small flocks. When perched, note the hunched shoulders; the bill often points slightly downward. They sit on conspicuous perches, from which they drop to the ground for insects. They also catch insects on the wing. In fall and winter bluebirds add berries to their diet. Nests are in natural cavities or bird boxes. Calls are given frequently in flight.

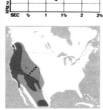

EASTERN BLUEBIRD   *Siália síalis*

Only bluebird east of the Great Plains, fairly common along roadsides and in farmyards and abandoned orchards. The male has a bright, entirely blue back and rusty throat and breast. The much larger Blue Jay (p. 222) is always crested and lacks the rusty breast. The Indigo Bunting (p. 312) and Blue Grosbeak (p. 310) are all-blue below; the Lazuli Bunting (p. 312) has wing bars. Recognize female and young as bluebirds by the hunched posture, eye ring, and the blue in wings and tail. Juvenile is spotted like a typical thrush; compare with juvenile Western and Mountain. Song and call are a melodious whistling, 30-40/min.

WESTERN BLUEBIRD   *Siália mexicána*

Fairly common. Adult male can be confused only with the Eastern Bluebird. The blue throat and rusty upper back are characteristic of the Western. The female and juvenile Westerns are browner above than the Eastern and have a grayer throat. Like other bluebirds, this species migrates by day, and generally is found in small flocks outside the nesting season. The usual song is a 3-fold or double whistle; a simple call note is typical. A more varied song is heard at dawn.

MOUNTAIN BLUEBIRD   *Siália currucoídes*

Fairly common. The sky-blue plumage of the male is diagnostic; neither sex has a rusty breast. The female can be recognized by its gray breast, and both sexes have a less hunched posture than the Eastern and Western Bluebirds. The juvenile is told from other bluebirds by its posture and by the paler blue of wings and tail. More than other bluebirds, this species hovers low over the ground hunting for insects. As its name implies, it is typical of high elevations in summer, being most common above 5,000' and wandering in late summer up to 12,000' and in winter to sea level. Generally silent except at dawn; song is a soft warbling whistle.

hrasher   thrush   bluebird   waxwing   shrike   starling

BLUEBIRDS

juv.   ♀   ♂

EASTERN BLUEBIRD
L 5½"

♀   ♂

WESTERN BLUEBIRD
L 5½"

juv.

hovering

♀   ♂

juv.

MOUNTAIN BLUEBIRD
L 6"

- **GNATCATCHERS AND KINGLETS** (*Family* Muscicapidae, *Subfamily* Sylviinae) are part of a large family of Old World warblers and flycatchers. Small, drab, and thin-billed, they are very active insectivorous birds. They have unspotted young, lay 4-8 spotted or speckled eggs.

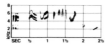

BLUE-GRAY GNATCATCHER *Polióptila caerúlea*
A common canopy species of moist forests, recognized by its blue back, eye ring, fly-catching habit, and the sideways twitching of its long tail. The next two species and the Painted Redstart (p. 292) of the Southwest are the only other small fly-catching birds with a long, dark, white-bordered tail. Its nest, which is coated with lichens, is easily found before leaves emerge. Its high nasal calls (65-85/min.) are more frequent than its soft vireo-like song.

BLACK-CAPPED GNATCATCHER *Polióptila nígriceps*
Rare and local breeder in southern Arizona (Sonoita Creek). Adult male in spring and summer is told by black cap and lack of eye ring. Winter male has a bluish cap and partial eye ring. Female is nondescript with bluish cap, no eye ring, and dark lores.

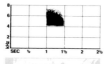

BLACK-TAILED GNATCATCHER *Polióptila melanúra*
Common in desert scrub, washes, and ravines. The male is easily told in spring and summer by its black cap. Female, young, and winter male are told by call and by large amount of black on the underside of the tail.

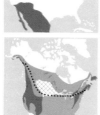

GOLDEN-CROWNED KINGLET *Régulus sátrapa*
Common; prefers conifers. Told from other tiny woodland birds by its brightly striped head. Female has a yellow crown. Song of 4 to 8 high notes, followed by a series of rapid, descending, chickadee-like notes, 4-8/min. Common call is 3-5 very high creeper-like notes.

RUBY-CROWNED KINGLET *Régulus caléndula*
Common. Told from Golden-crown by eye ring, and from vireos or fall warblers by its smaller size, short tail, and kinglet habit of flicking its wings. Ruby crown of the male may be concealed. Often hovers very briefly; prefers conifers. Gives a low-pitched, short, 2-note scolding call. Song is high and weak at the beginning and end, but has very loud ascending triplets in the middle.

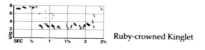

Ruby-crowned Kinglet

flycatcher chickadee gnatcatcher kinglet vi...

254

GNATCATCHERS AND KINGLETS

♀ ♂

BLUE-GRAY GNATCATCHER
L 4″

BLACK-CAPPED GNATCATCHER
L 4″

underside of tails

Blue-gray Black-capped Black-tailed

♀ ♂

BLACK-TAILED GNATCATCHER
L 4″

♀ ♂

GOLDEN-CROWNED KINGLET
L 3½″

♀ ♂

RUBY-CROWNED KINGLET
L 3¾″

ARCTIC WARBLER
Phylloscópus boreális

This drab Old World warbler breeds in Alaska and winters in Asia. Resembles our wood warblers in size and actions, and looks like an olive Tennessee Warbler (p. 274). Note the prominent pale eye stripe and the single wing bar. Sexes are alike. Song is a short high trill.

● **OLD WORLD FLYCATCHERS** (*Family* Muscicapidae, *Subfamily* Muscicapinae) are small, slender-billed, short-legged birds that sit erect in the open and sally after flying insects. Lay 4-9 blue or spotted eggs.

GRAY-SPOTTED FLYCATCHER
Muscicápa griseistícta

Spring vagrant in western Alaska. Note the prominent white eye ring, single faint wing bar, the distinct dark gray streaks on the white underparts, and plain dark tail.

● **WAGTAILS AND PIPITS** (*Family* Motacillidae) are sparrow-sized insectivorous birds with slender warbler-like bills and distinctive calls; they have dark tails with white outer feathers. They feed on the ground, walk leisurely, and wag their tails continually. They do not hop. They lay 4-7 eggs in a nest on the ground.

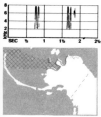

WHITE WAGTAIL
Motacílla álba

Rare local breeder in coastal western Alaska and Greenland; winters in Asia and Africa. Adult is told by its black cap, bib, and central tail feathers, and its white face, wing patch, and outer tail feathers. Immature is known by the black necklace, white breast and belly. Bobs head like a dove when walking. Call, *tschizzik*. The **Black-backed Wagtail** (*Motacílla lúgens*, L 6") from Asia is accidental in the Aleutians.

GRAY WAGTAIL
Motacílla cinérea

Spring vagrant in western Alaska. Note the very long tail and gray back. Male's throat is white in winter. Immature told from immature Yellow Wagtail by gray back, from White Wagtail by yellow rump and undertail coverts. Call, *stit-it*, like White Wagtail's but higher and shorter.

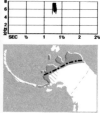

YELLOW WAGTAIL
Motacílla fláva

Locally common; breeds in arctic willow thickets and on tundra. Adult Yellow Wagtail is told from other arctic ground-walking birds by the long tail with white outer feathers, the white eye stripe, greenish back, and bright yellow underparts. Immature Yellow is buffy below. All wagtails have an undulating flight. Call, *tsweep*.

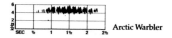

Arctic Warbler

ARCTIC WARBLER
L 4¼"

GRAY-SPOTTED FLYCATCHER
L 4"

WAGTAILS

WHITE WAGTAIL
L 6"

summer

im.

GRAY WAGTAIL
L 6"

♂ summer

winter

YELLOW WAGTAIL
L 5½"

im.

summer

BROWN TREE-PIPIT
Ánthus triviális

Accidental in western Alaska. Breeds in open woods in Eurasia, winters from Africa to India. Unstreaked rump, pink legs, yellowish wash on breast, and short, curved hind claw are diagnostic. Call, a coarse *teezee*.

OLIVE TREE-PIPIT
Ánthus hódgsoni

Spring vagrant to western Alaska and Nevada from southern Siberia. Told by coarse breast spots, broad buffy eye stripe, unstreaked rump, very finely streaked greenish back, pinkish brown legs. Call, *tseep*.

PECHORA PIPIT
Ánthus gústavi

Spring vagrant to western Alaska from Siberia. Told by pair of pale stripes down the dark back, heavily streaked nape and rump, buffy outer tail feathers, brownish flesh legs, and long hind claw. Call, *pwit*, given 3 times.

MEADOW PIPIT
Ánthus praténsis

Breeds on eastern Greenland tundra, winters in Old World. Has whiter breast than above pipits; rump is less streaked than back, legs are brown. Call, thin *zeep*.

RED-THROATED PIPIT
Ánthus cervínus

Uncommon tundra breeder on coastal mountains in Bering Strait area. In summer, male has rosy throat; duller in female. Told in winter by heavily streaked back and rump, heavily streaked breast contrasting with white background, and straw-colored legs. Call, a high, thin *tzeez*.

WATER PIPIT
Ánthus spinolétta

Common in flocks during migration and in winter on muddy shores and plowed fields; nests on tundra and in alpine meadows. Bobs white-edged tail rapidly. Told from sparrows and longspurs by its slender bill, from Sprague's by unstreaked back, dark legs, and voice. Rarely perches on trees or posts. Call, *pippit*, is given often in flight.

SPRAGUE'S PIPIT
Ánthus sprágueii

Unlike Water Pipit, stays hidden in tall grass. When flushed, it flies a few hundred feet, then drops into heavy cover. Told from Water Pipit by streaked back and flesh-colored legs. Nests on northern plains, where its weird hissing flight song is given high overhead, 5-6/min. Its sharp, squeaky, single-syllable call is distinctive.

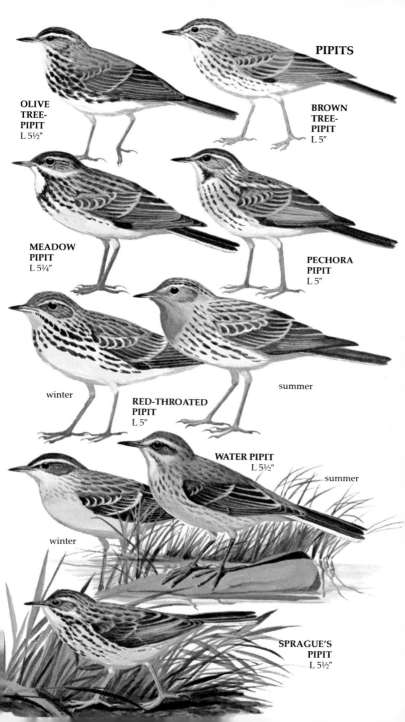

PIPITS

OLIVE TREE-PIPIT L 5½"

BROWN TREE-PIPIT L 5"

MEADOW PIPIT L 5¼"

PECHORA PIPIT L 5"

winter

summer

RED-THROATED PIPIT L 5"

WATER PIPIT L 5½"

summer

winter

SPRAGUE'S PIPIT L 5½"

258

● **WAXWINGS** (*Family* Bombycillidae), crested, gregarious birds with black masks and yellow tips to their short tails, are named for the red wax-like spots on the wings of adult. They eat fruits and berries; also catch insects as flycatchers do. In flight their silhouettes and flock formations resemble those of Starlings (p. 260). They lay 3-5 spotted eggs in a bulky shallow nest in late summer.

BOHEMIAN WAXWING   *Bombycílla gárrulus*
Abundant vagrant in large flocks except during the breeding season. Distribution is irregular, especially in eastern portion of winter range; may follow food supply. Recognized as a waxwing by the black mask, long crest, and yellow fringe to the tail. The cinnamon undertail coverts and distinctive yellow, black, and white wing markings identify it as the Bohemian. Females are similar to males. Young can be told by the tinge of cinnamon under the tail. Calls are similar to those of Cedar Waxwing, but recognizable with practice.

CEDAR WAXWING   *Bombycílla cedrórum*
Irregular in its wanderings, but at times abundant in compact flocks in berry-bearing trees and shrubs. Told from the grayer Bohemian Waxwing by the white undertail coverts, yellowish belly, and lack of conspicuous yellow and white markings on the wings. Sexes are similar. Young are grayer, with indistinct streaking below. Seldom seen alone except when nesting. Call is a very high thin monotone, generally with a slight quaver that distinguishes it from the Brown Creeper's (p. 234).

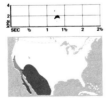

● **SILKY FLYCATCHERS** (*Family* Ptilogonatidae) are slim, dark, flycatching birds with long, pointed, erect crests and long tails. Gregarious, they often travel in small flocks. Thickly speckled eggs (2-3) are laid in a shallow loose nest.

PHAINOPEPLA   *Phainopépla nítens*
Common; in arid scrub, especially near streams. Recognized by its uniform dark color, tall crest, and long tail. In flight the male is best told by the white wing patch contrasting with the all-black body and tail. Female and immature are gray, with paler gray wing patches. Males generally outnumber females. Seen singly or in small flocks (15-20) eating berries (especially elderberries) or making short flights from a conspicuous perch after insects. Flight is slow and graceful. Call, a soft, short whistle.

thrasher   thrush   bluebird   waxwing   shrike

WAXWINGS, PHAINOPEPLA

BOHEMIAN WAXWING L 6¼″

im.

CEDAR WAXWING L 5¾″

im.

PHAINOPEPLA L 6¼″

♀

♂

♀

♂

● **SHRIKES** (*Family* Laniidae) are recognized by their heavy hooked beaks, black masks, large white wing patches contrasting with dark wings, and habit of pursuing insects, small birds, and rodents, which they impale on thorn trees or barbed wire. Shrikes perch alone, with tail held nearly horizontal, on treetops or telephone wires in open country. Their flight is low and undulating. Bulky nests with 4-6 eggs are in thorny shrubs or well hidden in small trees.

NORTHERN SHRIKE
Lánius excúbitor

An uncommon robin-sized bird that preys on small birds and mammals. Irregular winter visitor to northern states, where usually seen in brown immature plumage; immature Loggerhead Shrikes are gray after Aug. Told from Loggerhead by larger, heavier hooked bill, light base to lower mandible, pale body, faintly barred sides, and forward end of mask stopping at the bill. May hover over prey or pounce rapidly. Usually silent in winter, but has shrill cries and rattles.

LOGGERHEAD SHRIKE
Lánius ludoviciánus

Uncommon. Often confused with mockingbird (p. 240), as it is gray above and white below, but note its blacker wing, facial mask, heavy hooked bill, and undulating flight with wingbeats too fast to count. Song is a slow chat-like series of calls and trills, often unmusical, 20/min.

● **STARLINGS** (*Family* Sturnidae), introduced and widespread in North America, are short-tailed, dark, and fat-bodied. Gregarious and aggressive, they are especially abundant at roosting sites. Diets are varied. Blue eggs (4-6) are laid in nest hole.

EUROPEAN STARLING
Stúrnus vulgáris

Told from true blackbirds (p. 298) by its short tail and, in flight, by its browner wings. The yellow bill is diagnostic in spring and summer; winter plumage is heavily speckled. Spends the night in large communal roosts from late summer until spring. Often an abundant pest in city parks, suburbs, and farms. Song is largely of squeaky notes, but it imitates many bird calls.

CRESTED MYNA
Acridótheres cristatéllus

Introduced at Vancouver, British Columbia. Recognized by white wing patches contrasting with black wings and body and by short crest. Habits and song are like Starling's, but Crested Myna is much better imitator.

thrasher

thrush

bluebird

waxwing

shrike

im.

NORTHERN SHRIKE
L 8″

**SHRIKES,
STARLINGS**

juv.

**LOGGERHEAD
SHRIKE**
L 7″

winter

**EUROPEAN
STARLING**
L 6″

summer

im. European Starling

**CRESTED
MYNA**
L 9″

● **BANANAQUITS** (*Family* Emberizidae, *Subfamily* Coerebinae) are nectar eaters with long, pointed, generally downcurved bills and short tails.

BANANAQUIT
Coeréba flaveóla

Casual in southeast Florida. Tame; probes blossoms in gardens. Told by bright yellow rump and breastband, striking face pattern, white flash in wings and tail.

● **VIREOS** (*Family* Vireonidae) are plain-colored sluggish birds that pick crawling insects from the foliage of shade and forest trees. Some vireos have spectacles (eye rings with a connecting band) and wing bars; the others have eye stripes and no wing bars. Vireo bills are heavier than those of warblers and have a tiny hook at the end. Vireos are persistent singers. Eggs, 3-5, are laid in nests suspended from crotches of thin branches.

BLACK-CAPPED VIREO
Víreo atricapíllus

Locally common in cedar-oak thickets of central and west Texas. No other North American bird has white spectacles on a jet-black head. The female is told by the spectacles, the red eye, the buffy body, and the whitish wing bars. This tiny vireo is barely larger than a kinglet. Song is harsh but varied, suggestive of White-eyed Vireo's (p. 264).

GRAY VIREO
Víreo vicínior

Rare in pinyon-juniper and other arid scrub habitats. Drabbest of the wing-barred spectacled vireos; the single wing bar is faint. Easily confused with Bell's Vireo (p. 264), but rump is gray, as is back; tail is much longer; and Gray inhabits drier areas. This and Bell's are the only vireos that nervously twitch the tail as a gnatcatcher does. Song is slurred like Solitary's, but more rapid.

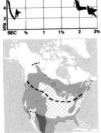

SOLITARY VIREO
Víreo solitárius

Common in mixed northern hardwood-coniferous forests. Its large size, prominent blue-gray or gray head, spectacles, and white throat are diagnostic. The gray-backed plumbeous form occurs in the Rockies. Its large white wing bars separate it from the Gray Vireo where ranges overlap, and the gray head rules out other vireos (p. 264) and kinglets (p. 252). Rather sluggish and tame. Song consists of slow, slurred, robin-like phrases, suggestive of Red-eyed Vireo's song (p. 266), but often with only 2 or 3 notes per phrase, 15-30/min.

kinglet   vireo   warbler

**BANANAQUIT, WING-BARRED
VIREOS 1**

BANANAQUIT
L 4″

♀

**BLACK-CAPPED
VIREO**
♂
L 4″

GRAY VIREO
L 4¾″

habitat of
Gray Vireo

Rocky Mt.
race

SOLITARY VIREO
L 4¾″

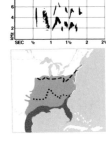

WHITE-EYED VIREO
Vireo gríseus

Common in dense moist deciduous thickets, wood margins, and hedgerows. The only vireo with a white iris (adult only). The bright yellowish sides distinguish it from all wing-barred vireos except the Solitary and Black-capped, both of which show sharp contrast between head and throat. The dark-eyed immature resembles Bell's Vireo, but has more yellow on the flanks and spectacles. *Empidonax* flycatchers (pp. 212-214) have dark eyes and light eye rings but no spectacles. The White-eyed Vireo is much easier to hear than see. Song is typically 5-7 loud notes slurred together, including an emphatic chip at the beginning and end, 6-12/min.

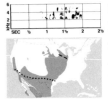

BELL'S VIREO
Vireo béllii

Common in moist thickets, wood margins, and mesquite. Western counterpart of White-eyed, but eye is always black. Note wing bars and narrow eye ring. Sexes are alike. Western Bell's are pale gray. Also similar to Gray (p. 262), which is darker gray with a longer tail, and Hutton's, which has broad wing bars and dull gray throat and breast. Easily told from both by its rapid warbling song, which ends alternately with rising and falling inflection, 10-15/min.

HUTTON'S VIREO
Vireo húttoni

Common in evergreen oaks; also found in pines and firs. Note the two distinct wing bars. Told from other vireos by incomplete spectacles that do not join above the eye; from Ruby-crowned Kinglet (p. 252) by its calls and its heavier bill, by having spectacles rather than an eye ring, and by its paler wing and sluggish actions; also by its distinctive song, which is a monotonous repetition of a 2-note phrase accented on the higher note, 60-75/min.

YELLOW-THROATED VIREO
Vireo flávifrons

Uncommon; in deciduous forests near water or in clearings; also in shade trees and mixed pine-deciduous woods. The only spectacled vireo with a distinct yellow throat and breast. Female and immature are similar to male. The heavy vireo bill and yellow spectacles distinguish it from the Pine Warbler (p. 286), which it most closely resembles in plumage. Yellow-throated Vireo has much larger nesting territories than most vireos do. Song is hoarse, a repetition of 4-5 slurred phrases given again and again in about the same order, 19-35/min.

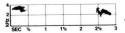

Yellow-throated Vireo

im.

WHITE-EYED VIREO
L 4½"

BELL'S VIREO
L 4¼"

Ruby-crowned Kinglet
for comparison

HUTTON'S VIREO
L 4"

Pine Warbler
for comparison

YELLOW-THROATED VIREO
L 5"

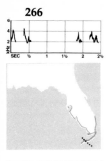

BLACK-WHISKERED VIREO — *Víreo altilóquus*

Common and easily found in its limited U.S. range in the Florida Keys and south Florida mainland, where it lives in mangroves and hammocks from Tampa to Everglades National Park. It is more easily recognized by its monotonous song than by its dark "whisker" marks. Song resembles Red-eyed Vireo's but with paired phrases and less variable pitch, 20-32/min.

RED-EYED VIREO — *Víreo olivâceus*

The most abundant bird in eastern deciduous forests. Red iris, prominent eye stripe, and blue-gray cap distinguish this bird from all others except in the limited areas where the preceding vireo occurs. Immature has a brown iris. The Yellow-green race, *V. o. flavovíridis*, formerly recognized as a separate species, is rare in woods and shade trees along the lower Rio Grande in southern Texas. It is told by its bright yellow sides and undertail coverts and less distinct eye stripe. Immature Red-eyed has buffy undertail coverts. Song of the species is robin-like, but phrases are separated by brief pauses; the song typically continues for many minutes without a long break, 35-70/min.

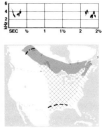

PHILADELPHIA VIREO — *Víreo philadélphicus*

Uncommon; in wood margins and deciduous scrub. This small elusive species is often mistaken for a Red-eyed Vireo when heard and for a warbler when seen. Its yellowish breast and unmarked wings tell it from all other vireos. The vireo bill should separate it from all warblers, but it may be confused in fall with the Tennessee Warbler (p. 274), which has a greener back, and the Orange-crowned Warbler (p. 274), which has obscure head markings and yellow undertail coverts. Song is like Red-eyed's, but higher pitched and slower.

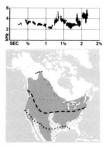

WARBLING VIREO — *Víreo gílvus*

This drab summer resident of tall deciduous shade trees is more easily detected by its song than by sight. Look for the vireo bill and broad white eye stripe, which is not outlined in black. This vireo is so well concealed by foliage that the male may sing from the nest. Immature has greener back, yellow flanks. Song is long and warbling, like a hoarse Purple Finch (p. 316), 6-11/min.

im.

**PLAIN-WINGED
VIREOS**

Yellow-green race

**RED-EYED
VIREO**
L 5″

im.

color
extremes

**PHILADELPHIA
VIREO**
L 4¾″

**WARBLING
VIREO**
L 4¾″

D-WARBLERS (*Subfamily* Parulinae) are small, very active, .ghtly colored songsters with slender, straight, pointed bills. Males in spring and early summer (through July) are fairly easy to recognize if you can get a good look at them. Because males do the singing, the great majority of birds seen in spring and summer are males in their breeding plumage. Look first for wing bars and characteristic head markings. Note the song patterns, which are diagnostic for most species.

Fall birds and spring females are difficult to tell at first. Most female plumage patterns bear some resemblance to those of spring males, but are duller. For comparisons of fall plumages see pp. 294-295.

Our warblers are divided into 16 genera. Those in the same genus have some similarity in habits as well as in plumage and structure, such as shape and size of bill. The genus *Seiurus* (Ovenbird and water-thrushes), for example, includes birds that teeter like the Spotted Sandpiper and walk on the ground in search of food. The genus *Oporornis* is composed of relatively sluggish warblers that feed on the ground. Members of the genus *Wilsonia* catch insects on the wing.

During the nesting season, warblers remain in or close to their preferred habitats. During migration they gather in mixed flocks, frequently in company with chickadees or titmice. Then nearly all species occur in wood margins, hedgerows, orchards, and wooded swamps, along streams, or even in desert oases. Warblers migrate mainly at

WOOD-WARBLERS WITHOUT WING BARS - SPRING MALES

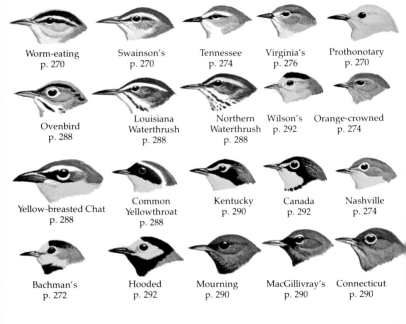

Worm-eating
p. 270

Swainson's
p. 270

Tennessee
p. 274

Virginia's
p. 276

Prothonotary
p. 270

Ovenbird
p. 288

Louisiana
Waterthrush
p. 288

Northern
Waterthrush
p. 288

Wilson's
p. 292

Orange-crowned
p. 274

Yellow-breasted Chat
p. 288

Common
Yellowthroat
p. 288

Kentucky
p. 290

Canada
p. 292

Nashville
p. 274

Bachman's
p. 272

Hooded
p. 292

Mourning
p. 290

MacGillivray's
p. 290

Connecticut
p. 290

night, but watch for them flying within 500′ of the treetops in early morning. Most winter in Mexico, Central America, or the West Indies.

The experienced observer can tell more than half the warblers just by their call notes. Learn the most distinctive chips first (such as those of Common Yellowthroat, Yellow-rumped, and Hooded); then study the chips of the common birds in your area. Some will be impossible to recognize, but awareness of a chip that is different will aid you in fall by drawing attention to the less common species in a mixed flock.

Warblers are almost entirely insectivorous. Most warblers nest on or within 10′ of the ground, but some, especially the parulas and some of the genus *Dendroica*, nest high in trees. Eggs, usually 4-5.

WOOD-WARBLERS WITH WING BARS — SPRING MALES

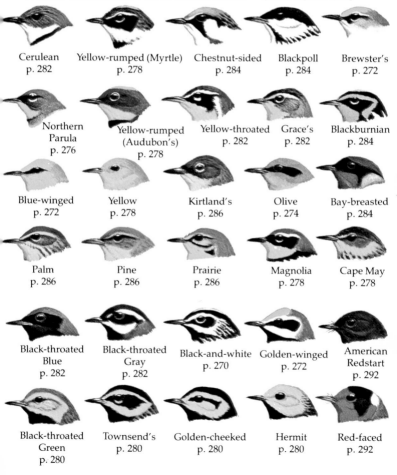

Cerulean
p. 282

Yellow-rumped (Myrtle)
p. 278

Chestnut-sided
p. 284

Blackpoll
p. 284

Brewster's
p. 272

Northern
Parula
p. 276

Yellow-rumped
(Audubon's)
p. 278

Yellow-throated
p. 282

Grace's
p. 282

Blackburnian
p. 284

Blue-winged
p. 272

Yellow
p. 278

Kirtland's
p. 286

Olive
p. 274

Bay-breasted
p. 284

Palm
p. 286

Pine
p. 286

Prairie
p. 286

Magnolia
p. 278

Cape May
p. 278

Black-throated
Blue
p. 282

Black-throated
Gray
p. 282

Black-and-white
p. 270

Golden-winged
p. 272

American
Redstart
p. 292

Black-throated
Green
p. 280

Townsend's
p. 280

Golden-cheeked
p. 280

Hermit
p. 280

Red-faced
p. 292

● **WOOD-WARBLERS** do not warble, but nearly all species have gay distinctive songs. Many species have 2 or more characteristic song patterns: frequently a longer song with a distinctive ending and a shorter one (heard more in late summer) that is harder to recognize. In general the more distinctive one is illustrated in Sonagrams. Many eastern species occur on the Pacific Coast in fall.

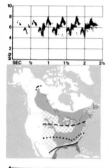

BLACK-AND-WHITE WARBLER *Mniotílta vária*
Common in deciduous woods. This, the Blackpoll Warbler (p. 284), and the western Black-throated Gray (p. 282) are the only warblers that are black and white. Neither of the others has the white streak through the crown, nor do they share the Black-and-white's habit of feeding primarily along the trunks and larger branches. In this behavior it is more like a nuthatch (p. 234), though its posture is different. The crown is striped in all plumages, but female and immature lack the black cheeks. Nests on the ground. Song is a high thin whistle, 4/min.

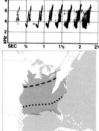

PROTHONOTARY WARBLER *Protonotária cítrea*
Common in wooded swamps and along streams. Golden head and plain blue-gray wings distinguish this brilliant bird in all plumages. Note also the long dark bill and white in and under the tail. Seldom seen far from water. Nests in tree cavity low over water. Song is loud and clear, of slurred ascending notes, 6-8/min.

SWAINSON'S WARBLER *Limnóthlypis swaínsonii*
Uncommon; in wooded swamps and canebrakes; rare and very local in rhododendron thickets in mountains. The plain brown back and wings, solid rusty cap, and plain underparts are diagnostic. Compare with Worm-eating and female Black-throated Blue (p. 282); other brown-backed warblers are heavily streaked below. Note large bill. Sexes and immature are similar. Inactive and hard to see. Song of about 5 clear slurred notes is suggestive of Louisiana Waterthrush's (p. 288), 5-8/min.

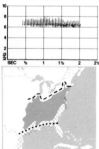

WORM-EATING WARBLER *Helmítheros vermívorus*
Uncommon; inconspicuous on deciduous slopes. Prominently streaked head, plain brown back and wings, and plain buffy underparts separate Worm-eating in all plumages from other warblers. Except for its slender bill, it resembles a sparrow. Often walks along limbs. Nests on ground. Song is much like Chipping Sparrow's (p. 338), but higher and generally more rapid, 4-6/min.

flycatcher
kinglet
vireo
warbler
sparrow

WARBLERS 1

BLACK-AND-WHITE WARBLER
L 4½″

♂

Blackpoll for comparison

♀

PROTHONOTARY WARBLER
L 4¾″

♀

♂

SWAINSON'S WARBLER
L 5″

WORM-EATING WARBLER
L 4½″

GOLDEN-WINGED WARBLER   *Vermívora chrysóptera*
Uncommon; in gray birch and other young deciduous growth and in abandoned pastures. Male looks like a chickadee, but has a yellow crown and yellow wing patch. Females and immatures always have enough of the male's pattern to identify them. No other warbler has the combination of black or gray throat and yellow wing bars. Song, which is given from a conspicuous perch, is buzzy: typically 1 note followed by 3 to 5 on a lower pitch, 6-10/min. Alternate song, *zi-zi-zi-zi-zeee*.

BLUE-WINGED WARBLER   *Vermívora pínus*
Uncommon; in old pastures overgrown with scattered saplings more than 10' tall. The narrow black eye line and white wing bars are diagnostic. Most of the other bright yellow warblers with unstreaked breasts have no wing bars. Female and immature Yellow Warbler (p. 278), which are common in migration at the same time as the Blue-winged, have much less contrast on the wing and have yellow tail spots. First note of the buzzy song is like Golden-winged's; its other high note is of more vibrant quality; 5-8/min.

● **HYBRIDS** occur locally where ranges of the above two species overlap. Several different plumages occur. The typical hybirds are known as Brewster's and Lawrence's Warblers. Brewster's, which is more frequently seen, is mostly white below with yellow (or occasionally white) wing bars. Lawrence's, with a black throat and yellow underparts, is extremely rare. Female Golden-wing can be mistaken for Brewster's, male Hooded (p. 292) for Lawrence's. Brewster's may have a pure white breast. Songs of the hybrids may be the same as either parent or may be a combination of the two songs.

BACHMAN'S WARBLER   *Vermívora báchmanii*
Rarest woodland warbler, very local in moist deciduous woodlands. The yellow forehead and face separate adult male's black crown from the black throat; its eye ring is yellow. There is no white in the tail. In the other plumages yellow or yellowish forehead, gray crown, and white undertail coverts will rule out similar species. Hooded Warbler (p. 292), which frequents the same habitat, has entirely different song and call notes. Bachman's sings from 20-40' up in the forest understory, giving distinct notes in a monotone, but with the quality of the alternate song of the Golden-winged Warbler. May be extinct.

EASTERN VERMIVORAS

♀

♂

GOLDEN-WINGED WARBLER
L 4¼"

♀

BLUE-WINGED WARBLER
L 4¼"

♂

Brewster's Warbler
hybrid L 4¼"

Lawrence's Warbler
hybrid L 4¼"

im.

♀

♂

BACHMAN'S WARBLER
L 4¼"

TENNESSEE WARBLER   *Vermívora peregrína*

Common in aspen and spruce woods. The only warbler except Lucy's (p. 276) with completely white underparts in spring. Its slender bill and bright greenish back separate it from sparrows. Similar to vireos (p. 262), but is slimmer and has a very slender bill. Female is washed with olive-green on the crown and yellowish on underparts. In fall the bright greenish back, white undertail coverts, and indistinct wing bar and eye stripe are diagnostic. Stays high in trees in spring. Song, of loud unevenly spaced chips, is more rapid at the end, 6-9 songs/min.

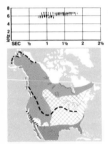

ORANGE-CROWNED WARBLER   *Vermívora celáta*

A nondescript warbler, common in West; rare in East except along the Gulf Coast in winter. Frequently forages in low trees and brush. The crown patch seldom is visible. Note the absence of white in all plumages. The very faint streaking on the sides of the breast helps distinguish this bird, especially in fall, when it is very similar to Tennessee Warbler (which has white or whitish undertail coverts). Most immatures approach the immature Tennessee in color; the one pictured here is the gray extreme. Song is a weak chippy-like trill.

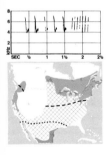

NASHVILLE WARBLER   *Vermívora ruficapílla*

Common in open second-growth deciduous woods and spruce bogs. Only North American warbler with the combination of bluish-gray head, white eye ring, bright yellow throat, and no wing bars. In fall it may be confused with dull Connecticut, Mourning, and MacGillivray's Warblers (p. 290), but these never have the bright yellow chin and throat. Reddish cap of male is often concealed. Song is in two parts: first half suggests Black-and-white's (p. 270), but notes are separate; the rest (sometimes omitted) is a lower-pitched, slow trill, 4-6/min.

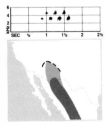
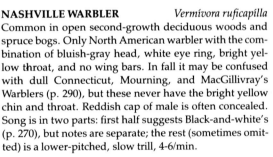

OLIVE WARBLER   *Peucédramus taeniátus*

The buffy brown head and black eye line of the male are diagnostic. Note also the broad white wing bars and dark wings and tail. The female is the only western warbler with broad wing bars and an unstreaked yellowish breast; note also the yellow triangle around the dusky eye patch. Uncommon; nests high up in sugar-pine and fir forests above 8,000'. The song is short; it consists of 2 to 5 pairs of loud, low-pitched slurred notes.

WIDESPREAD VERMIVORAS, OLIVE WARBLER

im.

summer ♂

TENNESSEE WARBLER
L 4¼"

ORANGE-CROWNED WARBLER
L 4¼"

gray race

NASHVILLE WARBLER
L 4"

im.

OLIVE WARBLER
L 4½"

♀ ♂

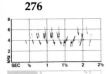

VIRGINIA'S WARBLER · · · · · · · · · · · · *Vermívora vírgíniae*

The unmarked gray back and wings distinguish this species and the two below from all except the gray-plumaged Orange-crowned Warbler (p. 274), which has an eye stripe rather than a white eye ring. Virginia's is told from Lucy's and the large Colima by its greenish-yellow rump and undertail coverts. Common in dense scrub at 6,000-9,000'. Song suggests Yellow Warbler's (p. 278).

COLIMA WARBLER · · · · · · · · · · · · · · · *Vermívora crissális*

Rare and local in young deciduous oaks and maples at Boot Spring (6,500'), in the Chisos Mountains of western Texas, and in adjacent Mexico. Very similar to Virginia's, but is larger, more robust, and heavier billed. The spring male can be told from Virginia's by the breast, which is mostly gray in Colima. Female and immature Colimas have more orange-yellow rump and undertail coverts, not greenish-yellow as in Virginia's. Song suggests Chipping Sparrow's (p. 338), but is much more musical and ends with 1 or 2 separate, slightly lower notes.

LUCY'S WARBLER · · · · · · · · · · · · · · · · *Vermívora lúciae*

Common in mesquite, generally nesting in cavities. Similar to the two species above, but can be told in all plumages by the white undertail coverts. The only warbler with a chestnut rump; immature has at least a trace of this color. Song is a series of musical chips (like Colima's) followed by 4-8 slower, slurred notes.

NORTHERN PARULA · · · · · · · · · · · · · · *Párula américána*

Common at all heights in mature deciduous and coniferous woods, especially river swamps in the Southeast. The only eastern warbler with yellow throat and blue back. Note also the yellow patch on the back, small size, narrow eye ring, and broad white wing bars. Builds its nest of Spanish moss when available. Song is a rising buzzy trill, dropping abruptly at the end; 6-7/min.

TROPICAL PARULA · · · · · · · · · · · · · · · *Párula pitiayúmi*

This southern counterpart of the Northern Parula is an uncommon summer resident in the lower Rio Grande Valley. Resembles Northern in plumage, song, and habits. Male is told by its distinct black mask and very faint rusty breastband. Wing bars of female are smaller than Northern's, and the eye ring is lacking.

WESTERN VERMIVORAS, PARULAS

im.

♂

VIRGINIA'S WARBLER
L 4¼"

♂

COLIMA WARBLER
L 4¾"

im.

LUCY'S WARBLER
L 4¼"

im.

♂

Lucy's nest in tree cavity

nest

juv.

♂

NORTHERN PARULA
L 3¾"

♀

♂

TROPICAL PARULA
L 3¾"

♀

- **GENUS DENDROICA,** a large group (pp. 278-286), includes primarily arboreal warblers with wing bars and tail spots.

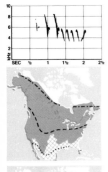

YELLOW WARBLER *Dendroíca petéchia*

Common in willow thickets, orchards, and suburban shrubbery. The only yellow-breasted warbler with yellow tail spots; no white in plumage. Note the rusty streaks on the male. Female and young are told from the similar Hooded and Wilson's (p. 292) by the yellow tail spots. Song has about 7 clear sweet notes, second half slightly faster, typically with the final note slurred upward, 4-10/min.

MAGNOLIA WARBLER *Dendroíca magnólia*

Common in moist hemlock and spruce forests. The only yellow-throated bird with a broad white tailband. The other dendroicas have spots on fewer tail feathers. Note the bright yellow rump and conspicuous wing bars. Immatures have a distinctive narrow gray breastband. Song is the quality of Yellow Warbler's, but is softer and limited to about 5 notes, 5-8/min. Sonagram below.

CAPE MAY WARBLER *Dendroíca tigrína*

Uncommon. Nests in spruce and fir. Yellow rump, chestnut cheeks, and large white wing patch of the male are diagnostic. The female has a yellow patch back of the ear and a yellow rump. In fall note the finely streaked breast, white belly and undertail coverts, olive-green rump, and small yellowish ear patch (usually visible). Song is a series of very high, thin, separate, slurred notes; 8-12/min.

Myrtle races

Audubon's races

YELLOW-RUMPED WARBLER *Dendroíca coronáta*

Abundant coastwise, especially along the Atlantic Coast during late fall and winter, when it is the commonest land bird in the thickets bordering tidewater. Nests in sprucefir forests in the North and East and in coniferous forests in the western mountains. The bright yellow rump and the yellow or dull orange side patches are diagnostic. Northern and eastern races (Myrtle Warbler) have a white throat, western breeding races (Audubon's Warbler) a yellow throat and more extensive white in the tail. Eats bayberries and poison ivy in cold weather when flying insects are not available. Song is a soft warble, 7-11/min.; call, a low-pitched *chuck*. Sonagram below.

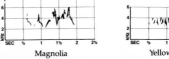

Magnolia

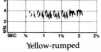

Yellow-rumped

YELLOW WARBLER
L 4"

♀ ♂

YELLOW-RUMPS

MAGNOLIA WARBLER
L 4¼"

♂

im. ♀

CAPE MAY WARBLER
L 4¼"

im. ♀

♀ ♂

YELLOW-RUMPED WARBLER
L 4¾"

♀ ♂

im. ♀

Yellow-rumped Myrtle race

Yellow-rumped Audubon's race

♀ ♂

im. ♂

- **GOLDEN-HEADED WARBLERS** Males of these four are easily recognized by the head patterns and back color. Breeding ranges are separate except in Washington. Females and especially immatures in fall pose identification problems in Southwest during migration.

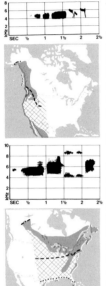

TOWNSEND'S WARBLER *Dendroíca tównsendi*
Common in coniferous forests. The dark cheek patch outlined in yellow should tell it in all plumages from all other warblers except female Blackburnian (p. 284), which is primarily eastern. The fall Black-throated Green and Golden-cheeked Warblers have only a suggestion of the dark cheek patch; their throats are white or pale yellow, not bright yellow. Song is slightly wheezy, often with 1 or 2 high clear notes at the end.

BLACK-THROATED GREEN WARBLER
Dendroíca vírens
Common, nesting high in northern conifers, oaks, and cypresses. The golden cheek is the most distinctive feature; no other eastern warbler has cheeks of this hue. Also note the black throat, white wing bars. Female is similar but duller, with the throat mottled darkly. Immatures lack the black throat but have the bold gold facial triangle and a distinctive yellowish vent area. Typical song is slow; third and fourth notes are a clear whistle; others are wheezy, 5/min. Second song has 4 similar notes, then 1 lower, 1 higher, all wheezy.

GOLDEN-CHEEKED WARBLER *Dendroíca chrysopária*
Uncommon and local; in virgin stands of mountain cedar, 25-40' high, on the Edwards Plateau, Texas. Only North American warbler with golden cheeks outlined in black (male). The similar Black-throated Green has olive-green crown and back. In fall, in the narrow zone of overlap with Black-throated Green and Townsend's, note that the males' face patterns are faintly present in all immatures. Song is similar to Black-throated Green's, but lower pitched, all notes wheezy.

HERMIT WARBLER *Dendroíca occidentális*
The unique male has an unmarked golden head and a small black bib. Female and immature have the entire face yellow, which distinguishes them from Townsend's; they are told from female and young Black-throated Green by their gray back. Common in tall conifers. Song is like Yellow Warbler's (p. 278), but is higher.

GOLDEN-HEADED
WARBLERS

winter ♂

♀

♂

im. ♀

**TOWNSEND'S
WARBLER**
L 4¼″

**BLACK-
THROATED
GREEN WARBLER**
L 4¼″

im. ♀

♀

♂

**GOLDEN-
CHEEKED
WARBLER**
L 4¼″

im. ♀

♀

♂

**HERMIT
WARBLER**
L 4¼″

im. ♀

♀

♂

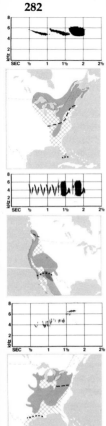

BLACK-THROATED BLUE WARBLER
Dendroíca caeruléscens

Common in evergreens (or deciduous undergrowth in the Appalachians). Adult and immature males are unique with their black cheeks and throat and blue-gray back. Wing patch of the female is frequently small, but is usually present. Note female's eye stripe, very dark face, lack of streaking, and junco-like chip. Song is slow, slurred, wheezy, and ascending.

BLACK-THROATED GRAY WARBLER
Dendroíca nigréscens

Common in dry western deciduous or coniferous scrub. The combination of dark cheek patches and very faintly streaked back distinguishes it in all plumages from the Black-and-white Warbler (p. 270) and Blackpoll (p. 284). The tiny yellow facial spot is hard to see, but diagnostic. Song is of slightly wheezy notes; pattern suggests Yellow rumped's (p. 278).

CERULEAN WARBLER   *Dendroíca cerúlea*

Locally common in deciduous woods in river bottoms and near streams. This is our only blue-backed, white-throated warbler. Note the thin black throat band of adult male. Female and young have a dull bluish-gray crown; this, together with a greenish tinge on the back and light buffy underparts, aids in identification. Song is typically of 6-8 buzzy notes, the middle ones rapid.

YELLOW-THROATED WARBLER   *Dendroíca domínica*

Common, high in pines or sycamores. Yellow throat, white belly, and black and white head are diagnostic. Black streaks border breast. Song is loud and clear, 4-6/min. **Sutton's Warbler** (*Dendroíca potómac*, L 4¼"), believed a Parula-Yellow-throated hybrid, resembles latter but has yellow back patch. Very rare; in eastern West Virginia. Song like Northern Parula's, but given twice.

GRACE'S WARBLER   *Dendroíca gráciae*

Locally common in pine-oak forests above 7,000'. The only western warbler with a yellow eye stripe and a yellow throat contrasting with the white lower breast and belly. Adults and immatures are similar. Compare head pattern with Yellow-throated, Townsend's (p. 280), and Blackburnian (p. 284). Song, a series of musical chips on the same pitch, slightly faster at the end.

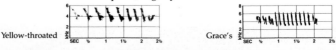

Yellow-throated   Grace's

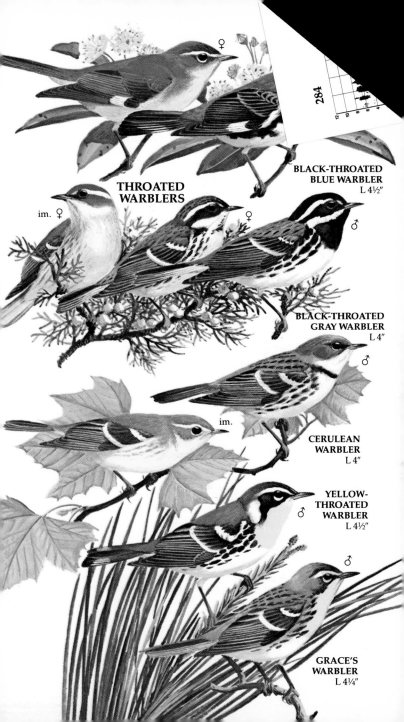

THROATED
WARBLERS

BLACK-THROATED
BLUE WARBLER
L 4½″

♀

im. ♀

♀

♂

BLACK-THROATED
GRAY WARBLER
L 4″

♂

im.

CERULEAN
WARBLER
L 4″

YELLOW-
THROATED
WARBLER
L 4½″

♂

♂

GRACE'S
WARBLER
L 4¼″

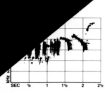

BLACKBURNIAN WARBLER   *Dendroíca fúsca*

A treetop warbler common in spruce-fir forests (in oaks in the Appalachians). The bright orange throat and head markings of the male are distinctive. Female and young have similar but paler markings; the only other eastern warblers with this face pattern are the Black-throated Green (p. 280) and Yellow-throated (p. 282). In West compare with female and immature Townsend's (p. 280). Song is very high and thin, often with an exceedingly high-pitched ending, 4-6/min.

CHESTNUT-SIDED WARBLER   *Dendroíca pensylvánica*

Common in deciduous brush. The yellowish crown and distinct chestnut sides identify both sexes in spring. The only other warbler with chestnut sides is the Bay-breasted. Immature females are without chestnut, but can be told by their bright unstreaked green back, yellow wing bars, white underparts, and narrow eye ring. Song is very similar to Yellow Warbler's (p. 278), but typically the next to last note is accented and final note slurred downward, 5-8/min. Another song lacks this ending.

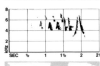

BAY-BREASTED WARBLER   *Dendroíca castánea*

Fairly common in northern coniferous forests. Chestnut sides, throat, and crown and buffy patch back of head are diagnostic of the spring male. The female is much duller. Fall birds often lack all traces of chestnut and are very similar to fall Blackpolls; the Bay-breasted is more buffy below, especially on the undertail coverts, and has black, not buffy yellow, legs and feet. Song is a very high weak one, like Cape May's (p. 278), but notes are more often run together rather than distinct.

BLACKPOLL WARBLER   *Dendroíca striáta*

Abundant in coniferous forests. Spring male has distinct black crown, white cheeks, and white throat, which distinguish it from the Black-and-white (p. 270) and Black-throated Gray (p. 282). Streaked back, buffy yellow feet and legs (legs sometimes dark), white undertail coverts, and prominent white wing bars on the olive wings are good field marks of the female and all fall birds. An abundant migrant in the Atlantic states, often seen on low branches. Song is high, thin, and distinctive; either fast or slow, but of separate notes in a monotone, often loud in the middle, soft at both ends, 4-7/min.

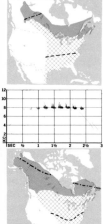

WARBLERS

im. ♀ ♀ ♂

BLACKBURNIAN WARBLER
L 4¼"

im. ♀ ♀ ♂

CHESTNUT-SIDED WARBLER
L 4¼"

♂

♀

BAY-BREASTED WARBLER
L 4¾"

im. Bay-breasted

♂

im. Blackpoll

BLACKPOLL WARBLER

♀

L 4½"

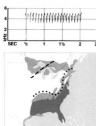

PINE WARBLER · *Dendroíca pínus*

Common in mature pines; during migration also in orchards and other deciduous trees. This large plain-backed warbler is highly variable in the amount of yellow on the underparts. Female and immature are hard to recognize when not in pines. Male resembles Yellow-throated Vireo (p. 264), but that vireo has prominent spectacles. Pine can be told in all plumages by the combination of large white wing bars, unstreaked back, white belly, faint eye stripe, and white tail spots. Immature Blackpoll and Bay-breasted (p. 284) are similar, but streaked on back. Song is a musical trill, slower than Chipping Sparrow's (p. 338), 4-7/min.

KIRTLAND'S WARBLER · *Dendroíca kírtlandii*

Rare and local, occurring only in large tracts of jack-pines, about 6-18' tall. Known to nest only in north-central Michigan. Believed to winter in Bahamas; almost never seen in migration. No other eastern tail-wagging warbler has a gray back. Note distinct black streaks on the gray back and along the yellow sides; also the black lores and white eye ring. Females are similar but duller. Compare with Magnolia Warbler (p. 278). Nests on ground. Very tame. Song is low, loud, 6-9/min.

PRAIRIE WARBLER · *Dendroíca díscolor*

Not found on prairies, but common in deciduous saplings (in heavily logged or burned areas), in young stands of pine (10'-30' tall), wood margins, and mangroves. This is the only tail-wagging warbler with an olive back. The chestnut streaks on the male's back are sometimes concealed. Note the eye and cheek markings, yellow and black in adult, gray and whitish in the immature. Streaking of underparts is restricted to the sides. Song, which may be fast (Sonagram) or slow, consists of buzzy notes ascending in a chromatic scale, 4-7/min.

PALM WARBLER · *Dendroíca palmárum*

Fairly common, nesting on the ground in bogs; in winter found at field edges. Bright yellow undertail coverts, bright olive rump, and tail-wagging habit identify this ground-feeding warbler. The rusty cap should be looked for in spring. Color of breast and belly varies geographically and seasonally from yellow to gray. Song is a rapid, slightly buzzy, junco-like trill.

WARBLERS

♀

♂

im. ♀

PINE WARBLER
L 4¾"

**KIRTLAND'S
WARBLER**
L 4¾"

♂

♂

im. ♀

♀

**PRAIRIE
WARBLER**
L 4"

im. ♀

Yellow race

Western race

♂

**PALM
WARBLER**
L 4½"

♂

OVENBIRD
Seiúrus aurocapíllus

Common in deciduous woods. Plain olive upperparts, the heavily streaked breast, and black stripes on the crown separate this common ground-walking species from all other warblers. Builds domed nest on ground. Sings from an exposed perch in the understory, a loud and clear *tea-cher* repeated about 10 times, louder and louder, 3-4/min. Flight song is given at dusk.

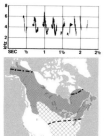

NORTHERN WATERTHRUSH
Seiúrus noveboracénsis

Common in northern bogs. Waterthrushes walk with bobbing motions like Spotted Sandpipers. Note the horizontal posture. Told from Ovenbird by head pattern. Northern is separated from Louisiana by its finely spotted throat and smaller bill. Northern's narrower eye stripe ranges from cream to yellow. Louisiana's is whiter and widens posteriorly. Feeds on ground near water. Song is loud and ringing, 3-8/min.

LOUISIANA WATERTHRUSH
Seiúrus motacílla

Uncommon; along rivers and in swamps. Sexes and immatures are similar. Note broad eye stripe, very white throat, cinnamon flank patch (see Northern). Song, about 3 slow, high, slurred notes followed by a rapid jumble in descending pitch, 4-12/min.

COMMON YELLOWTHROAT
Geóthlypis tríchas

Abundant in moist grassy or shrubby areas. Black mask distinguishes the male. Female's chin, throat, and breast are yellower than its dull white belly. Other similar species have an eye line extending both forward and backward from the eye. Seen near or on the ground. Song, *wichity* or *wichy*, is repeated several times, 4-6/min. **Gray-crowned Yellowthroat** or **Ground-chat** (*G. poliocéphala*, L 5″), a casual visitor to extreme south Texas, is intermediate in size and color between Common Yellowthroat and Yellow-breasted Chat. Underparts are all yellow, bill is chat-like. Male has gray head, black lores.

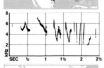

YELLOW-BREASTED CHAT
Ictéria vírens

Fairly common in deciduous thickets. Note the large size, heavy bill, white spectacles, plain olive-green upperparts, and bright yellow breast. Song is an amazing alternation of caws, whistles, grunts, and rattles, frequently given in flight and even at night; 12-28/min. Sonagram below.

Yellow-breasted Chat

OVENBIRD
L 5"

im.

**SEIURUS AND
MASKED
WARBLERS**

pale race

yellow race

**NORTHERN
WATERTHRUSH**
L 5"

im. ♂

**LOUISIANA
WATERTHRUSH**
L 5¼"

♂

**COMMON
YELLOWTHROAT**

L 4¼"

♀

**YELLOW-
BREASTED CHAT**
L 6¼"

290

- **OPORORNIS WARBLERS** are sluggish heavy warblers with rather short tails. They stay close to the ground except when singing. All are generally hard to see except the Kentucky, which often sings from an exposed understory perch.

KENTUCKY WARBLER *Oporórnis formósus*
Common; nests on the ground in moist deciduous woods with ample ground vegetation. The black mustache and yellow eye ring are diagnostic, but the black is largely concealed in immature. The male Common Yellowthroat (p. 288) has a black mask but its belly is white. Song, a loud *churree* repeated 7-10 times, is often mistaken for Carolina Wren's (p. 236); 4-5/min.

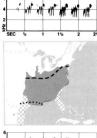

MacGILLIVRAY'S WARBLER *Oporórnis tólmiei*
Fairly common in dense thickets. The gray hood and broken eye ring are diagnostic except in fall, when it is impossible to separate this species from the immature and female Mourning Warbler in the limited area where both occur. The larger heavier Connecticut has a conspic-uous complete eye ring in all plumages, and in spring the Mourning has no eye ring at all. Song is similar to Mourn-ing's, 8-10/min.

MOURNING WARBLER *Oporórnis philadélphia*
Uncommon; in heavy underbrush. This eastern equiva-lent of MacGillivray's Warbler has the same gray hood and black throat (male), but lacks the eye ring in spring. A broken eye ring in fall confuses the female and imma-ture with the larger duller-colored Connecticut in the East and with MacGillivray's in the West. Song is short and soft, typically a 5-note warble, 5-8/min.

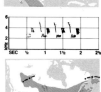

CONNECTICUT WARBLER *Oporórnis ágilis*
Uncommon and local; in moist woodlands with dense understory. The gray hood and conspicuous white eye ring are the best field marks in spring. The yellow under-tail coverts of this species are even longer than on the two above. Nashville Warbler (p. 274) has a yellow throat and short undertail coverts. In fall the immature Connecticut has a buffy eye ring and a more olive hood. The loud single chip resembles the softer double chip of Magnolia (p. 278). Song is very loud, clear, and jerky; suggests Common Yellowthroat's (p. 288) but is accented on last syllable, 5-7/min.

KENTUCKY WARBLER
L 4½"

im. ♀

♀

♂

OPORORNIS WARBLERS

MacGILLIVRAY'S WARBLER
L 4½"

im. ♀

♂

♀

MOURNING WARBLER
L 4½"

♂

♀

im. ♀

CONNECTICUT WARBLER
L 5"

im. ♀

♀

HOODED WARBLER
Wilsónia citrína

Common in moist deciduous woods with abundant undergrowth. Male is recognized by the yellow face and black hood; female by the yellow face pattern and white tail spots, which it displays as it often spreads its tail. Wilson's Warbler lacks tail spots. Nests close to ground. The loud musical chip is distinctive. Song is loud, clear, usually with an accented, slurred ending, 5-9/min.

WILSON'S WARBLER
Wilsónia pusílla

Fairly common in thickets, especially of willows. The male is recognized by the glossy black cap, the female by the plain bright yellow underparts, lack of tail spots, and yellow forehead. Song is of 15-20 musical chips, dropping slightly in pitch toward the end, 5-10/min.

CANADA WARBLER
Wilsónia canadénsis

Common in northern forest underbrush. Black necklace, usually present at least faintly, is best field mark; if this is lacking in fall, note yellow spectacles and plain gray back, wings, tail (with greenish cast). Song, rapid and varied, starting with low chip, 6-8/min. Sonagram below.

RED-FACED WARBLER
Cardellína rúbrifrons

Locally common in summer in pine and spruce forests above 6,500' in southeast Arizona and southwest New Mexico. Unmistakable; immature and female are like male. Jerks tail sideways. Song like Yellow Warbler's (p. 278), but thinner.

AMERICAN REDSTART
Setóphaga ruticílla

Common in deciduous forest understory, especially near water. An extremely active fly-catching warbler with prominent salmon or yellow patches in its long fanned tail; no other warbler has this wing and tail pattern. Song is a series of similar high notes, with or without a characteristic lower terminal note, 6-13/min.

PAINTED REDSTART
Myióborus píctus

Common at 5,000-8,000' in oak canyons. Adults and immatures are alike and unmistakable, with red breast, black head and throat, and large white patches on the wings and tail. Catches flying insects as American Redstart does. Song suggests that of Yellow-rumped Warbler (p. 278), but is more varied in pitch, 5-7/min.

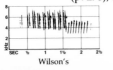
Wilson's

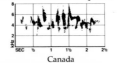
Canada

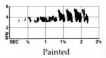
Painted

WILSONIA WARBLERS, REDSTARTS

♀

♂

HOODED WARBLER L 4½"

WILSON'S WARBLER L 4¼"

♂

RED-FACED WARBLER L 4½"

♀

♂

CANADA WARBLER L 4¾"

♂

AMERICAN REDSTART L 4½"

1st year ♂

♀

PAINTED REDSTART L 4½"

American Redstart

FALL WARBLERS Immature warblers in dull plumages generally outnumber adults in fall. Most adults are less brilliantly colored than in spring, but adult males (except the Blackpoll and Bay-breasted Warblers) retain distinctive patterns. Immatures, especially females, require careful study.

OLIVE OR YELLOW IMMATURES WITHOUT WING BARS ...

Seen near ground,
no tail spots

Connecticut
p. 290

Mourning
p. 290
♂ ♀

MacGillivray's
p. 290

Seen near ground,
no tail spots

Canada
p. 292

Kentucky
p. 290

Common Yellowthroat
p. 288
♂ ♀

Seen high or low

tail spots

tail spots

Prothonotary
p. 270

Hooded
p. 292

Wilson's
p. 292

Black-throated
Blue
p. 282

Very slender bill,
no tail spots

Virginia's
p. 276

Nashville
p. 274

Orange-crowned
p. 274

Tennessee
p. 274

Below are immature females (and a few immature males) of all warblers except: (1) those restricted to the Southwest, (2) those on pp. 270 and 288 that look much like the adults, and (3) American Redstart and the bluish-backed Northern Parula and Cerulean. Note the faint wing bars of the Palm (p. 286) and Tennessee (p. 274).

. . . WITH WING BARS AND TAIL SPOTS

Streaked backs ♂ ♀

Bay-breasted p. 284

Blackpoll p. 284

Blackburnian p. 284

Unstreaked backs

Pine p. 286

Chestnut-sided p. 284

Black-throated Gray p. 282

Townsend's p. 280

Black-throated Green p. 280

Yellow rumps

Yellow p. 278

Yellow-rumped (Myrtle) p. 278

Yellow-rumped (Audubon's) p. 278

Magnolia p. 278

Cape May p. 278

Tail waggers

Kirtland's p. 286

Prairie p. 286

Palm

(Yellow race) p. 286

(Western race) p. 286

● **OLD WORLD SPARROWS** (*Family* Passeridae) are a large family represented in North America by two introduced species. Both resemble our native sparrows, but have shorter legs and thicker beaks. They are non-migratory. They nest in bird boxes or on buildings or make bulky, woven grass nests in trees; lay 4-7 eggs.

HOUSE SPARROW *Pásser doméstics*

Abundant on farms and in cities and suburbs. The male is recognized by his black bib and bill and white cheeks. The female often is confused with other sparrows or female buntings; the unstreaked dingy breast, the bold buffy eye line, and the streaked back are the best field marks. Often seen in flocks. Song is a long series of monotonous musical chirps, 30-120/min.

EURASIAN TREE SPARROW *Pásser montánus*

Locally common around St. Louis, Missouri, and nearby Illinois. Told in all plumages by bright chestnut crown, black ear and throat patches. Calls like House Sparrow's.

● **BLACKBIRDS AND ORIOLES** (*Family* Emberizidae, *Subfamily* Icterinae) are medium to large, heavy-billed birds, mainly iridescent black or black with yellow or orange. Some walk on the ground; others are arboreal. The upper ridge of the bill parts the feathers of the forehead. Eggs, 3-6.

BOBOLINK *Dolichónyx oryzívorus*

Locally common in hayfields and in fall migration in large flocks near marshes. Spring male is only North American land bird dark below, light above. Female and fall male resemble large sparrows, but have buffy crown stripes, buffy breast, and narrow pointed tail feathers. Song is long, loud, and bubbling, 5-15/min.

EASTERN MEADOWLARK *Sturnélla mágna*

Common in fields and on fences. Adults and immatures known by black V on bright yellow breast, and white outer tail feathers. Gregarious. In flight it alternately flaps and sails. Song, a clear slurred whistle, 5-11/min.

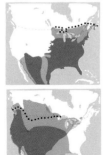

WESTERN MEADOWLARK *Sturnélla neglécta*

Common, and similar to Eastern Meadowlark in plumage, habits, and habitat, but yellow of throat extends farther onto cheek. Where both occur together in winter flocks, Western can be told by its paler back and tail. Song is loud and flute-like, 4-8/min.

Eastern Meadowlark   Western Meadowlark

Song Sparrow

House Sparrow

starling

oriole

grackle

♂
im.

HOUSE SPARROW
L 5¼″

♂

♀

im.

ad.

EURASIAN TREE SPARROW
L 5″

BOBOLINK, MEADOWLARKS

♀

summer

BOBOLINK
L 6″

♂

fall ♂

il feathers

WESTERN MEADOW-LARK
L 8½″

W.   E.

EASTERN MEADOW-LARK
L 8½″

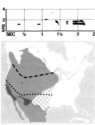

YELLOW-HEADED BLACKBIRD

Xanthocéphalus xanthocéphalus

Locally common to abundant in cattail and tule marshes. No other North American bird has yellow head and black body. White wing patch is lacking in females and first-year males. The brownish females are easily overlooked in large flocks of blackbirds. Look for the unstreaked yellowish throat. Song of low rasping notes ends in a long descending buzz, 3-5/min. Call is a distinctive low hoarse croak.

RED-WINGED BLACKBIRD

Agelaíus phoeníceus

Abundant in marshes and fields. The red-shouldered male can be confused only with the western Tricolored Blackbird. Females and immature males resemble large sparrows, but are longer-billed and more heavily streaked, often with a tinge of red on shoulder or throat. Feed, fly, and roost in huge flocks. Song, a squeaky *kong-ka-ree*, 4-9/min.

TRICOLORED BLACKBIRD

Agelaíus trícolor

Common in flocks in cattails or tules. Male is told from Red-winged by the darker red of the shoulders and the white border; female by the solid dark belly and lower back (obscuring the streaking). Song, quite different from Red-winged's, is harsh and unmusical.

RUSTY BLACKBIRD

Eúphagus carolínus

Fairly common in wooded swamps; rare in fields with other blackbirds. Size and shape of Red-winged, but has a slightly longer tail. Adult is told from cowbird (p. 300), Red-winged, and female Brewer's by its light eyes, rusty edges to undertail coverts, and lack of iridescence. Bill is more slender at base than in other blackbirds. Brown eye of young Rusty is yellowish by October. Song is high, squeaky.

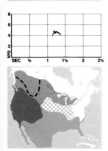

BREWER'S BLACKBIRD

Eúphagus cyanocéphalus

Common around farms, fields, and roadsides, especially in West. Spring male can be told in good light by light eye, purplish sheen on head, and greenish tint on body. Note similarity to both cowbirds (p. 300) and to Common Grackle (p. 300). Female is told from female Rusty by dark brown eye and in winter by absence of rusty wash. Starling (p. 260) is much shorter-tailed. Song is soft hoarse whistle. *Chack* note resembles Rusty's.

BLACKBIRDS

♂

♀ Yellow-headed

Red-winged

♀

im. ♂

Rusty

♀

♀

♂ fall

♀

♂

♂

YELLOW-HEADED BLACKBIRD
L 8½"

♂

RED-WINGED BLACKBIRD
L 7¼"

TRICOLORED BLACKBIRD
L 7½"

RUSTY BLACKBIRD
L 8"

BREWER'S BLACKBIRD
L 8"

GREAT-TAILED GRACKLE
Quíscalus mexicánus

Common in southwestern towns, mesquite, and arid farmlands. Male (16″), much larger than female (12″), is about length of Fish Crow (p. 226). Its very long slender V-shaped tail widens at the end. A distant flock can be recognized by the contrast in size and color between sexes. Both sexes have the bright yellow iris and the male has unbarred purple iridescence. Female is browner than female Common Grackle. Song of stick-breaking noises, whistles, and rattles is long, loud, and varied.

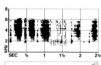

BOAT-TAILED GRACKLE
Quíscalus májor

Common on shores and in coastal marshes, and (in Florida) along inland waters. Best told from Great-tailed by locality and song, but Gulf Coast males have dull yellow or brown eyes, iridescence tends to be mainly blue, and neck more puffy when displaying. Song is a distinctive mixture of ascending squeaky calls and guttural gurgles.

COMMON GRACKLE
Quíscalus quíscula

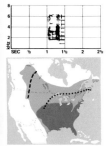

Abundant on farmland; nests in evergreens if present. Long keel-shaped tail is broader at the end. Flocks with cowbirds, Red-winged Blackbirds, and starlings. Head iridescence may appear green, blue, or violet. Inland and northern males have unbarred bronzy backs; southeastern ones have iridescent bars. Female is smaller, but has the long keel-shaped tail. Young have brown eyes until October. Song is a loud ascending squeak.

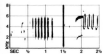

BROWN-HEADED COWBIRD
Molóthrus áter

Common on farmland, often in mixed flocks with Red-winged and Brewer's Blackbirds or Common Grackles. Note its heavier bill, slighter build, and uptilted tail when it walks. The plain mouse-gray female lays its speckled egg in the nests of other species. Young resemble female but have faint breast streaks; they beg noisily for food from their foster parents. Song is a thin whistle.

BRONZED COWBIRD
Molóthrus aéneus

Locally common on farms, where it flocks with other blackbirds. Larger and much longer-billed than Brown-headed Cowbird, it is more like Brewer's Blackbird (p. 298), but told from it by red eye and shorter bill. In poor light both sexes appear uniformly dark. Both sexes have an inflatable ruff on the hind neck. Song is similar to Brown-headed's, but notes are shorter and wheezier.

GREAT-TAILED GRACKLE L 12-16"

BOAT-TAILED GRACKLE L 16"

♂

♀

♂

Bronzed race

♀

GRACKLES AND COWBIRDS

♂

COMMON GRACKLE L 10-12"

BROWN-HEADED COWBIRD L 6½"

Purple race

♂

Brown-headed removing egg

♀

♀

♂

BRONZED COWBIRD L 7"

● **ORIOLES** are colorful arboreal icterids, quite different in habits, appearance, habitat preference, and nest structure from their ground-feeding relatives. All North American orioles have the same basic pattern. Adult males and most first-year males are strikingly marked with brilliant breasts, bellies, and rump patches that contrast with black wings, black throats or heads, and in many species black, rounded tails. Most females are similar to one another and pose a real problem in the Southwest, where several species occur. All have conspicuous wing bars and very sharply pointed beaks. Female tanagers (inset) have heavier, lighter-colored beaks and notched tails. Orioles migrate primarily by night, but loose bands of 5-10 may sometimes be seen just above the treetops in the early morning.

ORCHARD ORIOLE *Ícterus spúrius*

Locally common in unsprayed orchards, wood margins, shade trees. Adult male is our only brick-red oriole and (except in south Florida) the only oriole east of the Mississippi River with a solid black tail. First-year male has a well-defined black bib. Female is the only eastern oriole with greenish-yellow rather than orange-yellow breast. Migrates south early (July-Aug.). Song is a medley of melodious whistles and flute-like notes, quite different from short phrases of Northern (p. 304), 4-8/min. Call, a soft low *chuck*, is distinctive.

AUDUBON'S ORIOLE *Ícterus graduacáuda*

Uncommon; in dense woods and thickets. The only North American oriole with combination of black head and yellow (male) or olive-green (female and young) back. All our other adult male orioles have black or black-streaked upper back. Young of both sexes get the black head in Aug.; black wings and tail appear the second fall. In spite of its large size, it often goes undetected because of its retiring nature, preference for heavy cover, and infrequent singing. Song is a soft low whistle.

SCOTT'S ORIOLE *Ícterus parisórum*

Common in joshua trees, yuccas, pinyons, and junipers of Southwest. No other adult male oriole in its range is black and yellow. Note the redstart tail pattern (p. 293). Black throat of first-year male is poorly defined in contrast to similar Orchard's and Hooded's (p. 304). Female closely resembles these two species, but can be identified by its straight heavy bill and prominently streaked back. Scott's Oriole is 1" longer than Orchard. Song is suggestive of Western Meadowlark's (p. 296).

robin

oriole

tanager

grosbeak

YELLOW ORIOLES

♀ ♂

ORCHARD ORIOLE
L 6"

♂

1st year
♂

♂

♀

AUDUBON'S ORIOLE
L 8"

♂

tanager for comparison

1st year ♂

SCOTT'S ORIOLE
L 7"

♀

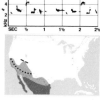

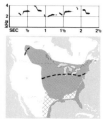

Baltimore race

Bullock's race

HOODED ORIOLE *Ícterus cucullátus*

Common in palms where present, otherwise in cotton-woods and other tall trees with shrubby undergrowth, often in residential areas. Golden crown and solid black tail separate the adult male from all but the much larger Altamira. The bill is more decurved than in our other orioles. Compare first-year male with Scott's and Orchard Orioles (p. 302). Female Hooded is greener than female and young Northern and has a more rounded tail. Song is soft and warbling, interrupted by harsh metallic trills. Call, an ascending *sweep*.

NORTHERN ORIOLE *Ícterus gálbula*

Common in tall elms and other shade trees, where its deep pendant nest is a familiar sight. The other orange North American orioles have graduated tails and (on adult males) orange crowns. Adult males of the eastern Baltimore race are told by black head and black T on the tail. The western Bullock's race has an orange eye stripe and inverted T on the tail. Female of Baltimore race typically has orange-yellow belly and streaked back; female Bullock's has gray belly and unstreaked pale gray back. Intermediate plumages occur in Great Plains. Song is of clear flute-like whistles, either singly or in varied series of 4-15. Call, a rapid chatter.

ALTAMIRA ORIOLE *Ícterus guláris*

Rare resident near Brownsville, Texas. Adult is told from the male Hooded by larger size, heavier bill, and broad yellow upper wing patch. Females and young males (after their Aug. molt) are duller, with dark grayish-brown wings and yellowish-olive back. Song is 1 or more separate whistles interrupted by harsh notes.

STREAK-BACKED ORIOLE *Ícterus pustulátus*

Casual in southern California and Arizona (all seasons). Similar to Altamira but smaller, and upper back streaked with black, heavily so in adult male. Calls like Northern but slightly higher and faster.

SPOT-BREASTED ORIOLE *Ícterus pectorális*

Introduced resident in eastern Dade County, Florida. Native to Central America. Female is duller than male, but both are recognized by the black spots on the sides of the breast and by the black tail and the large amount of white on the wing. Song is loud, varied, and more continuous than those of most orioles.

ORANGE ORIOLES

HOODED ORIOLE L 7"

♀

♂

1st year ♂

1st year ♂

♀

nest

Baltimore race

Baltimore race

NORTHERN ORIOLE L 7"

♀ ♂

Bullock's race

ALTAMIRA ORIOLE L 8½"

♂

SPOT-BREASTED ORIOLE L 7½"

STREAK-BACKED ORIOLE L 7½"

- **TANAGERS** (*Family* Emberizidae, *Subfamily* Thraupinae) are brilliant thrush-sized forest birds whose "swollen" beaks are thicker than the slender pointed beaks of orioles and longer than the conical ones of grosbeaks. Males often sing from the topmost branch. Eggs, 3-5.

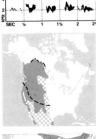

WESTERN TANAGER   *Piránga ludoviciána*

Fairly common in Douglas fir, spruce, pine, and aspen forests. Note the male's red head or face, yellow body, and black wings and tail. Head is yellow-green in fall, but wings and tail remain black. Female and young are told by their wing bars, pale tanager beak, and notched tail. Song is robin-like, but hoarse with a pause after each phrase. Call, an ascending *pit-ik* or *pit-er-ik*.

SCARLET TANAGER   *Piránga olivácea*

Common in deciduous and pine-oak woods. No other North American bird has red body with black wings and tail. First-year males occasionally are orange instead of red. In July-Aug. greenish feathers gradually replace red ones, but black wings are retained. Females are told from female Summer Tanager by yellow-green plumage and smaller darker bills. Song of 6 or 7 hoarse continuous robin-like phrases; 4-7/min. Call is low toneless *keep-back*.

SUMMER TANAGER   *Piránga rúbra*

Common in southern oak-pine woods; in the Southwest in willows and cottonwoods along streams at low elevations. Adult male remains red all winter. Young male resembles female. Female is orange-yellow in contrast to yellow-green of Scarlet, and has longer yellowish bill. Song is robin-like, not hoarse, as in other tanagers, 3-5/min. Call is a low, rapid, descending *chicky-tucky-tuck*.

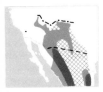

HEPATIC TANAGER   *Piránga fláva*

Uncommon; in pines and oaks of mountain canyons at 5,000-7,000'. The dark bill and dark cheek distinguish the brick-red male from the Summer Tanager. Female and young are told from Western and orioles (p. 302) by lack of white wing bars; from Summer by the dark bill, dark cheek patch, and call, *chuck*, repeated several times. Song is like Scarlet's, but slightly lower.

STRIPE-HEADED TANAGER   *Spindális zéna*

Vagrant from West Indies to s. Florida. Note head stripes and parula pattern of male. Plain-bodied female has same wing pattern. Song of paired high notes.

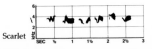

Scarlet

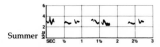

Summer

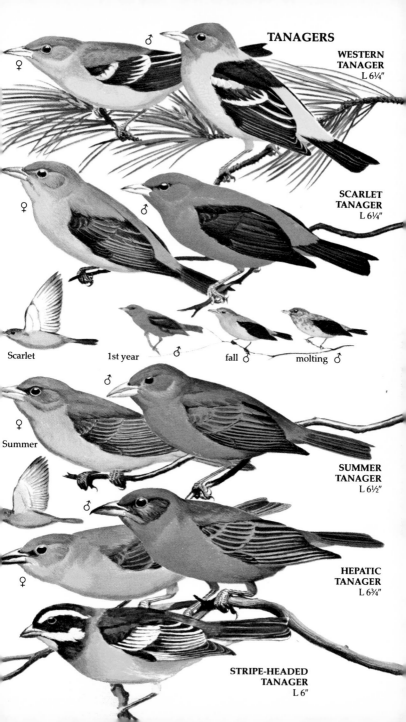

TANAGERS

WESTERN TANAGER L 6¼"

♀
♂

SCARLET TANAGER L 6¼"

♀
♂

Scarlet

1st year

fall ♂

molting ♂

♂

♀
Summer

SUMMER TANAGER L 6½"

♂

♀

HEPATIC TANAGER L 6¾"

STRIPE-HEADED TANAGER L 6"

● **GROSBEAKS, SPARROWS, AND BUNTINGS** (*Family* Emberizidae, *Subfamilies* Cardinalinae and Emberizinae) and **CARDUELINE FINCHES** (*Family* Fringillidae, *Subfamily* Carduelinae) comprise a large group of seed-eating birds. The cardueline finches include the Evening Grosbeak and all species from Hawfinch (p. 314) through the crossbills (p. 322). The best field mark is the short heavy conical beak. Only Old World sparrows, Bobolinks, and cowbirds have similar beaks. In the grosbeaks, finches, buntings, longspurs, Dickcissel, seedeater, and some of the towhees the males are much brighter than the females and young. In the other towhees and the sparrows the sexes are similar at all seasons. Crossbills and Pine Grosbeaks prefer evergreens; other grosbeaks, deciduous trees. Male buntings, goldfinches, and Blue Grosbeaks often perch on wires. Towhees scratch among fallen leaves. Finches and northern grosbeaks often call or sing during their undulating flight. Northern species are highly migratory or erratic wanderers. In winter the smaller finches prefer weed seeds. Eggs, 3-6.

feeding shelf in winter

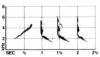

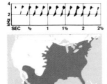

NORTHERN CARDINAL   *Cardinális cardinális*
Common in hedgerows, wood margins, suburbs, and desert washes. Our only crested bird with a conical beak except in the Southwest, where it is replaced in part by the Pyrrhuloxia. Bright red male with black throat is unmistakable. Both male and female have pointed crests and thick red (or dusky in immature) beaks. Song is a repetition of loud slurred whistles, 5-10/min.

PYRRHULOXIA   *Cardinális sinuátus*
Fairly common in Southwest. Nests to 3,500'. The male is gray above except for its red crest. The female is told by its stubby yellow beak with an abruptly curved upper mandible, and by its gray back and tail. Usually feeds on the ground and remains near cover. Song and calls often are indistinguishable from Cardinal's.

pine
woods

wire near
hedgerow

oak woods

shrubs in
Southeast

weed
patch

brush

♀   ♂

**NORTHERN
CARDINAL**
L 7¾"

im.

♀

♂

PYRRHULOXIA
L 7½"

ROSE-BREASTED GROSBEAK *Pheúcticus ludoviciánus*
Common in northern deciduous woods, suburbs and old orchards. Rose bib of adult male is diagnostic. In flight note the rose wing linings and white wing patch. Female resembles Purple Finch (p. 316), but is much larger, with proportionately heavier beak and broad white or buffy midline through the crown; orange-yellow wing linings are conspicuous in flight. No other grosbeak except female Black-headed has streaked breast or sides. Song is a long continuous robin-like whistle, 4-9/min. Call, a single loud sharp *peek*, is easily recognized.

BLACK-HEADED GROSBEAK

Pheúcticus melanocéphalus

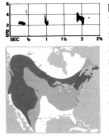

Common in open woodlands, especially deciduous. Male is easily recognized by its orange underparts, black head, and white wing patches. Female is best told from female Rose-breasted Grosbeak by extremely fine streaking on sides, unstreaked breast, and bright lemon-yellow wing linings. Many females have a yellow wash on the belly in spring. Towhees (p. 324) lack head streaks. Song and call are similar to those of the Rose-breasted, with which the Black-headed hybridizes.

EVENING GROSBEAK *Coccothraústes vespertínus*
Locally abundant in conifers. Irregular (sometimes common) in southern part of its winter range. Partial to sunflower seeds at feeding stations. Male is told by its large size, huge beak, yellow body, and large white wing patches. Female has yellow on nape and sides. Bill varies from chalky white in winter to pale green in spring. Usually flies in loose flocks; note the undulating flight and the short tail. The most frequent call (at right in Sonagram) is a loud House Sparrow-like chirp.

BLUE GROSBEAK *Guiráca caerúlea*

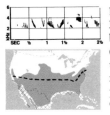

Fairly common, especially in hedgerows. Our only other blue bird with a conical beak is the little Indigo Bunting (p. 312). Both are commonly seen on roadside wires. Note the much heavier beak, broad rusty wing bars and, in the male, the deeper, almost violet blue of Blue Grosbeak. In poor light either sex could be mistaken for Brown-headed Cowbird (p. 300) if wing bars are not noticed. Seen singly or in family groups; watch for occasional tail-flicking. Song is long, rich, and warbling, more like Purple Finch's (p. 316) than Indigo Bunting's, 4-7/min.

Rose-breasted Grosbeak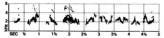

GROSBEAKS

ROSE-BREASTED GROSBEAK
L 7¼"

im. ♂

♀

♂

Rose-breasted
♀

♂

Black-headed
♀

Evening
♂

♀

BLACK-HEADED GROSBEAK
L 7¼"

♂

♀

EVENING GROSBEAK
L 7¼"

♀

♂

Indigo Bunting
for comparison

♀

♂

BLUE GROSBEAK
L 6¼"

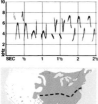

INDIGO BUNTING
Passerína cyánea

Common in hedgerows and wood margins; perches on wires during nesting season. Male resembles Blue Grosbeak (p. 310), but is much smaller, more brilliant, almost iridescent blue, and darker on the crown, with a sparrow-like beak and no wing bars. The plain brown female and immature have a tinge of blue on the tail and shoulder. The unstreaked back separates them from all sparrows. Note the very fine blurred streaking on sides. Young have faint wing bars. Seen in flocks during migration. The song, especially conspicuous at midday, is long and varied, with most phrases paired, 5-9/min.

LAZULI BUNTING
Passerína amoéna

The common western counterpart of Indigo Bunting, which it resembles in its habits. Found in scattered deciduous or scrub growth, especially near water. The pattern of the male suggests a bluebird (p. 250) except for the wing bars, but the short conical beak and sparrow-sized body are diagnostic. Female and young are told from all sparrows by the plain, unstreaked, brown back; from Indigo Buntings by the broad whitish wing bars and the rich, buffy wash on the breast. Song, faster than Indigo's, has a few scratchy notes, 4-8/min.

VARIED BUNTING
Passerína versícolor

Uncommon and local along the Mexican border in thickets, generally near water. Male looks uniformly dark in poor light, but its purple body, bluish rump, and the bright red head spot leave no doubt when it is well seen. Female and young are similar to Indigo Bunting, but are grayer above and have no trace of faint streaking on the sides. Because of variation in Indigo's plumages, the female Varied is not safely separable in the field outside its normal range. Song resembles Indigo's.

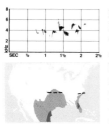

PAINTED BUNTING
Passerína círis

Locally common in thickets, but is hard to see except when the colorful male sings from an exposed perch. No other bird has red underparts and a blue head. The red breast and rump may suggest a Purple Finch (p. 316), but note the difference in color. Female Painted is a brilliant yellow-green, quite unlike the color of any other North American bird except escaped cage birds. Note its yellowish belly, sparrow-like beak, narrow eye ring, and lack of wing bars. Song is a rather soft warble.

TROPICAL BUNTINGS

juv.

♀

summer ♂

INDIGO BUNTING
L 4½″

molting ♂

♀

♂

LAZULI BUNTING
L 4½″

♀

♂

VARIED BUNTING
L 4½″

♀

♂

PAINTED BUNTING
L 4½″

314

● **STRAGGLERS TO FLORIDA OR ALASKA**

BLACK-FACED GRASSQUIT · *Tiáris bícolor*
Casual visitor to southern Florida from the Bahamas. The male of this tiny greenish-backed finch is recognized by its black head and underparts. On the nondescript female and immature, look for the uniform dull green underparts, rounded tail, and pale ear patch. Prefers brushy habitats; eats grass seeds. Song is a weak buzzing *chip-chip-zeee*.

MELODIOUS GRASSQUIT · *Tiáris canóra*
Casual visitor to southern Florida from Cuba. Bred in N. Miami in 1961. Told from Black-faced Grassquit by yellow collar. Habits and habitat are similar. Song is very different, a soft warble, *chibiri-wichii*.

BRAMBLING · *Fringílla montifringílla*
Rare migrant in the Aleutians, casual elsewhere in Alaska and Northwest. White rump, white and orange wing bars, and orange breast are diagnostic. Song is a slow nasal *tweeee*; flight call, a nasal *chek, chek*.

HAWFINCH · *Coccothraústes coccothraústes*
Rare spring vagrant in the Aleutian and Pribilof Islands. Wary, but recognized at a distance by its huge beak and very broad white wing bar. The beak, steel-blue in spring, pale horn in winter, is outlined in black. In flight, heavy body and short tail suggest Evening Grosbeak (p. 310), but white-tipped tail is not notched. Call is a metallic *tpik*.

EURASIAN BULLFINCH · *Pýrrhula pýrrhula*
Rare vagrant, all seasons, in western Alaska. Easily recognized by black cap, chinstrip, wings, and tail. Note the broad wing bar and broad white rump. Song is a low-pitched piping warble; call, a soft *peu, peu*.

COMMON ROSEFINCH · *Carpódacus erythrínus*
Rare spring vagrant, western Aleutians and St. Lawrence Island; casual elsewhere in western Alaska. Male is told from male Purple Finch (p. 316) by narrow dark eye line, dark bill, and lack of prominent streaks on back. Female closely resembles female House Finch (p. 316), but has unstreaked white lower belly and undertail coverts and a trace of the dark eye line; breast streaking may be very faint. Call is a soft repeated *screet*.

ORIENTAL GREENFINCH · *Carduélis sínica*
Rare spring vagrant in the outer Aleutians. Green cheeks, forehead, and breast, brown back and flanks, and prominent yellow on wings, tail, and abdomen are diagnostic. Also note the heavy pinkish beak. Song, a long nasal *dweee*; call, a distinctive, twittering *kyrr, kyrr*.

♀

♂

**BLACK-FACED
GRASSQUIT**
L 3¾″

♀

♂

**MELODIOUS
GRASSQUIT**
L 3¾″

♂

winter

summer

BRAMBLING
L 5″

♀

♂

♂

♂

♂

HAWFINCH
L 6″

♂

♀

**COMMON
ROSEFINCH**

♂

L 5″

L 5″

**EURASIAN
BULLFINCH**

♀

♀

♂

♂

L 4¾″

ORIENTAL GREENFINCH

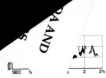

PURPLE FINCH
Carpódacus purpúreus

Common in open woodlands and suburbs, often at feeding stations. The wine-colored male is more uniformly colored than other red finches. West of the Great Plains, compare with the brighter-crowned Cassin's. The heavily streaked female and immature resemble a sparrow except for the heavier beak, deeper tail notch, and undulating flight. Female is told from female House Finch by the broad white line back of the eye and the larger beak. The sharp musical chip of the Purple, often given in flight, is distinctive. Song is a long, loud, rich warbling, 4-8/min.

CASSIN'S FINCH
Carpódacus cássinii

Fairly common in western conifers. Where its range overlaps Purple or House Finch, Cassin's is often recognized by its call note or song before plumage differences can be studied. Best mark of male Cassin's is the brilliant crown, contrasting with browner hind neck. Female has narrower streaks below than Purple and stronger head markings than House. Bill profile of Cassin's is straight and wing tips extend halfway out the tail. Song is more varied than Purple's.

HOUSE FINCH
Carpódacus mexicánus

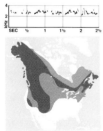

Abundant in bottomlands, canyons, suburbs, and ranches in the West; becoming common and spreading in East, especially at feeders. Nests to 7,000'. Red of male is much more restricted than in Cassin's or Purple Finch, and sides are streaked with brown. Female is plain-headed, without an eye stripe or dark mustache, and with a smaller bill than Purple or Cassin's. Tail is less notched than in other finches. Call suggests House Sparrow's (p. 296). The warbling song has a few harsh notes.

PINE GROSBEAK
Pinícola enucleátor

These tame birds are locally common in northern forests of spruce and fir. Male is like a large Purple Finch, but has white wing bars contrasting with dark wings. White-winged Crossbill (p. 322) is much smaller and has shorter tail. Female in poor light looks plain gray except for wing bars; olive on head and rump are characteristic. In flight Pine Grosbeak is told from Evening Grosbeak (p. 310) by its long tail. Feeds on seeds and fruits. Song like low Purple Finch's. Call, 3 high weak whistles suggesting Greater Yellowlegs' (p. 120).

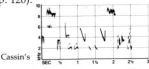

Cassin's

RED FINCHES

PURPLE FINCH
L 5½"

♂

♀

CASSIN'S FINCH
L 6"

♀

♂

HOUSE FINCH
L 5¼"

♀

♂

PINE GROSBEAK
L 7¾"

♀

♂

1st year ♂

● **ROSY FINCHES** nest in western Arctic and above timberline in western U.S. and Canada. These tame birds spend much time on the ground, gleaning seeds and insects from snowbanks. Rosy wings and rumps of males show both at rest and in flight. Pink of female is visible at close range. No other reddish finches have unmarked dark breasts.

Gray-crowned races

Black race

Brown-capped race

ROSY FINCH   *Leucostícte arctóa*

Locally common. Nests above 7,000' (in Washington) and winters in lowlands. The Gray-crowned race (*L. a. tephrocótis*) is told from the Black race by the brown back and breast and from the Brown-capped by the well-marked gray headband. Some female Gray-crowns with little gray over the eye closely resemble the Brown-capped, but have a browner body.

The dark blackish-brown breast and back of the uncommon Black race (*L. a. atráta*) distinguish this bird from other Rosy Finches.

The Brown-capped race (*L. a. austrális*) is locally common, breeding above timberline in the central and northern Rockies. It is most easily found on Mt. Evans, Colorado. Winters in nearby lowlands. All plumages lack the gray headband, as do some female Gray-crowns. Calls of Rosy Finches are low and hoarse, or high sharp chips.

● **REDPOLLS** wander south irregularly in winter, sometimes in huge flocks. They feed on weed seeds in snow-covered fields; also eat alder and birch catkins. They are sparrow-like but have a black chin spot, red crown, deeply notched tail, and undulating flight.

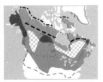

HOARY REDPOLL   *Carduélis hórnemanni*

Uncommon in Far North; rare near Canadian border. Occurs with flocks of Common Redpolls, whose geographic variations make identification of a Hoary risky except under ideal conditions. Examine flock for pale-backed birds with short, curved mandibles; then look for the unstreaked rump and undertail coverts, which are the Hoary's only reliable field marks. Calls are like Common Redpoll's.

COMMON REDPOLL   *Carduélis flámmea*

Irregularly common in snow-covered weedy fields, where it feeds much like goldfinches. The black chin and red cap are diagnostic. Common call, a hoarse *chit-chit-chit*, given frequently in flight, suggests a White-winged Crossbill's (p. 322) but is more rapid.

Common Redpoll

tanager grosbeak finch bunting sparrow longspur

Gray-headed race ♂

ROSY FINCHES, REDPOLLS

Gray-crowned race

♀

ROSY FINCH
L 6"

♂

♀

Black race

♂

♀ Brown-capped race

♂

HOARY REDPOLL
L 5"

♀

♂

juv.

COMMON REDPOLL
L 5"

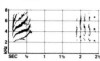

PINE SISKIN · *Carduélis pínus*

Irregularly common in large flocks, especially in conifers. Amount of yellow at the base of the tail and in the wings varies greatly. Note the heavily streaked underparts, deeply notched tail, and slender sharp bill. Siskins, smaller and slimmer than female Purple Finches (p. 316), are more finely streaked below, and lack the dark patch at the side of the throat. In form and actions they resemble goldfinches, with which they often flock. Tame. Wheezy voice is diagnostic.

AMERICAN GOLDFINCH · *Carduélis trístis*

Common in flocks in weedy fields, bushes, and road-sides, and in seed-bearing trees. Fond of thistles, sun-flowers, and dandelions. Our only other bright-yellow bird with black cap and wings is the much larger Evening Grosbeak (p. 310). Female and young can be told by the unstreaked back and breast, stubby finch bill, wing bars, notched tail, whitish rump, and roller-coaster flight. Male in winter and immature resemble female. Song is long, high, and sweet. Call, *per-chik-o-ree*, is diagnostic of this species. Both are given in flight.

LESSER GOLDFINCH · *Carduélis psáltria*

Common in flocks in same or drier habitats than Ameri-can Goldfinch. Breeds up to 7,500′. Both a black-backed and a green-backed race occur. Males of both races are easily told from American by the dark rump and, in flight, by the large white wing patch. Females are told by lack of contrast between back and rump. Song is more scratchy than American's; call, a descending whistle.

LAWRENCE'S GOLDFINCH · *Carduélis láwrencei*

Locally common, but erratic. They flock at times with other goldfinches but prefer drier habitats. The flesh-col-ored bill of the male contrasts with his black face and throat at all seasons. Head and back of female are grayer than in other goldfinches, wing bars are yellower, and the song is lower pitched, with distinctive harsh notes. Flight call is high and bell-like.

EUROPEAN GOLDFINCH · *Carduélis carduélis*

Introduced and rare in New York and New Jersey; not well established anywhere in North America. Face pattern of adult is distinctive, as is wing pattern of immature. Song suggests American's.

SISKINS AND GOLDFINCHES

♂
♂

PINE SISKIN
L 4¼″

♂
summer

flight pattern

♀

im.

♀

winter ♂

AMERICAN GOLDFINCH
L 4¼″

green-backed race

im.

LESSER GOLDFINCH
L 3¾″

♀

black-backed race

♂

winter

♂

♀

summer ♂

LAWRENCE'S GOLDFINCH
L 4¼″

juv.

juv.

ad.

EUROPEAN GOLDFINCH
L 4½″

● **CROSSBILLS** are irregular vagrants partial to conifers, in which they may nest at any season. They are especially fond of salt and are very tame. Only when they are close can one notice the crossed bill. Like other northern finches, they call frequently in flight.

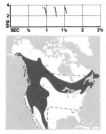

RED CROSSBILL
Lóxia curviróstra

Unpredictable but common at times in pine woods. The brick-red plumage of the adult male is distinctive; immature is more orange-red. All plumages lack wing bars on their blackish wings. The female, heavier billed and distinctly larger than a goldfinch, has a yellow rump like some subadult Purple Finches' but lacks the heavily streaked breast. They cling to pine cones, from which they noisily extract seeds with their peculiar bills. Call, *kip-kip-kip*, is frequently given in flight.

WHITE-WINGED CROSSBILL
Lóxia leucóptera

Less common and more irregular than Red Crossbill. Prefers spruces, pines, and larches. Distinctive pinkish color and broad white wing bars identify the adult male. Similar wing bars are best mark of female and young male. Note also bright rump and fine streaking on flanks. In flight, has 3- or 4-note call suggesting redpolls' (p. 318). Song is long and canary-like, 5-10/min.

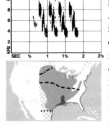

DICKCISSEL
Spíza americána

Abundant in grainfields and weed patches, but variable from year to year. The black-bibbed male sings from a conspicuous perch; the sparrow-like female is seldom noticed. The chestnut wing patch, narrow streak at side of throat, and trace of yellow separate winter Dickcissel from House Sparrow (p. 296). Migrates in enormous flocks. Stray birds reach the Atlantic Coast or winter with sparrows at feeders. Song is 1 or 2 *dick*s followed by a guttural trill; in flight a low *br-r-r-r-rt*.

WHITE-COLLARED SEEDEATER
Sporóphila torqueóla

Resident, rare and local in flocks in weed patches in Rio Grande Delta. This tiny Mexican finch is much smaller than the sparrows with which it flocks. The stubby bill is the best field mark. Seedeaters are slimmer bodied, longer tailed, and much buffier than goldfinches, and lack the notched tail. Most birds seen are females or immatures. The loud song has 4 or 5 upward slurred notes followed by fewer notes on a lower pitch.

tanager

grosbeak

crossbill

bunting

sparrow longspur

im. ♂

♀

♂

RED CROSSBILL
L 5½″

im.
♂

♀

WHITE-WINGED CROSSBILL
L 5¾″

CROSSBILLS

♀

im. ♂

♂

DICKCISSEL
L 5¾″

House Sparrow
for comparison

♀

♀

♂

♂

subadult

WHITE-COLLARED SEEDEATER
L 3¾″

- **TOWHEES**, large ground-feeding sparrows with long rounded tails, are often seen scratching for insects and seeds under shrubbery or brush. They hop and kick with both feet together; usually fly close to the ground, pumping their tail. Young are finely streaked below.

GREEN-TAILED TOWHEE   *Pípilo chlorúrus*
Fairly common in underbrush or chaparral. They nest up to 9,000'; are found to 11,000' in fall. The clear white chin and greenish tinge of the upperparts separate it from all other towhees. Call is a soft mew.

RUFOUS-SIDED TOWHEE   *Pípilo erythrophthálmus*
Common in brush, heavy undergrowth, wood margins, and hedgerows. Note the rufous sides, white belly, and long rounded tail with its large white spots. In the female, black is replaced by brown. In the West, the back is spotted with white. Juvenile loses its streaking in early fall. Adult's iris is red in most of North America but may be white or orange in the Southeast; iris of immature is brown. Call is a slurred *chewink* (nasal *wheee*, West). Song, *drink-your-tea*, 7-12/min., the last note trilled (descending dry trill, West).

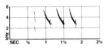

BROWN TOWHEE   *Pípilo fúscus*
Common near dense shrubbery in residential areas, and in chaparral and stream borders with shrubby growth. Male and female are alike, colored much like thrashers (p. 240) but distinguished by the conical beak and smaller size. Juvenile is streaked and sparrow-like. Where range overlaps Green-tailed's, note the plain brown back and tail. Female Blue Grosbeak and cowbirds have shorter notched tails. Call is a musical finch-like *peenk*. Song of loud chips and then often a trill.

ABERT'S TOWHEE   *Pípilo áberti*
A common towhee in brushlands of the arid Southwest. More secretive than the Brown Towhee, from which it is told by its black face and buff underparts. Song is similar to Brown's, with the final trill more guttural.

OLIVE SPARROW   *Arremónops rufivirgátus*
Locally common in southern Texas in brushy areas. The unstreaked body, olive upperparts, and rounded tail make this bird look more like a Green-tailed Towhee than a sparrow. Note median stripe through crown and lack of a white chin patch. Song is a series of musical chips.

TOWHEES

juv.

GREEN-TAILED TOWHEE L 6¼″

♂ western race

eastern race

RUFOUS-SIDED TOWHEE L 7¼″

♂

eastern race

♀

White-eyed race

♂

juv. ♀

Rocky Mt. race

BROWN TOWHEE L 7¼″

juv.

Brown Towhee Pacific race

ABERT'S TOWHEE L 7¾″

OLIVE SPARROW L 5¾″

● **SPARROWS** are small brown-bodied birds with streaked backs and short conical beaks. Their food, mostly seeds except during the nesting season, is obtained on or near the ground. When not nesting, most are seen in flocks. Each species has its own habitat preferences; these may be diagnostic. Head and breast patterns are most helpful for identification; note also the length and shape of the tail. In most species females are very similar to males. Heads of adult males of most species are shown on this spread. The juncos and longspurs are represented by one head each; the striking Lark Bunting, the Snow Bunting, the towhees, and the Olive Sparrow are omitted. Immatures of some species are much duller, especially those species with black or rufous on the head. Songs and chips of sparrows are often more easily distinguished than are their plumages. See pp. 328-345 for further details.

STREAKED BREASTS

Vesper
p. 332
(white outer tail)

Song
p. 342

Lincoln's
p. 342

Savannah
p. 328

Le Conte's
p. 330

Sharp-tailed
p. 330

Henslow's
p. 328
(rufous wing)

Baird's
p. 328

Purple Finch
for comparison
p. 316

Seaside
p. 330

Fox
p. 342
(rufous rump)

Sage
p. 332

UNSTREAKED BREASTS

Dark-eyed Junco
p. 334
(white outer tail)

Black-chinned
p. 338

Black-throated
p. 332
(white outer tail)

Lapland Longspur
p. 344

White-crowned
p. 340

White-throated
p. 340

Golden-crowned
p. 340

Harris'
p. 340

American Tree
p. 338

Field
p. 338

Chipping
p. 338
(gray rump)

Swamp
p. 342

Brewer's
p. 338

Clay-colored
p. 338
(brown rump)

Grasshopper
p. 328

Rufous-crowned
p. 336

Lark
p. 332
(white tail fringe)

Rufous-winged
p. 336

Cassin's
p. 336

Bachman's
p. 336

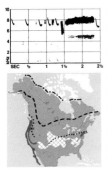

SAVANNAH SPARROW   *Passérculus sandwichénsis*
Common in large fields with short or sparse grass or weeds. The heavily streaked breast without a central spot and the short notched tail are characteristic of most populations, but some western races have a central breast spot. The yellow lores, when present, are also a good field mark. Extremes of geographic variation are illustrated. When flushed, it flies for a short distance and usually returns to the ground. The rare Ipswich race, formerly considered a separate species, is of special interest because of its limited geographical range. It nests only on Sable Island, Nova Scotia; winters in coastal dunes from Massachusetts to Georgia. Larger and paler than other eastern races of Savannah, Ipswich race walks or runs, rarely hops; other races typically run or hop. Savannah's song consists of 2-6 faint musical chips followed by 1 or 2 thin trills, 4-8/min.

GRASSHOPPER SPARROW   *Ammódramus savannárum*
Common in hayfields and weedy fallow fields. The unstreaked buffy breast is characteristic of adult. At close range note the yellow at bend of the wing, the yellow lores, and the unique back color. The tail is very short and narrow. Sings from a tall weed or utility line. When flushed, the Grasshopper flies a short distance, then descends suddenly to the ground and disappears. The relatively large flat-topped head is thrown far back when singing. The song is grasshopper-like: 2 or 3 *ticks*, then an insect-like trill, 4-8/min.

BAIRD'S SPARROW   *Ammódramus baírdii*
Uncommon on the high plains. The broad orange-brown median stripe through the crown separates this bird from the solid-capped Sharp-tail (p. 330), the white-striped Le Conte's (p. 330), and the faintly striped Savannah. Note also the finely streaked breastband. Song is 3 short ticks followed by a musical trill, 5-9/min.

HENSLOW'S SPARROW   *Ammódramus hénslowii*
Rare and local in broomsedge fields east of the Appalachians; more common in the Mississippi valley. No other sparrow has an olive head that contrasts strongly with a brown back. This large-headed short-tailed bird sings its insignificant song from such a low perch that often it is not visible. Song is ventriloqual, an unmusical *ssllick*.

SHORT-TAILED GRASS SPARROWS

a pale race

SAVANNAH SPARROW
L 4¾″

a dark race

Ipswich race
L 5½″

Ipswich

GRASSHOPPER SPARROW
L 4½″

juv.

BAIRD'S SPARROW
L 4½″

juv.

HENSLOW'S SPARROW
L 4½″

juv.

330

LE CONTE'S SPARROW   *Ammódramus lecónteii*

Common in tall marsh grass in summer, rare in dry fields in winter. Broad purplish collar, bright orange breast and eye stripe, and white stripe through crown distinguish this sparrow from all others. The gray cheek and sharp contrast between the orange breast and white belly help rule out a young molting Grasshopper Sparrow (p. 328). Henslow's (p. 328) has an olive head, Sharp-tailed an unstreaked crown. Most easily recognized by its insect-like song, *tickity-tshshshsh-tick*, 6-9/min.

SHARP-TAILED SPARROW   *Ammódramus caudacútus*

Common in short grass salt marshes and locally common inland in fresh marshes. The broad orange triangle on the face is diagnostic. Note the unstreaked crown. Sharp-tails spend most of their time on the wet ground. If flushed they fly weakly for a short distance, then drop back into the marsh. In flight, they appear smaller and browner than the Seaside Sparrows with which they often associate. Song is a high faint trill preceded by almost inaudible chips, 6-10/min.

SEASIDE SPARROW   *Ammódramus marítimus*

Common in short grass tidal marshes with scattered shrubs. Seaside Sparrow is recognized by its dark gray head and body, very long bill, and the yellow line before the eye. Its tail is short and narrow for the size of the bird. Like the Sharp-tailed, when flushed it flies short distances and drops back into the marsh. It eats fewer seeds and more insects and crustaceans than other sparrows. The endangered Dusky race, which was formerly resident locally in salt marshes of eastern Orange and northern Brevard Counties (Merritt Island area), Florida, may now be extinct in the wild. This blackest race of the Seasides was the only one breeding in its range. If found, it can be recognized by the heavy black streakings on its breast and back. The endangered Cape Sable race is restricted to southern Florida (Ochopee marshes to Shark River basin

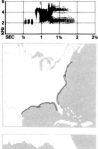

to vicinity of Everglades National Park headquarters). Destruction of marshes by hurricanes threatens its existence. It is the only race of the Seaside Sparrow in southern Florida. Note the greenish tinge on the back and the more distinct streaking below, contrasting with the white background. Seaside's call is a low *chuck*; song is like a distant Red-winged Blackbird's (p. 298).

Dusky race

Cape Sable race

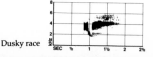

Dusky race

MARSH SPARROWS

LE CONTE'S SPARROW L 4¼"

juv.

inland race

northeastern race

eastern race

SHARP-TAILED SPARROW L 5"

Sharp-tailed Sparrow im.

SEASIDE SPARROW L 5½"

juv.

Dusky race

Cape Sable race

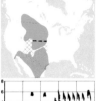

LARK BUNTING   *Calamospíza melanócorys*
Common on or near the ground in short grass prairie;
irregular near margins of its range. Spring and summer
male can be confused only with Bobolink (p. 296). Heads
of female and winter male resemble female Purple Finch's
(p. 316). Note broad white wing bars, rounded tail, white
tips to tail feathers, crisp streaking of underparts. Gregarious. Song, often given in flight, is long and varied, with
trills and repeated single notes, 2-6/min.

VESPER SPARROW   *Pooécetes gramíneus*
Fairly common in meadows, pastures, hay and grain
fields. Told from all other brown sparrows by white outer
feathers of notched tail. Note narrow eye ring and chestnut shoulder. Lark Sparrow has white around tip of its
rounded tail. Pipits have white outer tail feathers but
warbler-like bills, and are more often seen in dense flocks.
Song suggests Song Sparrow's (p. 342), but is recognized
by 2 longer, slurred, introductory notes.

LARK SPARROW   *Chondéstes grámmacus*
Fairly common in West (local east of Mississippi River) in
dry fields near brush or trees. Told by the rounded white-
tipped tail, black breast spot, and chestnut head markings. Immature lacks breast spot but has white tail margin
and dull face pattern. Song is melodious notes and trills,
interrupted by unmusical buzzes, 4-10/min.

BLACK-THROATED SPARROW   *Amphispíza bilineáta*
Common desert bird of cactus, sage, and mesquite. Gray
with white underparts; other black-bibbed sparrows have
streaked backs. Immature is told by the finely streaked
breast, face pattern, dark rounded tail with white on outer
feather, lack of wing bars. Song is high, sweet, and trilled,
much like Bewick's Wren's (p. 236).

SAGE SPARROW   *Amphispíza bélli*
Fairly common in sagebrush and chaparral. This large
dark-headed sparrow is recognized by its single breast
spot and its habit of flicking its dark tail. Look for the
white spot below the ear. The narrow white margin on the
outer tail feather may be lacking. The streak-breasted
immature suggests a Lark Sparrow but has a dark head, a
plain crown, and much less white on its tail. Song of 4-7
high thin notes, third note highest.

Lark Sparrow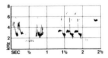

WHITE-TAILED SPARROWS

♀

LARK BUNTING
L 6"

♂

VESPER SPARROW
L 5½"

Lark
Sparrow
juv.

LARK SPARROW
L 5¾"

juv.

BLACK-THROATED SPARROW
L 4½"

♂

♂

juv.

SAGE SPARROW
L 5"

- **JUNCOS** are common to abundant, rather tame sparrows with light pink bills, gray or black hoods, white outer tail feathers, and, in the West, rusty backs or pinkish sides. Often in large flocks, they hop on the ground and pick up small seeds but seldom scratch with their feet. Streaked juveniles on breeding ground resemble sparrows except for tail and voice.

White-winged race

Slate-colored races

Oregon races

Gray-headed races

DARK-EYED JUNCO
Júnco hyemális

The White-winged, Slate-colored, Oregon and Gray-headed Juncos are now considered conspecific, but several populations that are recognizable in the field are discussed separately. The large White-winged race is common in its restricted range in yellow pine forests in the Black Hills; no record east of Great Plains. This race is told by the two white wing bars, broad pale margins on its secondaries, and excessive white on the tail (at least 3 feathers on each side are completely white).

The typical Slate-colored bird is abundant in brushy clearings and borders of coniferous forests in summer, and in weedy fields, brush, and wood margins in winter. Head, back, and breast are uniformly slate-gray. Immatures, especially in or from far Northwest, have varying amounts of pink on the sides and may be confused with the Oregon races.

The Oregon races are abundant in western conifers, and in winter in suburbs, farmyards, and fields. Plumage and size vary geographically. Some races have a black breast and head, contrasting sharply with the rusty back. Others have a pale gray head and breast with no head-back contrast, and a broad pink stripe down the sides.

The Gray-headed races are common in coniferous forests in the Rockies. They are told from other races by their gray head and pale gray breast and sides, contrasting with rusty upper back. Lores are dark gray or black. Told from adult Yellow-eyed Junco by its dark eye. A Rocky Mountain race has a light bill and a Southwest race a dark upper mandible.

Song is a simple slow trill, more musical than Chipping Sparrow's (p. 338), 5-l2/min. Sonagram below.

YELLOW-EYED JUNCO
Júnco phaeonótus

Locally common in coniferous and pine-oak forests above 5,000'. Bright yellow eye of adult is the best field mark. The entire underparts are whitish; the lores are black. Generally walks instead of hopping. Tame. Song is varied for a junco; call is like Chipping Sparrow's (p. 338).

Dark-eyed Junco

tanager

grosbeak

crossbill

bunting   sparrow

longspur

JUNCOS

DARK-EYED JUNCO
White-winged
race
L 6″

Slate-colored
race

im.

♀

♂

♂

Slate-colored
race
L 5¼″

juv.

Pink-sided
Oregon race

♂

Oregon race
L 5¼″

Southwest race

Gray-headed races
L 5½″

Rocky Mt.
race

**YELLOW-EYED
JUNCO**
L 5½″

FIVE-STRIPED SPARROW
Amphispíza quinquestriáta

Local in southern Arizona in thick bushes on steep hillsides, 3500-4000', especially in canyons that flow into the Rio Magdalena in Mexico. Note white and black throat stripes, black spot on gray breast.

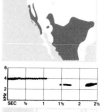

RUFOUS-WINGED SPARROW
Aimóphila carpális

Rare and local in tall grass amid thorny desert shrubs. Looks like a large dusky Field Sparrow with a gray stripe through the crown. Unlike Field and Chipping (p. 338), it has a black whisker mark and a rounded tail. Small rusty shoulder patch can be seen (except in juvenile) at close range. Song, towhee-like, about 2 notes, and a trill.

RUFOUS-CROWNED SPARROW
Aimóphila rúficeps

Locally common on steep slopes with scattered bushes. Told by its unstreaked deep rufous crown, black whisker mark, lack of wing bars, obscure back streakings, dusky breast, and rounded tail. Other rusty-capped sparrows are on pp. 338-342. Song is a jumble of short rapid notes, like House Wren.

CASSIN'S SPARROW
Aimóphila cássinii

Fairly common on dry plains with short grass and scattered low brush. Recognized by its plain breast, finely streaked crown, gray-brown back, and dark gray tail. Compare with Grasshopper (p. 328), Brewer's (p. 338), and Botteri's Sparrows. Cassin's often sings in flight, a high musical trill preceded and followed by 1 or 2 short notes.

BOTTERI'S SPARROW
Aimóphila bótterii

Rare and local summer resident in the tall grass of brushy coastal prairies of Texas and in portions of southeast Arizona deserts. Similar to Cassin's, it occurs with it in Arizona. Note at close range the rusty tinge of the wings and tail, the pale buffy breast and sides, and the heavier black streaking on the back. The song, always given from a perch, is 2 to 4 notes followed by a trill.

BACHMAN'S SPARROW
Aimóphila aestivális

Uncommon and local; in abandoned fields with scattered shrubs, pines, or oaks, usually in dense ground cover. Told from Field Sparrow (p. 338), which often occurs with it, by the yellow bend of the wing, dark upper mandible, purplish back, darker crown, and dark tail. Song is beautiful and varied, 4-10/min.

Bachman's Sparrow

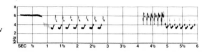

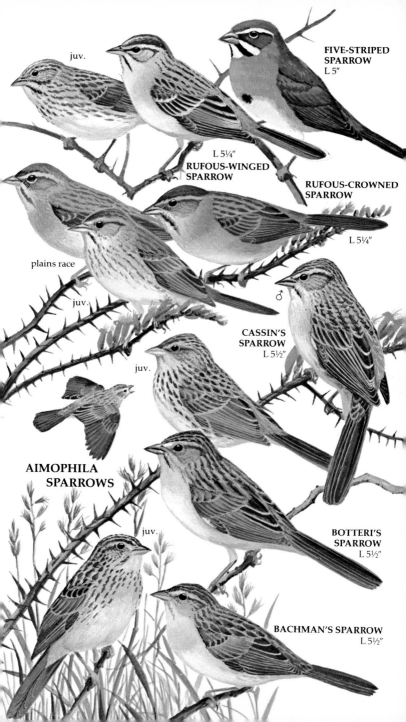

juv.

**FIVE-STRIPED
SPARROW**
L 5"

L 5¼"
**RUFOUS-WINGED
SPARROW**

**RUFOUS-CROWNED
SPARROW**

L 5¼"

plains race

juv.

♂

**CASSIN'S
SPARROW**
L 5½"

juv.

**AIMOPHILA
SPARROWS**

juv.

**BOTTERI'S
SPARROW**
L 5½"

juv.

BACHMAN'S SPARROW
L 5½"

AMERICAN TREE SPARROW   *Spizélla arbórea*

Common in willow thickets, weedy fields, and hedgerows. This brightest and largest of the rusty-capped sparrows is seen in large flocks in winter. It is the only one with a large central breast spot. Note also 2-tone bill and dark legs. Immature is like adult. Song has pattern of Fox Sparrow's (p. 342), but is higher, thinner, and softer. A musical 2-note twitter is diagnostic in winter.

CHIPPING SPARROW   *Spizélla passerína*

Common on lawns or sparse grass under scattered trees. In winter it flocks with other sparrows in hedgerows and weedy fields. Black bill and very white eye stripe separate spring adults from other rusty-capped sparrows. Immatures and winter adults, with lighter bills and dull streaked crowns, are told by contrast between gray rump and brown back. Song is of rapid chips, 5-9/min.

CLAY-COLORED SPARROW   *Spizélla pállida*

Locally common in open brushland. Brown cheek patch and light median streak through crown are distinctive. If rump color is not seen it may be mistaken in fall for Chipping Sparrow. Song is a distinctive series of 2-5 identical, slow, low-pitched buzzes, 5-10/min.

BREWER'S SPARROW   *Spizélla bréweri*

Common; in sage and desert scrub. The pale brown crown, finely streaked with black, lacks a median line. Note the small size, slim build, eye ring, and clear breast. Song is a varied series of rapid trills (Sonagram below).

FIELD SPARROW   *Spizélla pusílla*

Common; in abandoned fields with tall grass or scattered saplings. Told by its pink bill and legs, unstreaked crown, and lack of dark eye line. Song is a series of slurred whistles in increasing tempo, 4-6/min.

BLACK-CHINNED SPARROW   *Spizélla atroguláris*

Uncommon; in chaparral and sage. Pink bill contrasting with gray head and breast make it appear junco-like, but Black-chinned is easily told by the streaked back and absence of white on the tail. Song suggests Field Sparrow's, but is higher pitched and more rapid.

Brewer's Sparrow

SPIZELLA SPARROWS

AMERICAN TREE SPARROW
L 5¼"

CHIPPING SPARROW
L 4¾"

im.

CLAY-COLORED SPARROW
L 4½"

im.

BREWER'S SPARROW
L 4½"

juv.

FIELD SPARROW
L 5"

im.

♂

BLACK-CHINNED SPARROW
L 5¼"

HARRIS' SPARROW *Zonotríchia quérula*

Fairly common. Breeds at timberline; in winter it prefers hedgerows, wood margins, and brush. Our largest sparrow; recognized by the combination of the pink bill, black or blotched bib, black crown, and streaked sides. No other pink-billed sparrow has streaked sides. The sexes are alike. Song consists of 2-4 identical high whistles; repeated on a different pitch.

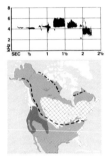

WHITE-CROWNED SPARROW *Zonotríchia leucóphrys*

Abundant in West, in thickets, hedgerows, or wood margins adjacent to fields or open areas. Recognized by its pink or yellowish bill, erect posture, gray throat and breast, and prominently streaked crown. Adult and immature are told from White-throated Sparrow by posture, bill color, and lores. Geographic races show minor differences in head pattern and bill color. Gambel's race breeds in Alaska and northwestern Canada. The White-crowned shuns the woodland thickets so favored by the White-throated Sparrow. Song is of clear whistles and buzzy trills; it varies geographically.

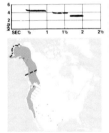

GOLDEN-CROWNED SPARROW *Zonotríchia atricapílla*

Fairly common, breeding at high elevations near timberline and at openings in stunted spruce forests. Often seen in winter with the White-crowned Sparrow, which it most closely resembles. Golden-crowned is best told by the crown pattern and dusky bill. Immature and fall adult can be mistaken for immature White-throated except for the plain throat, larger size, and lack of a buffy median crown stripe. Song consists of 3-5 clear whistles, descending scale *Oh dear me*.

WHITE-THROATED SPARROW *Zonotríchia albicóllis*

Abundant in dense undergrowth and brush; seldom found far from dense cover. The well-defined white throat is the best field mark. The yellow lores are diagnostic, but are inconspicuous in immatures and some fall adults. The dark bill and short-necked posture separate it from the White-crowned in all plumages. The similar immature Swamp Sparrow has a white throat and dingy breast, but is smaller and has rufous wings and a rounded tail. White-throated usually feeds on the ground. Song is a clear high whistle, *Old Sam Peabody Peabody Peabody*.

White-throated Sparrow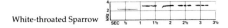

CROWNED SPARROWS

im.

♂

**HARRIS'
SPARROW**
L 7"

im.

**WHITE-CROWNED
SPARROW**
L 5¾"

Gambel's
race

im.

2nd
winter

fall ♂

**GOLDEN-CROWNED
SPARROW**
L 6¼"

♀

juv.

**WHITE-THROATED
SPARROW**
L 5¾"

spring ♂

FOX SPARROW *Passerélla ilíaca*

Common in dense coniferous thickets and deciduous brush. It is recognized by its heavily streaked underparts and in the East (where it is the largest sparrow) by its bright orange-brown rump and tail. Like the Song Sparrow, it has a central breast spot. It feeds by scratching, towhee-fashion, with both feet. Western Fox Sparrows are a deep chocolate or dark gray-brown, almost devoid of head and back markings. They may be confused with Hermit Thrush (p. 248) and with large northwestern races of the Song Sparrow, except for the yellow lower mandible and slightly notched tail. Song is loud and clear, starting with characteristic slurred whistles.

LINCOLN'S SPARROW *Melospíza líncolnii*

Fairly common in thickets along bogs and streams; uncommon in East. In migration and winter it prefers brush piles and wood margins. Note the fine neat streakings on the buffy breastband and the semblance of a tiny eye ring. Its gray face and longer rounded tail separate Lincoln's from grass and marsh sparrows. Secretive. Seldom sings in winter or migration. Note junco-like chip. Song suggests House Wren's (p. 236), 3-6/min.

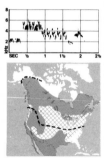

SWAMP SPARROW *Melospíza georgiána*

Common in bogs and marshes but not heavily wooded swamps; in migration it is also seen in weedy fields. Adult is told by its red cap, gray eye stripe and gray face, white throat, and solid dark bill. Immature is grayer breasted than Lincoln's and lacks the clear-cut breast streakings. Also note the rusty wings in all plumages. Feeds on or near the ground. Song is a slow trill of similar slurred liquid notes, suggestive of a Chipping Sparrow's (p. 338) but much more musical and slower, 4-6/min.

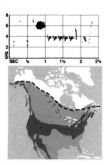

SONG SPARROW *Melospíza melódia*

Abundant in East, locally in West in moist areas with bushes, hedgerows, and wood margins. Told by the heavily streaked breast with a central spot, by lack of yellow or buffy color, and by long slightly rounded tail which it "pumps" in flight. Geographic races vary from rusty to gray and light to dark. Short-tailed juvenile, which lacks central breast spot, can be mistaken for Savannah (p. 328). Song is lively and varied, of many short notes and a trill near the end, 4-6/min.

FOX AND ROUND-TAILED SPARROWS

eastern race

FOX SPARROW
L 6¼″

western race

LINCOLN'S SPARROW
L 4¾″

im.

SWAMP SPARROW
L 5″

brown race

gray race

juv.

SONG SPARROW
L 5½″

344

● **LONGSPURS AND SNOW BUNTINGS** are gregarious sparrow-like ground birds of open fields, tundra, and dunes. Adult male plumage seldom is seen outside the nesting ground. Watch for distinctive patterns on the rather short tails.

McCOWN'S LONGSPUR   *Calcárius mccównii*
Less common than Chestnut-collared on arid plains. The tail is mostly white, with only narrow median and terminal bands. The only longspur with rusty bend of wing (often concealed). Note the gray hind neck. Flight song is a long twittering warble; call, a dry rattle.

CHESTNUT-COLLARED LONGSPUR
Calcárius ornátus
Common in fallow plains and short grass prairies. Told in all plumages by the dark triangle on the white tail and by lack of a well-defined ear patch. Song is like a faint Western Meadowlark's (p. 296), 3-8/min. Call is finch-like, 2 syllables; does not give the typical longspur rattle.

LAPLAND LONGSPUR   *Calcárius lappónicus*
Abundant in Arctic and locally in interior; uncommon in East. Flocks with Horned Larks (p. 218), Snow Buntings, or other longspurs. Winter male is told by chestnut hind neck and gray throat blotch. Tail with white outer feathers is like pipit's (p. 256) or Vesper Sparrow's (p. 332). Flight calls, a dry rattle and a short, clear whistled *pew*.

SMITH'S LONGSPUR   *Calcárius píctus*
Uncommon and local; winters on short grass plains and airports. Told from other longspurs by the buffy body and flesh-colored legs and male's broad white wing bar (shared by Chestnut-collared). Rapid clicking in flight.

SNOW BUNTING   *Plectróphenax nivális*
Common on tundra; local on beaches, dunes, and in short grass; often seen with Horned Larks (p. 218) or longspurs. Most readily identified in flight by large white wing patches; no other flocking songbird in its range has these. Flight call is a short descending whistle.

McKAY'S BUNTING   *Plectróphenax hyperbóreus*
Common breeder on Bering Sea islands. Winters in coastal western Alaska. Female is told by pure white head and male by white head and back. Song is like American Goldfinch's (p. 320).

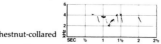

Chestnut-collared

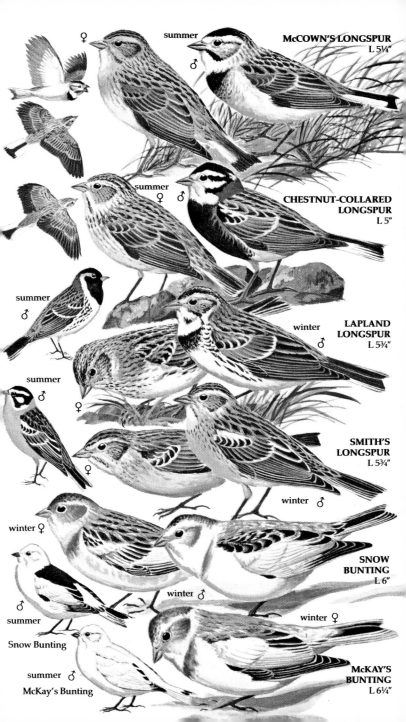

McCOWN'S LONGSPUR
L 5¼"

summer ♀

summer ♂

CHESTNUT-COLLARED LONGSPUR
L 5"

summer ♀ ♂

summer ♂

winter ♂

LAPLAND LONGSPUR
L 5¾"

summer ♂

♀

SMITH'S LONGSPUR
L 5¾"

♀

winter ♂

winter ♀

SNOW BUNTING
L 6"

winter ♂

winter ♀

♂

summer
Snow Bunting

McKAY'S BUNTING
L 6¼"

summer ♂
McKay's Bunting

BIBLIOGRAPHY

Hundreds of books on birds are published each year. Many states and provinces have books on where to find birds as well as books covering occurrence and life history. Here are some of the most important and readily available books on birds of North America and nearby regions.

American Birding Assoc. *A.B.A. Checklist*, 2nd ed. Austin, Tex., 1982.

American Ornithologists' Union. *Check-list of North American Birds*, 6th ed. expected 1983. Washington, D.C.

Bellrose, F. C. *Ducks, Geese and Swans of North America*, rev. ed. Harrisburg, Pa.: Stackpole, 1981.

Bent, A. C. *Life Histories of North American Birds*, 20 vols. Washington, D.C.: U.S. National Museum, 1919-1967.

Bond, J. *Birds of the West Indies*, 4th ed. Boston: Houghton Mifflin, 1980.

Bruun, B. *Birds of Britain and Europe*. N.Y.: Larousse, 1978.

Bull, J. *Birds of New York State*. N.Y.: Doubleday, 1974.

Garrett, K. *Birds of Southern California*. Los Angeles: Artisan, 1981.

Godfrey, W. E. *Birds of Canada*. Ottawa: Nat'l Museum of Canada, 1979.

Griscom, L., and A. Sprunt. *Warblers of America*. N.Y.: Doubleday, 1979.

Harrison, H. H. *A Field Guide to Birds' Nests Found East of the Mississippi*, 1975; *A Field Guide to Western Birds' Nests*, 1979; both Boston: Houghton Mifflin.

Hickey, J. J. *A Guide to Bird Watching*. N.Y.: Dover, 1975.

Kessel, B., and D. D. Gibson. *Status and Distribution of Alaska Birds*. Lawrence, Kans.: Allen Press, Studies in Avian Biology 1, 1978.

Oberholser, H. C. *Bird Life of Texas*, 2 vols. Austin: Tex. Univ., 1974.

Palmer, R. S. (ed.) *Handbook of North American Birds*, vols. 1-3, loons through waterfowl; 1962, 1976, 1976. New Haven: Yale Univ. Press.

Peterson, R. T. *A Field Guide to the Birds*, 4th ed., 1980; *A Field Guide to the Birds of Texas and Adjacent States*, 1979; *A Field Guide to Western Birds*, 1961; *A Field Guide to Mexican Birds*, 1973; *A Field Guide to the Birds of Britain and Europe*, 3rd ed., 1975; all Boston: Houghton Mifflin.

Pettingill, O. S. Jr. *A Guide to Bird Finding East of the Mississippi*, 2nd ed., 1977; *A Guide to Bird Finding West of the Mississippi*, 2nd ed., 1981; both N.Y.: Oxford. *Ornithology in Laboratory and Field*, 4th ed. Minneapolis: Burgess, 1970.

Phillips, A. R. *Birds of Arizona*. Tucson: Ariz. Univ. Press, 1964.

Pough, R. H. *Audubon Land Bird Guide*, rev. ed., 1951; *Audubon Water Bird Guide*, 1951; *Audubon Western Bird Guide*, 1957; N.Y.: Doubleday.

Rickert, J. E. *A Guide to North American Bird Clubs*. Elizabethtown, Ky.: Avian Publications, 1978.

Roberson, D. *Rare Birds of the West Coast of North America*. Pacific Grove, Calif.: Woodcock, 1980.

Sprunt, A. Jr. *Florida Bird Life*. N.Y.: Coward-McCann, 1954.

Terres, J. K. *Audubon Society Encyclopedia of North American Birds*. N.Y.: Knopf, 1980.

Van Tyne, J. *Fundamentals of Ornithology*, 2nd ed. N.Y.: Wiley, 1976.

INDEX

Individual species names, both common and scientific, are indicated with the text page only when the illustration is on the facing page, as it is for most birds. For orders, families, and other groups inclusive page numbers are usually given.

Names formerly used on a wide scale for common birds are indicated by "*see*" references leading to the currently accepted name.

The boxes at the left of the common names can be used for checking the birds you have identified.

MEASURING SCALE (IN INCHES)